Sensing Sacred

Studies in Body and Religion

Series Editors: Richard M. Carp, Saint Mary's College of California, and Julia Huang Lemmon, National Tsing Hua University, Taiwan

Studies in Body and Religion publishes contemporary research and theory that addresses body as a fundamental category of analysis in the study of religion. Embodied humans conceive of, study, transmit, receive, and practice religion, with and through their bodies and bodily capacities. Volumes in this series will include diverse examples and perspectives on the roles and understandings of body in religion, as well as the influence and importance of religion for body. They will also move conversation on body and religion forward by problematizing "body," which, like "religion," is a contested concept. We do not know exactly what religion is, nor do we know exactly what body is, either; much less do we understand their mutual interpenetrations. This series aims to address this by bringing multiple understandings of body into an arena of conversation.

Titles in the Series

Sensing Sacred

Exploring the Human Senses in Practical Theology and Pastoral Care

Edited by Jennifer Baldwin

LEXINGTON BOOKS
Lanham • Boulder • New York • London

Published by Lexington Books
An imprint of The Rowman & Littlefield Publishing Group, Inc.
4501 Forbes Boulevard, Suite 200, Lanham, Maryland 20706
www.rowman.com

Unit A, Whitacre Mews, 26-34 Stannary Street, London SE11 4AB

British Library Cataloguing in Publication Information Available

Library of Congress Cataloging-in-Publication Data
The hardback edition of this book was previously catalogued by the Library of Congress as follows:

Names: Baldwin, Jennifer, editor
Title: Sensing sacred : exploring the human senses in practical theology and pastoral care / edited by
    Jennifer Baldwin.
Description: Lanham : Lexington Books, 2016. | Series: Studies in body and religion | Includes
    bibliographical references and index.
Identifiers: LCCN 2016026381 (print) | LCCN 2016026596 (ebook)
Subjects: LCSH: Senses and sensation--Religious aspects. | Human body--Religious aspects.
Classification: LCC BL65.B63 S46 2016 (print) | LCC BL65.B63 (ebook) | DDC 233/.5--dc23 LC
    record available at https://lccn.loc.gov/2016026381

ISBN 978-1-4985-3123-8 (cloth : alk. paper)
ISBN 978-1-4985-3125-2 (pbk.: alk. paper)
ISBN 978-1-4985-3124-5 (electronic)

♾™ The paper used in this publication meets the minimum requirements of American
National Standard for Information Sciences Permanence of Paper for Printed Library
Materials, ANSI/NISO Z39.48-1992.

Printed in the United States of America

Contents

Preface

Making Sense

Jennifer Baldwin

Sensing Sacred: Exploring the Human Senses in Practical Theology and Pastoral Care is an edited volume that explores the critical intersection of "religion" and "body" through the "religious" lens of practical theology with an emphasis on sensation as the embodied means in which human beings know themselves, others, and the divine in the world. The manuscript argues that all human interaction and practice, including religious praxis, engages "body" through at least one of the human senses (touch, smell, hearing, taste, sight, kinestics/proprioception).

Lisbeth Lipari's monograph *Listening, Thinking, Being: An Ethics of Attunement* notes the relationship among culture, bodies, and sensation. She writes,

> Culture [and religion] is a living being, and its habitat is the body. Embodied in the five senses, the cultured body lives and breathes in moving corporeality, enacting and reenacting itself moment by millimeter, with every gaze and passing sigh, moving with the rhythmic pattering of gestures, posture, and everyday talk. We humans are embodied beings—we live in and with and from our bodies. [1]

She explicitly highlights the oft forgotten reality that human bodies are the means and consumers of all expressions of all social life and culture. From embodied movements in the art of ballet to the movement practices of religious traditions either through liturgical practice or meditation and yoga practice, religious expression, epistemology, community, and traditions are sensuously corporeal. Unfortunately, body and, more specifically and ironically, sensation are eclipsed in contemporary academic scholarship that is inherently bent toward the realm of theory and ideas. This is unfortunate because it neglects bodies, physical or communal, as the repository and generator of culturally conditioned ideas and theory. It is ironic because all knowledge transmission minimally requires several senses for accurate communication. For instance, I cannot write my ideas without touching a keyboard and "hearing" my thoughts. You cannot receive my ideas without utilizing sight to read the words or hearing to hear my verbal communication or your own internal "hearing." At a more inclusive level, all communication is formed within the "body" of the community that frames our linguistic structures and symbols, teaches us how to function in the world, and supports bodily living. In the practice of religion, sensation is often blindly invoked in the sight of reading and hearing of religious texts, in the taste, touch, and smell of religious meals and rituals. Overall, as sensuous, religious, and cultural beings, we fail to receive and recognize our full embodiment as a means of interacting with self, world, and the sacred.

Moreover, religious scholars who do attend to body often do so as a site of particularity within the social realm. "Body" is a limited category alongside other categories of sexuality, community interaction and inclusion/exclusion, familial connection, site of violence, or matrix of affect. Body is rarely attended to as the necessary subject of knowing and being in the world and being in relationship with self, others, and the sacred. Without body sensation, we are each floating in a nondescript vacuum, alone and without the connections needed to survive, much less flourish.

Sensing Sacred seeks to fill the gap in contemporary religious, and more specifically practical theology, scholarship by placing the senses as the honored subjects of care and attention. The senses are essential for living in the world, identifying internal body functions and placement, and accessing the divine across religious traditions and spiritual practices. The human senses are the focus of this volume as subject and as an avenue toward religious and spiritual expression, relation, and reception.

One of the strengths of the text is in generating a choral effect in which many voices with differing tones and timbres join together in a shared chorus or song. Each author provides a distinctive voice, focus, and range while all share a focus on the Christian expression of confession, faith, and practice. The chorus of authorship provides attention to a depth and breadth of knowledge of Christianity while also sharing in the specialty of practical theology. Practical theology, as a lens distinct from systematic and constructive theologies, expands the reach of this volume into the fields of cultural studies, anthropology, sociology, psychology, and social sciences in general. Due to the blending of robust academic attention with practical lenses and practices, *Sensing Sacred* offers a novel approach to the study of body and religion and offers a polyvocal addition to the Studies in Body and Religion Series.

Sensing Sacred is organized into two parts. The first section devotes a chapter to each human sense as an avenue of accessing religious experience; while the second section explores religious practices as they highlight the multisensory dimensions of religious experience. The overarching aim of the volume is to explicitly highlight each sense and utilize the theoretical lenses of practical theology to bring to vivid life the connections between essential sensation and religious thinking and practice.

In the introduction, Bonnie Miller-McLemore provides an informative survey of the physical body in religious scholarship.[2] She notes that relig-

ious scholarship invokes "embodiment" frequently but rarely incorporates the physical body as a subject/object of attention. Rather, religious
scholars over the past two decades have attended so much to the cultural
conditioning of bodies that the physical body is rendered invisible. Her
introductory chapter provides a foundation for thinking about practical
theology and practices involving the body with an attunement to the role
of sensation in religious thinking and ritual practice. She does so by providing an overview of practical theology's attention (or lack thereof) to
the physical body in religious practices, an appeal to biological learnings
about the physical body in terms of human infancy development, emotion and empathy, and social experiences of care and formation. Finally,
she argues the need for a weaving of biological and cultural learnings
about the physical and cultural body that retain the centrality of the
physical body in scholarship without losing the particularity of the body
in the cultural formation of social bodies.

Part I of *Sensing Sacred* is devoted to each of the six human senses:
smell, touch, taste, hearing, sight, kinesthetic. Each chapter presents one
of the human senses as a means of engaging in full-bodied participation
with the divine.

Martha S. Jacobi offers connections between olfaction, memory, and
ritual practices in her chapter "Smelling Remembrance." She begins with
a brief overview of the physiology of smell and its connection to the
limbic and cortical systems of the brain and types of memory formation
and mood. She then offers a rich theological and spiritual question, "How
might we smell God?" Jacobi argues, on one hand, that smells permeate
sacred texts and contemporary religious practices and are almost ignored; however, on the other, smells are always all around us, engaging
our mind/spirit/bodies with every inhalation of respiration. How is our
religious and spiritual life expanded by attending to the knowledge of
the nose?

Shirley S. Guider's chapter "Embodying Christ, Touching Others" explores the sensation of touch in rituals of care. She discusses the biology
of touch via the body's largest organ, the skin, the role of touch for health
and vitality, social connections, and flourishing. From the perspective of
Protestant Christianity, Guider argues that the Christian religious tradition contains both sanctions against touch and examples of healing touch.
Ultimately, she argues in favor of thoughtfully engaged rituals of touch
and including intentional touch in the practices of care and community.

"Savoring Taste as Religious Praxis: Where Individual and Social Intimacy Converge," by Stephanie N. Arel, investigates the sense of taste and
accompanying acts of eating in religious practices. She examines a variety
of religious traditions, including the Abrahamic traditions, Hinduism,
and ritual meals from Hawaii and Africa, in order to elucidate the connections between the sense of taste, community cultivation, and connection to the divine. Arel traces taste through biology, experiences that link

the physical, cognitive, affective, and epistemological and rituals of individual participation and community affiliation.

In "Akroatic, Embodied Hearing and Presence as Spiritual Practice," Jennifer Baldwin advocates for an expansive understanding of the sense of hearing as a full-bodied practice. She argues that attending hearing does not just occur though the ear but includes the whole body reception of verbal, nonverbal, and energetic information. Additionally, she offers a framework for hearing and presence that focuses on the components of communication reception, interpretation, and response. Baldwin makes the claim that this form of attending to self, others, and God is a spiritual practice that can infuse multiple dimensions of life and practice.

Sonia Waters's chapter, "Devotional Looking and the Possibilities of Free Associative Sight," combines insights from psychoanalytic notions of "experiential free association" with "visual piety" from visual studies to explore devotional practices of spiritual gazing. She argues that sight is not a unidirectional process but is constructed through the combination of the object of sight, personal histories, and social traditions. After exploring the theoretical, personal, and social lenses, Waters offers a case study to illustrate how spiritual gazing is generated through the particularities of the chosen image, personal experiences and associations, and social frames of narrative, thought, and praxis.

Emmanuel Y. Lartey invites us to explore the epistemological, hermeneutical, and ontological dimensions of the sense of human movement. He argues that proprioception and kinesthetic sensations are essential for being human and experiencing self, community, and the divine. Lartey partners with African religious traditions in Africa and through the Diaspora, arguing that African traditional healers have much to teach Western religious scholars about the ways in which physical movement impacts an individual's health, communal dance and music bonds members of a society together, and religious dances invite God to speak to the community just as the participants are gathered into communal worship.

Having granted focused attention on each of the senses in part I, part II of *Sensing Sacred* focuses on specific religious practices of worship, devotion, and care and their particular relation to human sensation. Several of the chapters in this section model the ways in which senses are rather difficult to isolate and largely function in cooperation to allow each of us a more complete experience of self, community, and the divine.

Most of the time, spiritual practices are considered to be limited to the space of religious buildings and communities. John C. Carr invites us to expand the context of spiritual practices to include the regular use of hot tubs as means of invoking the sensations of touch and proprioception. Carr begins with a survey of the physiological and psychological benefits of hot tub use and warns against some of the risks inherent in hot tub use. He then continues by exploring the intent and focus of spirituality as an individual, as well as communal, seeking of connection to the divine. He argues that intentional use of hot tubs can be a spiritual practice that quiets the mind, soothes the soul, and enlivens the body. Drawing from his own practice of hot tub, Carr presents a model of hot tub use that is, for him and others, a deeply meaningful spiritual practice.

In "Word Made Flesh: Using Visual Textuality of Sign Languages to Construct Religious Meaning and Identity," Jason Hays investigates hegemonic power structures within religious communities that function to silence and ignore persons who are deaf. Hays demonstrates, through the sensory intersectionality of sight, hearing, and kinesthetics, the challenges inherent in Protestant Christian communities who singularly preference the omni-importance of the spoken "Word." He presents a vital critique of hearing-centric practices and the active exclusion of sign language as a means of constructing communal religious meaning and spiritual identity.

Christina Jones Davis's chapter "A Laying On of Hands: Black Feminist Intimations of the Divine and Healing Touch in Religious Practice" provides a helpful survey of the impact and prevalence of sexual violence and harmful touch. Utilizing relational psychoanalytic frames, Davis offers a lens for understanding the role of pastoral leaders and religious communities as agents of healing and transformation. A component of this role in facilitating recovery from sexual violence is the offering of "healing touch" through rituals of consensual care. By employing choreopoetry as the voice of survivors of sexual trauma, Davis weaves movement, speech, and hearing in and through her analysis of restorative touch.

Kenya J. Tuttle explores the relationship between the sense of taste and cultural influences of religious practice, care for the body, and systems of oppression and food scarcity. In her chapter, she notes a reciprocal relationship between taste/health and religio-cultural narratives that inform which bodies in society are worthy of care and provision. Tuttle claims that theological constructs which disregard the body in favor of soul-development combine with systems of race and class oppression to generate food deserts that limit access to healthy and nutritious food. When highly processed foods high in sugar and salt are the only options available, individuals and communities lose their "taste," metaphorically and literally, for distinguishing between healthy and damaging foods. This loss of taste discernment has metabolically disastrous consequences. Tuttle offers folk healing and religious resources for attending to the urgent need to regain healthy, body-nourishing, life-affirming taste.

In "Holy Transitional and Transcendent Smells: Aromatherapy as an Adjunctive Support for Trauma in Pastoral Care and Counseling," Jennifer Baldwin advocates for a focused and balanced growth in the awareness and understanding of traumatic exposure, response, and recovery for religious care givers. Recognizing that traumatic experience is far more common than recognized and the nearly complete lack of trauma training in seminaries and communities of faith, Baldwin makes a case for the importance of trauma awareness and offers a robust frame for the use of aromatherapy as one resource for pastoral care in attending to individual and community survivors of trauma.

Sensing Sacred: Exploring the Human Senses in Practical Theology and Pastoral Care highlights the impact of the human sense in the cultivation of spirituality and explores the weavings of sensations through spiritual practices. Within the buffet of disciplinary traditions and fields, the human senses have historically been the purview of medicine as object of inquiry, science (generally) as research tool, and, more recently, cultural studies as subject; however, the human senses have largely been missing as anything more than a literary device in theology and religious studies. Christian theology has a long rhetorical tradition of the "body" as a metaphor for communal religious life and elevated confession of "incarnation" as a cornerstone of faith and proclamation. Nevertheless, despite the multitude of sacred texts employing people of faith to taste, hear, see, touch, dance, and smell, religious scholarship has largely neglected the role of the human senses in faith and practice.

The exclusion of the human senses as a subject of being, knowing, and connecting is rooted in and furthers the mind/body dualism that rends spirit from flesh, human from nature, female from male, and sensuality from holiness. Throughout the text, individual authors have argued for the importance of attending to the human senses as the means through which we experience connection to one another and to the divine. As a chorus of sensuous voices, this volume expands the scope of scholarly attention to the body to include the biological physicality of the body and in the variety of communal religious and spiritual practices that connect human beings to one another and to the divine.

The real gift of this volume is to begin anew an enlarged tending to beauty of the sensuous as a necessary dimension of full humanity and fully em-body-ed and incarnated spiritual relationality. The human senses are on ripe soil for scholarly attention by those in theology (systematic, historical, constructive, and practical) and religious studies. The expansion of sensuous scholarship is imperative especially in the fields of religious theory and praxis precisely due to the ways in which religion has facilitated the elevation of the mind and spirit and demonization of the physical and the body. *Sensing Sacred: Exploring the Human Senses in Practical Theology and Pastoral Care* ultimately invites further creative and openly curious inquiry into the beautiful, vibrant, and luscious world available through the human senses and the multitude of avenues they open up to the spiritual and divine, within, among, and beyond.

NOTES

1. Lisbeth Lipari, *Listening, Thinking, Being: Toward an Ethics of Attunement* (University Park: Penn State University Press, 2014), 30.

2. The introduction of this text is reproduced "[w]ith kind permission from Springer Science+Business Media: *Journal of Pastoral Psychology*, "Embodied Knowing, Embodied Theology: What Happened to the Body?," Volume 62, 2013, Bonnie Miller-McLemore, License number 3696251323469."

REFERENCES

Lisbeth Lipari, *Listening, Thinking, Being: Toward an Ethics of Attunement*, University Park: Penn State University Press, 2014.

Acknowledgments

I would like to thank Richard Carp, Rebecca Sachs Norris, and Julia Huang Lemmon, the editors of this series, for their belief in this edited project, support through the changes, patience within the pauses, and comments that helped to clarify and refine the vision and shape of this volume. Thank you to Sarah Craig at Rowman & Littlefield for her comments and guidance in moving this manuscript through the process and Kenneth Kao (Pole Ninja Photography) and Marlo Fisken (Flow Movement) for use of their beautiful photograph on the cover of the volume. I'd like to thank the Society for Pastoral Theology (SPT) for providing a common space for pastoral theology scholars to meet, work, play, and imagine. SPT was the central ground for gathering together all of the contributors in this volume, which would not exist apart from this community of scholarship. Finally, I extend, on behalf of myself and the other contributors, gratitude to our families and friends who sacrificed moments, or days, with us so that we could devote time and attention to this project.

Introduction

Embodied Knowing, Embodied Theology: What Happened to the Body?

Bonnie Miller-McLemore

Today, scholars in religion and theology often use the term *embodied* interchangeably with *cultural embeddedness* or *cultural constructions* of the body.[1] As a nice example, religion scholar Sam Gill[2] contributes a noteworthy chapter entitled "Embodied Theology" to an edited book on the academic legitimacy of religious and theological studies, an issue that has troubled the modern university at least since nineteenth-century attempts to reconcile Christianity with the Enlightenment. He argues for a non-religious or nonconfessional approach to religious study, in contrast to one biased by religious convictions, even though he admits that such a theologically free stance is impossible because Christian theology is so embedded in Western society. Hence, his title. However, putting aside problems with his reductive view of theology as "belief that is outside our usual frame of propositionality,"[3] I am curious about his use of the term *embodied*. He talks about the body, but largely in terms of how it is formed by culture and history rather than how being in actual bodies forms culture or history.[4] Oddly the body itself, its literal physicality, almost drops out of the picture. In other words, culture has the high road in a new kind of Platonism despite Gill's own intent otherwise.

This cultural reading of the term *body* and *embodied* is actually quite widespread. Today religion and theology scholars talk all the time about embodied knowing or embodied theology but with little thought or attention to what is being said about bodies themselves, especially with regard to what it means to inhabit a physical or biological body. That is, we talk a lot about *embodied* theology or *embodied* knowing but less so about the *body* itself or what it means to know in and through material bodies. Ironically, the term *embodied* seems impaled on the very dualism between flesh and spirit, body and soul, body and culture that many scholars hoped to disrupt in using the term.

This chapter is a preliminary investigation into how biology and physicality shape human knowing. In one way, this is a new research interest. But in another way, I have been thinking about this question for

1

a long time. My interest is also part of a larger effort to understand practical knowledge or how people know in and through practice more generally. So I want to trace briefly the progression of my thought to acknowledge disciplinary areas that have given attention to bodies and shaped my own reflection, noting a few conclusions I have reached and developed in greater depth elsewhere, before I turn to selected research on evolution, biology, and bodies in anthropology and the biological sciences.

I know that "looking to the biological sciences has been for a long time taboo among feminist thinkers," as Jewish studies scholar Mara Benjamin[5] observes. Indeed, feminist theorist Susan Bordo, well known for her study of the impact of cultural stereotypes on bodies, describes the feminist politics of the material body as an "extended argument against the notion that the body is a purely biological or natural form."[6] I proceed nonetheless. Please do not mistake my interest in the physical body as a desire to return to some kind of arrested determinism that ignores culture or presumes or implies that our bodies are our destinies. I realize that defining the body in relationship to culture is a difficult, if not fruitless, enterprise, and that returning to biology for some kind of foundational explanation about human behavior is hazardous (from a feminist perspective) and epistemologically wrongheaded (from a hermeneutical and postmodern perspective). The body is not simply a physical entity; it is always already shaped by culture. I am not interested in adjudicating complicated philosophical questions about definitions of body or culture, their relationship, or the weight given biology/culture in human development. I also know that Westerners such as myself are shaped by a long history of dualism between body and mind, body and culture, out of which none of us can easily step just by quoting an overused aphorism among theologians these days that "we not only have bodies, we are bodies."[7] Westerners lie in the bed our history has made.

Nonetheless, I am interested in gaining a greater understanding of how physical (sensual, somatic, visceral, material, carnal, mortal, fleshly, vulnerable—I search for appropriate adjectives here) dimensions of our bodies inform our thought and knowing. What is the relationship between this dimension of human bodies and human knowledge? And how do actual physical bodies shape religious and theological knowledge? If there is an argument behind this initial examination, it is that there has been lapse in attention to physical bodies in the unreflective employment of the phrase *embodied knowing/embodied theology*, especially among practical theologians who have particular interest in understanding how theology operates on the ground. Simply stated, I want to put the physical body back into embodied knowing and theology.

A DIS-BODY-ED EMBODIED THEOLOGY

Religion and theology scholars might be surprised to know that for many scholars in the sciences the word *embodied* carries a close connection to human physiology, biology, and material goods. When a source like *Wikipedia* defines *embodiment*, it lists the uses of *embodied* in cognitive science, for example, as focused on how the body shapes the mind or on the interplay between brain, body, and world; in law, as directed toward putting conceptual ideas into actual bodily practice; in theater training, as a reconnection of body and mind; and in economics, as related to a material good or product.[8] Whether law, cognitive science, theater, or economics, physicality has a prominence when the term *embodied* is employed that it often lacks in the study of religion. Moreover, in recent years there has been renewed interest across disciplines in mind-body-brain connections, research that has only begun to find a comparable home among scholars in religion.

In one sense, it is odd that the body or at least its physiological dimensions have dropped out of sight in religious and theological study. At least one powerful origin of the term *embodied* in theological studies is theological ethicist James Nelson's[9] challenge to Christian theological body/soul dualism, *Embodiment: An Approach to Sexuality and Christian Theology*. In his work, the term *embodied* refers almost entirely to human sexuality.[10] He was among the first to attack Christianity's devaluation of the body, particularly its negative repressive approach over the course of Western history to sexual bodies—bodies that become aroused, bodies that engage in sexual activities, bodies that birth children, and bodies that are attracted to bodies of the same sex. Interest in the body has mushroomed in decades since his book, influencing, if not directly spawning, the creation of the phrase *embodied knowing* or *embodied theology*.

In another sense, however, the collapse of the word *embodied* into its cultural connotations makes perfect sense. In the years since Nelson's groundbreaking effort to put sexuality back into the common Christian lexicon, attention has turned increasingly toward controversial politics surrounding the cultural construction of bodies, such as those of race, disability, orientation, gender, and body commodification and modification. Feminists and poststructuralists have shown how culture marks and manipulates bodies, foisting on particular populations restrictive expectations grounded in narrow perceptions of biological normativity and (so called) naturalness, whether ideals of female maternal instinct, heterosexual mating desire, masculine aggression, and so forth. Over two decades ago, British and Australian sociologist Bryan Turner said, "In recent developments of social theory, there has been an important reevaluation of the importance of the body, not simply in feminist social theory, but more generally in the analysis of class, culture and consumption."[11] Sociologist Pierre Bourdieu and those shaped by his work, such as Michel de Cer-

teau, have had great appeal among religion scholars in particular because
Bourdieu and others understand *habitus* as much more than the Aristote-
lian character formation assumed by a prior generation shaped by Alas-
dair MacIntyre's and Edward Farley's use of the term. *Habitus* for Bourdieu involves ways in which the "body ingests and digests and assimi-
lates, physiologically and psychologically" cultural ideals at a prereflex-
ive, prediscursive level. [12]

Nonetheless, there are problems with limiting the meaning of the term
embodied to the body's social habituation, even for those who agree, as I
do, with the importance of analysis of political and cultural constructions
of bodies. In a book on *Sensuous Scholarship*, anthropologist Paul Stoller
identifies "two salient features of this new embodied discourse" that
"weaken its overall scholarly impact." First, the body is transported to
the literate, verbal world of Western academics where it becomes merely
a text "that can be read and analyzed," stripped of "its smells, tastes,
textures and pains—its sensuousness." [13] The ears of scholars shaped by
pastoral theology's twentieth-century history should perk up here. Is
there something potentially reductive or restrictive in Anton Boisen's
characterization of human beings as textual *documents* in his pioneering
work in clinical education? Can living subjects be adequately understood
when turned into linear texts?

The second concern that Stoller names is equally suggestive. "Recent
writing on the body," he observes, "tends to be articulated in a curiously
disembodied language." [14] He names Judith Butler's classic work, *Gender
Trouble*, [15] as an example—not to diminish its immense significance in
showing just how deeply cultural constructions of both sex and gender
run—but to note the irony that such Foucault-like efforts to contest the
tyranny of Cartesian rationalism actually reinforce in their "dense mosaic
of abstract analysis" the "very principle they critique—the separation of
mind and body, which . . . regulates and subjugates the very bodies they
would liberate." [16] So, ironically, the body disappears in abstraction in the
very effort to release it from entrapping hegemonic mores that constrict
its expression.

TRACING BODY INTEREST ACROSS INTERSECTING DISCIPLINES

A few years ago, I did a plenary address on method in theology and the
social sciences for a Society of Pastoral Theology conference on cognitive
neuroscience. Although my focus was more on method than neuroscience, [17] I began reading recent literature in this expanding field and ran
across books that triggered thought, such as Shaun Gallager's *How the
Body Shapes the Mind* [18] and Raymond Gibbs's *Embodiment and Cognitive
Science*. [19] I was struck specifically by the complicated nature of the brain
as matter (or deeply in-bodied) and of thinking as never solely a cogni-

tive process but one deeply influenced by embodiment—"matter over mind" to reverse the modern cliché. I wondered what more could be learned from the burgeoning field of brain science about the role of the body in practical knowing and in how one learns to perform a practice (such as pastoral care or ministry or religious faith more generally).

My interests go further back, however, to early research on motherhood in which I attempt to articulate what difference it might make in knowing to inhabit a woman's body capable of carrying a fetus, birthing a child, and nursing an infant.[20] At that time, I read books worth returning to once again by feminist scientists and philosophers like Evelyn Fox Keller, Sandra Harding, Sara Ruddick, and Susan Bordo.[21] In different ways, they all tried to articulate alternative patterns of knowing that undermine conventional approaches to what philosopher Charles Taylor describes as the modern "thrall of intellectualism."[22] They provided plenty of conceptual support for my own argument that I might know differently through experiences such as nursing a child. Certain tactile experiences of mothering vividly relocate thinking within the body.

My research on maternal knowing was sparked in particular by a request to speak at another Society for Pastoral Theology conference twenty years ago on the theme of epistemology. Since I had two young sons and a third on his way, colleague and friend Herbert Anderson encouraged me to address whether I knew anything distinct from maternal embodiment. His question and the Society's concern about epistemology in general were provoked by the impact of feminist scholarship on modern truth claims and ways of knowing. A wealth of work in the late twentieth century protests the exclusion of women's thought and experience—in essence, their bodies—from sacred spaces within academic and ecclesial institutions. Feminist scientists and philosophers as well as feminist theologians all worked to undermine dualisms of mind (man) over body (woman) and articulate other ways of knowing. Feminism is only one among many movements in the past century that have shifted our attention to the power and place of the body in knowing.[23] But, "open talk about one's body" (2010) and reclaiming control over it were key to the development of second wave feminism, according to Jean Baker Miller, one of the first psychologists to address women's experience.[24] As Latina theologian Mayra Rivera Rivera says so well, "Feminists have argued for decades that the devaluation of flesh contributes to the subordination of women and thus we work to rescue the body and materiality from patriarchal deprecation."[25]

As if feminist theory and cognitive science are not sign enough that modern conceptions of disembodied knowing are coming undone, one could point further back to a foundational influence on twentieth-century pastoral theology's emergence, Sigmund Freud himself. This is not the place to evaluate the contributions of either development in the detail it deserves. How Freud understood the relationship between body and knowledge is an interesting question in itself that others such as religion scholar Naomi Goldenberg have explored. However, it would be a grave oversight not to recognize Freud's efforts to understand how the body speaks, whether his early neurological interests and study of hysterics and paralysis or his later work on slips of the tongue and the very mechanics of psychological development around erogenous zones. As psychoanalysts Peter Fonagy and Target point out, the "rootedness of symbolic thought in sensory, emotional, and enacted experience with objects" stands at the heart of much psychoanalytic thought.[26] Although later proponents and critics, such as Norman Brown, exaggerate the promise of a psychoanalytic resurrection of the body, they are correct to note Freud's powerful message that bodily desire drives human behavior more than people in Western civilization have admitted.

Nonetheless, although Freud, Brown, and later analysts sought to overcome the psyche-soma split in theory and clinical practice, it is less clear that the body gained validation even though it gained visibility. That is, the body remains the horse, the ego is the rider, and the hierarchy of "higher and lower"—to use Brown's words—goes fundamentally undisturbed.[27] In psychoanalytic perspective, people are pulled and pushed—even driven—by bodily desire, but the body—the horse—has little valid knowledge of its own. It is still just an animal, and Freud remains ambivalent about and cautious, even distrusting, of animals, children, women, the primitive, emotions, and the body, all of which need guidance, oversight, and control, if not by religion's oppressive forces, then at least by more mature scientific discovery. A disturbing paradigmatic instance of his valuation of mind over body appears in his revision of his early seduction theory; it is not, he comes to believe, actual bodily molestation that shapes later pathology, just fantasies in the mind of the child. In the years since, findings on actual physical and sexual abuse have shown the serious consequences of real experiences and early social environment. Nonetheless, at least the body is foregrounded in Freud, even if still devalued. In the post-Freudian shift away from Oedipal drives and psychosexual development to pre-oedipal relationships in object relations theory and self-psychology, the body slowly disappears from analysis. "Psychoanalysis to some measure has been desexualized," say Fonagy and Target.[28]

There are, of course, many scholars in religion who do in fact write about the body in a literal sense, and this work has also shaped my own thought. Influenced by Freud's psychoanalytical legacy and with a focus on care directed at bodies (e.g., ill, dying, traumatized, etc.), pastoral theologians have naturally included the body among their many research interests. The first edited book on pastoral care and women,[29] for example, contains a chapter on women's bodies as well as chapters indirectly related to bodies, such as battering and sexual abuse. Also illustrative is research such as that of Ralph L. Underwood on chronic pain and mortality, which cannot help but locate reflection in acute relationship to the body. And of course, beyond pastoral theology, there are many religion scholars, particularly in race, sexuality, gender, and disability studies as suggested above, who have given serious attention to bodies, too many to name and cover here.[30] However, only a few scholars both within and beyond pastoral theology give explicit attention to questions about knowledge and bodies. As curious, many exemplify the pattern of collapsing embodied knowing into concern about how bodies are shaped by culture and show little interest in how physical bodies shape ideas. So there is not much research on literal bodies, and the work on literal bodies does not go far enough in terms of exploring questions of epistemology.

BODIES AND LEARNING A PRACTICE

More recently, the prominence of the body in social theory emerges in theories of practice in sociology, such as the work of a Bourdieu-influenced French sociologist, Loïc Wacquant, *Body and Soul: Notebooks of an Apprentice Boxer*.[31] There is a lot going on in his book, such as his creative redefinition of the boundaries of ethnography and his investigation into social dynamics of racism and classism. More relevant for this chapter, however, is his demonstration of the body/mind dynamics in his own novice entry into learning boxing and his claims about body knowledge gleaned from this experience. In his account of personal "initiation into a bodily craft," he fashions a "carnal sociology" that captures the "taste and ache of action," a sociology "not only *of* the body . . . but also *from* the body" (p. viii, his emphasis). At some visceral, prerational level, the body learns and knows, and thought follows. His work is suggestive in my own search for a more "carnal theology."

Do ministers experience anything similar in learning ministry? This question is actually the most immediate instigator of this chapter. The concern has arisen for me largely as a result of recent research in practical theology. The reinvigoration of practical theology as a discipline in the last three decades in the United States and internationally originated in a concern over an abstract disembodied conceptualization of theology removed from everyday practice. Practical theology distinguishes itself in its emphasis on lived religious practices from what has been variously called dogmatic, systematic, philosophical, or constructive theology, historically focused on the study of conceptual belief. Practical theologians explore the complicated elusive dissonance between stated belief (e.g., doctrine, creeds) and everyday practice (e.g., rituals, daily life) and sustain an abiding interest in the materiality of human religiosity (e.g., material culture, bodies, everyday practices, ethnographies of local communities, the dynamics of place and time, and so forth). Although some U.S.

pastoral theologians hold practical theology's scholarly development suspect as further abstracting theology from its context or pastoral theology from its roots in the study of the self and psychology, it has been practical theology's investment in living theology that most attracts me. Research on bodies is therefore also partly an extension of my involvement in this discussion.

Since the publication of a collaborative book, *For Life Abundant,*[32] I have worked with four colleagues—Dorothy Bass, Kathleen Cahalan, James Nieman, and Christian Scharen—on a second book on a subject we touched on in the earlier book but did not explore sufficiently—the kind of knowledge that both arises from practice and makes good practice possible or, to put it another way, the practical wisdom that is crucial to the life of Christian faith, ministry, and theological education. We have varied in how we describe our primary subject matter, using in turn words with diverse and complex histories, such as *phronesis* (hard to do better in parsing knowledge than Aristotle's threefold characterization of intellectual virtue as *phronesis, techne,* and *episteme*), wisdom (a loaded cultural and religious term if there ever was one), know-how (an aptitude sadly devalued in the 1980s "clerical paradigm" hype about merely teaching ministerial skills), and practical knowledge (as contrasted perhaps too simplistically and sharply with theoretical knowledge). When we deliberated about what each of us could contribute to a work-in-progress, I identified my interest in bodies and embodied knowing as one aspect of the kind of knowing distinct to faith, practical theology, and *phronesis.* I had begun to notice that when practical theologians use the term *embodied* to mean *theology in practice,* the actual body often drops out of sight.

As we considered the fullness of what we hoped to explore about alternative ways of knowing in theology, we thought a prototypically academic approach of "telling" or analyzing would not do justice to the subject. So we experimented with other writing styles, trying to "show" or display through narrative and image rather than "telling," thereby changing the usual disproportion in academic prose of the conceptual over the depictive, analysis over images. I ventured into the murky waters of narrative and attempted a "show" chapter on body knowing. To my surprise, composing that chapter turned into one of the more rewarding ventures of my writing life.

In a way, the "tell-oriented" chapter you are reading is a companion to my "show" chapter on Christian phronesis and the body. In "showing," argument is indirect—between the story lines so to speak—although my proclivity for scholarly footnoting inevitably led me to document my portrait, even if only through research on other peoples' stories of embodiment and knowing. If one believes that a picture tells a thousand words, distilling key ideas from this "show" chapter is not really possible. Nonetheless, there are a few conclusions worth carrying forward here.

The chapter has three movements on bodily knowing in worship, intimate relationship, and the practice of care respectively, but at the moment I find myself most compelled by reflection on worshipping bodies and "knowing God." So I focus my remarks here. My own religious practice has been indelibly shaped by a free or low-church tradition where liturgy remains informal and elaborate rituals around praying, reading scripture, partaking in communion, and so on are few. This is even truer in smaller congregations, which are in the majority. We are not exactly the Presbyterian "frozen chosen," whom some describe as actively repressing bodily expression like clapping or dancing,[33] but we did not leave everything behind in breaking away from this strand of the Reformed tradition in the U.S. Protestant revival movement of the 1800s. Members of the Christian Church (Disciples of Christ) sit, stand, sing, and close eyes and bow heads during prayer but do not cross ourselves, process with a cross or Bible, utter set responses to scriptural reading or prayer, lift up the Bible, stand for the Gospel reading, kneel for prayer, raise arms in praise or prayer, and so forth, unless particular ministers and congregations decide to imitate other traditions, which Disciples are free to do. This is not to say we do not have body habits. Rather bodily gesture is purposively downplayed and almost completely ignored. People do not think it matters.

Hence, perhaps, my interest. What does it mean, for example, to bow to God and to each other as a repeated lifelong body practice for Benedictine monks at St. John's Abbey in Minnesota near the research center where I spent sabbatical time? Or, in my wandering religious life, now adrift from the Disciples congregation where my membership resides, what does it mean to process forward and hold out your hands to receive the Eucharist from a priest in a university Episcopalian congregation versus sitting and passing a communion plate, taking bread, and then serving your neighbor in my own tradition? Does it shape how and what one knows or even how one conceives of the divine, especially when one practices certain body motions over a lifetime?

One of the more striking findings when sociologist of religion Susan Ridgely Bales studied children's understanding of First Communion in three Roman Catholic congregations in North Carolina is the impact and centrality of sensory experience. To her surprise, her conversations with children in the weeks leading up to and following First Communion do not center on white dresses and parties, much less on the concepts adults thought they were teaching about transubstantiation or joining the Catholic Church universal, but on the "taste of Jesus' body."[34] Taste preoccupies children in the days before First Communion and in the hours after it. One child even explains her understanding of transubstantiation through taste, saying that the real bread tastes better than the practice bread.[35] Moreover, in their evolving theologies of taste and sensory movement, children experience their separation and membership not in terms of doctrinal belief but as centered on action. They are hypervigilant about movement; they want to teach "their bodies to move as the adults moved during the liturgy."[36] Thus, "things which seemingly had so little to do with their initiation into the Body of Christ," at least for adults, "in many ways, defined it" via their bodies.[37]

Adults are not all that different from children, although we like to think we are. We do not leave sensate experience and knowing behind, even though Western doctrinal and intellectual history implies that such detachment is possible and even admirable. Our own religious convictions are more deeply buried in our bodies and bodily practices than we realize. In *Worship as Theology*,[38] liturgical theologian Don Saliers observes that "bodily signs carry theological convictions at a deeper cultural level than do rationally expressed 'beliefs.'" In fact, "the more directly the body is involved, the more theological conflict there is likely to be between traditions." Protestants, for example, "may have more trouble with . . . genuflection than with more explicitly doctrinal differences with Roman Catholics."[39] In other words, Christian faith becomes deeply entangled right here, in the smallest of bodily movements with their multiple, highly elusive, seemingly negligible meanings as much as or more than in the big conceptual frameworks laboriously worked out over the centuries by church leaders, scholars, and denominations. This might surprise educators who put such stock in our words and ideas. This does not negate the value of systematic doctrinal reflection or formal learning. But the devil, so to speak, or the divine, is in the corporeal details.

In Western society, detachment from bodies is often considered a sign of intellectual and spiritual maturity and a mark of true science and morality. So, late twentieth-century experts on moral and faith development who have had significant influence on pastoral theology, such as Lawrence Kohlberg and James Fowler, agree with cognitive development theorists that concrete thinking denotes immaturity rather than, for example, an imaginative or philosophically astute way of seeing the world. Does this view, I wonder in my "show" chapter, "harbor unwarranted prejudice against material religion, bodies, children, laity, ritual, and the knowledge within physical acts of faith?"

A BIOLOGICAL ACCOUNT OF PSYCHOSOCIAL DEVELOPMENT

Having situated my thinking in a rough overview of a variety of disciplinary developments that support reflection on bodies and knowing, I want to make what may seem like an abrupt change of course and turn to the biological sciences to see what might be learned from paying greater attention to research on bodies and human development. Recently, when asked by Princeton's Center of Theological Inquiry (CTI) to participate in a symposium on Melvin Konner's book, *The Evolution of Childhood*, I agreed, knowing I would learn more about new research in biology but without realizing the magnitude of the task. Readers begin 530 million years ago (mya) with the "creature . . . close to the root of all vertebrates"[40]—a "simple tubelike structure" in which the "genetics and chemistry governing major CNS [central nervous system] domains was in place."[41] By chapter 5, we have progressed (only) to 18 mya when our most likely ancestor diverged from chimpanzees and bonobos, mammals with whom we share 96 percent of our DNA. There are still thirty chapters and several hundred pages to go (plus seven interludes, three transitions, a reprise, and an epilogue). In his four-part movement from phylogeny to ontogeny to social and cultural evolution, the Emory professor of anthropology and neurology nearly "explain[s] everything"—"Up to a point" as he says.[42]

My response to Konner centered on this phrase—*up to a point*—and invited consideration of tougher questions implicit in but not tackled by the book (and the book tackles big questions): How does one use this amassed knowledge and, more important, to what end? If "improving the human condition" is the "aim of scientific activity," as he himself indicates in his prologue, then these are important questions that cannot be fully answered within the realm of science alone, although Konner seems to assume that cumulative empirical discoveries in and of themselves can have a salutary affect (the more we know, the better we will behave, and, if we keep going, we will know more and more). In other words, my questions were less about the book's argument and more about the relationship of the sciences and the humanities and the nature of theological inquiry in CTI's new venture in interdisciplinary research in science and religion (a question that goes beyond his book).

I turn to Konner here, despite such moral and philosophical uncertainties, because he wants to make anthropologists, developmental psychologists, and perhaps even religion scholars more "cognizant of biology," to put it simply.[43] His book is partly a response to what he characterizes as the "anthropological veto"[44] to cross-cultural commonalities, something I encountered vividly at an interdisciplinary consultation on childhood studies several years ago when a prototypical anthropologist decried the essentialism of the psychologist across the table and insisted there are absolutely *no* universals. Konner insists, by contrast, that although understanding cultural variation remains central, anthropologists still need to elucidate the "enduring and biologically informative facts about our species."[45] In his view, more anthropologists in recent years are coming to see the truth of this position. His desire as an anthropologist to understand the "behavioral biology of psychosocial development"[46] is also relevant for scholars in religious and theological studies who have become so enamored with theories about cultural construction (of selves, illness, sexuality, motherhood, and lots more) that biology is often ignored.

Although I see problems with the weight given to evolutionary biology in what Konner calls his "deterministic interactionism" between biology and culture,[47] the book is not, as his phrase itself reflects, a flat assertion of the "laws and facts of biology."[48] He strives for a nuanced reading of the interconnections. Although he sees biology as setting the parameters within which culture operates (e.g., the "mind is bathed in culture because biology makes it so, and biology does that with clear guidelines"[49]), he also stresses, "nothing in biology is 100 percent." "If it's a biological law, it's fuzzy around the edges; all the rules are probabilities."[50] This does not prevent him or others from drawing normative conclusions from the sweeping distillation of research in sociobiology, behavior genetics, brain studies, neural and neuroendocrine development, and the ethnology of primate and human societies. But it does allow him to compile data worth our consideration. I name here just a few illustrative findings that theologians might consider as we strive to understand human behavior, childhood, and practical knowledge.

As is commonly known, infant dependency among humans, unlike other animals, requires extraordinary care on the part of adults for an extended period of time. Konner offers further elucidation. In the final chapter of part I on the evolution of vertebrates and mammals, he traces increases in human brain size and cultural complexity over the last two million years. Compared to other primates and mammals, humans are distinctive in their prolonged rapid postbirth brain growth. Brain size more than doubles in volume during the first twelve postnatal months, and nearly doubles again in the next twelve months, suggesting that infant behavior in the first weeks after birth is "as much a kind of postnatal neuroembryology as a learning process"[51] or what he later labels "postnatal gestation."[52] In other words, "humans should be born about twelve months later than we are, in terms of brain growth rate."[53]

Our nine-month rather than the twenty-one-month gestation that would be optimal for the infant is a compromise made necessary by the disproportion between neonate head size and changes in female pelvic anatomy that accompanied upright posture. We see here an early instance of mother-offspring conflict that characterizes childrearing more broadly. That is, there is a weighing even at this point between maternal welfare and mortality and that of the infant, so "expulsion occurs at a time that is not ideal for the neonate," at a lower than optimal birth weight, but at a time that provides an obvious advantage for the mother.[54]

A similar tension arises around a development distinctive to mammals—infant crying. Crying is a "vital built-in survival mechanism," a "distress call" that was critical to mammalian emergence[55] and likely coevolved with lactation and maternal care as middle ear bones allowed mammals to hear sounds at a higher frequency than was audible by reptilian predators.[56] In human infants, the ability to emit a high-pitched noise designed to provoke a reaction actually forms a "developmental bridge" between immaturity at birth and the aptitude for attachment that does not develop until five months. The caregiver's route to ending crying through holding, rocking, nursing, and so forth tests dramatically the "best interest," if not the patience, resilience, and resourcefulness, of the caregiver.[57] So, crying, which comes at some irritation and cost to the parent, elicits nutrition, warmth, and protection from predation during a time when adults often find themselves less attracted or attached to an expressively limited neonate. Its pattern follows a cross-culturally valid inverted U-shaped curve that peaks at two to three months[58] and declines at about the same time that other distinctively human means for securing a response emerge, such as smiling and mutual gaze. Especially notable, in a study of 591 infants the pattern of shaken baby syndrome among adult caregivers followed the same inverted U-pattern of crying, peaking in the first few months and thus indicating a potential correlation between heightened crying and aggressive adult response.[59] Such knowledge, alongside findings that abuse is more likely to be perpetuated by non-genetically-related adult males than related kin, has obvious implications for prevention and care.

The bulk of part II on maturation looks at just these kinds of "relatively fixed sequences of psychosocial development, drawing on cross-cultural and cross population studies" and relating this data to "neural and neuroendocrine development"[60] Also of interest, Konner describes research on a notable "social bias" in infants that challenges the view of the neonate's "relative lack of social responsiveness" and leads Konner and some pediatricians to call the first weeks postpartum the "fourth trimester."[61] Supported by fairly advanced visual capacities at birth, a neonate can actually "follow a sketch of a face" nine minutes after birth. They prefer the mother's voice at a few hours, "look longer and differently at their mother's face" at forty-five hours, and by two or three weeks can "mimic two facial gestures—tongue protrusion and mouth opening."[62] Particularly fascinating are studies of mirror neuron development that make imitation possible. A region in the lateral frontal cortex becomes active in monkeys and humans watching others perform actions. These neurons also fire when doing the action. In fact, it may be necessary to "mirror action (at the premotor level) to understand it."[63] As Konner concludes, "It is likely that both the phylogeny and ontogeny of intersubjectivity begin with the ability to interpret the actions of others through our own incipient action or preparedness for action, a less purely cognitive but more realistic view of intersubjectivity."[64]

Such findings on the human ability to grasp the intentions and mind of the other person are relevant not only for those who want to understand human development but also for those interested in practical

knowledge and embodied knowing. They correspond to more recent research that appeared after Konner's book confirming that the use of Bo-
tox to erase facial wrinkles not only impedes the expression of emotion
but its comprehension. That is, "people comprehend emotional language
in part by involuntarily simulating emotions with their facial nerves and
muscles."[65] The inability to replicate the emotion physically impedes
ability to understand it.

In part III on socialization, Konner reviews research on the impact of
early social experience, moving through studies of rodents, monkeys,
and humans on the effects of early handling, stress, stimulation, social
deprivation, isolation, and separation from mothers. With Harlow's monkeys, for example, "numerous efforts at rehabilitating the most deprived
monkeys failed or fell short." At the same time, studies of deprived children reveal "resilience even in severe deprivation."[66] The brain has the
capacity to recover "significantly from either biological or psychosocial
trauma."[67] In studies of rat pups, some changes caused by disruption in
care "persist into adulthood" and, particularly significant, may actually
be "passed on to offspring genetically," indicating, "maternal care can
reach into the genome of the young." This finding has "implications we
have barely begun to understand."[68] Intriguing research on such "epige-
netics" has continued since Konner's book publication, suggesting that
environmental effects can be passed on to progeny not just through the
mother in utero but also through the male genome.[69] So biology and
culture are in real interactional flux.

Equally informative and simultaneously inconclusive are the many
studies of childrearing and new findings on the significant evolutionary
role of *allocare* or caregivers related to the mother. Konner argues that
"there is no human society in which males have primary or even equal
responsibility for the care of offspring,"[70] even though some contemporary societies test the limits here. At the same time, research reveals the
extent to which humans are "cooperative breeders." That is, mothers
predominate in infant care but nonmaternal care by men, children,
grandmothers, and extended family networks is substantial. Among
hunter-gatherers, infants still spend the majority of their time in closest
proximity to their maternal caregiver, but mothers are rarely alone with a
crying child.[71] A survey of extended family helping in vertebrates, mammals, hunter-gatherers, and humans confirms that cooperative breeding
"has probably made a difference between us and our last common ancestor" in terms of evolutionary and reproductive success.[72]

So, in contrast to former anthropological and psychodynamic views,
comparative studies with nonhuman species reveals that "we can no
longer believe . . . there is one basic relationship—that with the mother—
from which all others are derived."[73] High levels of allocare also allow
for patterns typical of hunter-gatherers and even intermediate-level societies but difficult in industrial societies of high indulgence, continuous

physical contact, frequent nursing, close sleeping distance, late weaning, and regular nonphysical interactions (visual, vocal). Several other findings are of related interest: Only female humans "live for decades beyond their reproductive years,"[74] affording a unique place for grandmothers who often play a key role in fostering the welfare of offspring; among males in other species, such as Mongolian gerbils, lower testosterone levels are related to increased time spent delivering allocare;[75] humans are unique in having an extended period of slow growth between five to seven years old and puberty, a period when massive enculturation occurs and children begin caring for younger children; and a study of children in Kenya where boys were assigned chores typically given to girls indicates changed behavior. In particular, "boys who did a lot of baby tending showed very little aggression."[76]

This is just a small list, covering a fraction of the book's findings and obviously shaped by my own interests in understanding practical knowledge and promoting shared responsibility and greater male involvement in childcare—all of which I am more than happy to see Konner affirm "scientifically" as a necessity of evolution! And here's the rub. Other readers likely have their own lists of favorites based on their interests. Indeed, one major concern I have is Konner's neglect of interests that drive research. He seldom situates the research he reports and the interests that drive it historically, contextually, or politically. This leaves the impression that research stands on its own, even though all research presumes money, power, constituencies, alliances, funders, personal histories, biases, values, goals, and hopes. Even Freud is presented in a way few scholars in the humanities read him anymore, although Konner cannot help but acknowledge at least in passing the influence of Freud's Victorian context. Konner also overlooks the fine line between fact and value. "We cannot derive 'ought' from 'is,'" he says, "but we have to know what is."[77] I agree. But in the centuries since David Hume, we have learned that there is no simple separation of fact from value, knowledge from knowledge use, results of empirical study from application.

As I read Konner's book, I could not help but wonder how biological "laws and facts" might be co-opted around controversial issues—maternal nurture and paternal neglect; male violence; gender orientation. One of his more speculative questions is especially illustrative in this regard: "Could our marked departure" from early patterns of childrearing "be producing a discordance" comparable to our departure from the lifestyle but not the diet heavy in fat of our hunter-gatherer predecessors?[78] This must be important to him because he repeats the suggestion in his reprise.[79] However, are changes in parenting today as foreboding or comparable in their consequences as the hardening of the arteries that has become the leading cause of most deaths in Western countries? To be fair, earlier he has noted that "different patterns of child care and attachment are not necessarily better or worse for infants; they are strategies for maximizing reproductive success in different environments."[80] I am more receptive to facts and laws that broaden our empathy than those that heighten (punitive) judgment. At the same time, there are topics that Konner opens up where judgment seems warranted and is lacking, such as male violence and female genital cutting. Once again, this simply illustrates the complexity of trying to ferret out the facts and laws on which everything else rests. Even he has to admit that many human activities reveal the limits of such scientific reasoning, such as language development,[81] human adoption of other nonbiological children,[82] play,[83] grief,[84] and social learning,[85] to name just a few. Nonetheless, with each such complex behavior, there are still benefits to knowing its biological and evolutionary dynamics.

Conversation with Konner made clear to me that quite different philosophies of mind shape science and the humanities. Scholars in the humanities are indelibly shaped by epistemologies that question the idea of pure or objective science—two centuries of German and French hermeneutics (e.g., Hegel, Heidegger, Merleau-Ponty, Wittgenstein, Gadamer, Habermas), twentieth-century Foucaultian poststructuralism, and feminist and other liberationist theories. For all three intellectual streams, there is no uninterpreted fact. As Charles Taylor remarks, "Even in our theoretical stance to the world, we are agents."[86] We cannot "form disinterested representations any other way."[87] Nor can we find "basic empirical experiences on which we can ground everything else,"[88] an idea Konner assumes in the ordering of his book itself from biology at the bottom to culture at the top. In some ways, scientists and humanities scholars live in rather different thought worlds.

A FINAL NOTE ON THEOLOGY AND BODIES

To his credit, Sam Gill—the religious studies scholar with whom I began who illustrated the cultural use of the term *embodied*—does give the body its due later in his historical analysis of the current state of theological studies. Using the "robed, heavily garbed body" of both professor and cleric as paradigmatic, his chapter offers a vivid, even if a bit oversimplified, portrait of the typical Western view of the body. Our academic and liturgical robes reflect and enact, he suggests, "our deepest cultural and religious beliefs" about the body. "Such garments transform the human body into a cloth-covered pedestal on which is prominently displayed the all-important head, the domain of mind and spirit."[89] Everything else from the neck down is under suspicion and so "its articulation, its sexuality, its fleshiness, is to be covered, suppressed, denied."[90] Similarly, academic institutions themselves discipline the body to "'sit still and pay attention'" (one hears Foucault here, but he goes unmentioned). "Educational architecture and furniture are designed to disembody" and "limit body mobility"[91] with desks lined up, bolted to the floor, and facing forward toward the teacher "thus establishing in the body a hierarchy of learning" and proclaiming the "utter uselessness of the body."[92] "Academic bodies are not natural bodies; they are bodies disciplined from their earliest days of school to privilege the head part and to develop agnosia with respect to everything from the mouth down."[93]

Indeed, we might speculate that part of the thrall of intellectualism is the relief from entanglement with bodies. The "monological subject" of the modern scientific mindset, to borrow Taylor's term,[94] still predominates. In this view, the "mind" operates independently of body and other people. The hubris of the modern mind sustains a certain disdain for our mammalian bodies and the knowledge gained through them. So, centuries after Greek Platonic thought shaped early religious history, basic perceptions of bodies remain relatively unchanged. The physical world, like the body, is still "a place of transit, a temporary and dangerous place to be overcome and transcended."[95]

Gill's portrait is a little overdrawn and presents as monolithic realities that have more than one meaning. But he still captures a problem in religion with bodies. His critique of two renowned scholars in the 1960s and 1980s, Mircea Eliade and Jonathan Smith, is telling. Eliade grounds his highly influential theory of religion, which Smith later refutes, in aboriginal examples that neither one witnessed. That is, they never actually went to Central Australia to study aborigines. Instead, they reconstruct aboriginal life entirely from textual sources. "The physical bodied existence of aborigines is of no concern to either scholar. Aborigines exist as texts, writing, examples, not as bodied people."[96] "Rather, both considered the texts, even in their opacity, even in their disembodying their subjects, completely sufficient."[97]

Willie Jennings, theological scholar at Duke Divinity School, might consider this an inevitable consequence of a twentieth-century European-American Christianity shaped by a four-century history of conquest, enslavement, colonization, and displacement. His powerful portrait of this history, *The Christian Imagination*,[98] stands alongside the work of another Duke colleague, Mary McClintock Fulkerson's *Places of Redemption*,[99] as unusual in their close attention to bodies and place. I note them briefly here only to raise them up as intriguing exceptions to the rule Gill outlines about body negation. Both are painstaking in the care with which they engage bodies and place, Jennings through a meticulous reading of historical documents, Fulkerson by immersion in a congregation attempting inclusivity of race and ability. It is hard to read either book and not see religious and ecclesial life through different eyes, eyes more attuned to the physicality and materiality of practical theological construction. Theologians have begun to see and analyze the raced body, the disabled body, bodies whose physical attributes matter, bodies whose place in time and space make a difference.

As theologians continue to reengage bodies, we would do well to keep the physical body in mind. One avenue to doing so is to attend to research in the sciences and their investigation of physical bodies, both as a source of insight and as dialogue partners. And the sciences continue to need the hermeneutical and normative resources of the humanities to guide appropriate use of their burgeoning discoveries about human brains, hormones, genetics, and evolution. This chapter is a preliminary and suggestive effort in this direction, raising more leads than it can follow, hoping thereby to elicit interest and pave the way for further research. At the very least, we have witnessed the complexity and necessity of taking physicality, biology, evolution, and neurology more seriously.

NOTES

1. I am grateful to the *Journal of Pastoral Psychology* for permission to reprint an article that appeared a few years ago (volume 62, 2013, pp. 743–758). I am even more appreciative of all the authors who contributed chapters to this book and, most especially, Jennifer Baldwin for all the work she did to imagine and then create a volume that addresses so well the role of physicality and sensory knowledge in the construction of theology and the practice of faith. The chapters that follow go a long way to correct a problem I recognize—neglect and inattention to real bodies. They demonstrate the value of taking physical embodiment more seriously in our exploration and understanding of belief and religious practice.

2. Sam Gill, "Embodied Theology," in *Religious Studies, Theology, and the University: Conflicting Maps, Changing Terrain*, ed. by L. E. Cady and D. Brown (New York: State University of New York Press, 2002), 81–92.

3. Ibid., 83.

4. For example, he says he wants to "trace specific body histories to show how bodies are variously and differently constructed and, in turn, how such body histories correspond with and even determine how the world is encountered and seen as meaningful" (p. 84).

5. Mara Benjamin, "Jewish Thought, Feminist Ethics, and the Obligated Self," paper presented at Stanford University, February 28, 2011, 17; S. B. Hrdy, *Mother Nature: A History of Mothers, Infants, and Natural Selection* (New York: Pantheon Press, 2000); S. B. Hrdy, *Mothers and Others: The Evolutionary Origins of Mutual Understanding* (Cambridge: Harvard University Press, 2011).

6. S. Bordo, *Unbearable Weight: Feminism, Western Culture, and the Body*, 10th edition (Berkeley: University of California Press, 1993, 2003), 33.

7. M. A. May, *A Body Knows: A Theopoetics of Death and Resurrection* (New York: Continuum, 1995), 18; B. Morrill, ed., *Bodies of Worship: Explorations in Theory and Practice* (Collegeville: Liturgical Press, 1999), 12; Stephanie Paulsell, *Honoring the Body: Meditations on a Christian Practice* (Grand Rapids: Eerdmans, 2002), 16, 18.

8. http://en.wikipedia.org/wiki/Embodiment, consulted September 10, 2012.

9. James Nelson, *Embodiment: An Approach to Sexuality and Christian Theology* (Minneapolis: Augsburg Press, 1978).

10. He writes, "The question before us now is the positive significance of our physical bodies, and hence our sexual bodies, in Christian *theologizing*. The wording is significant. We are not simply asking what theology has to say *about* the body . . . from some superior vantage point by discarnate, disembodied spirits. We are asking what it means that we as body-selves . . . reflect upon—theologize about—that reality [of God]" (1978, p. 20, his emphasis).

11. Brian Turner, "Recent Developments in the Theory of the Body," in *The Body: Social Process and Cultural Theory*, ed. by M. Featherstone, M. Hepworth, & B. S. Turner (San Francisco: Sage, 1991), 11.

12. Pierre Bourdieu, *Distinction: A Social Critique of the Judgment of Taste* (Cambridge: Harvard University Press, 1984), 201.

13. Paul Stoller, *Sensuous Scholarship* (Philadelphia: University of Pennsylvania Press, 1997), xiv.

14. Ibid.

15. Judith Butler, *Gender Trouble: Feminism and the Subversion of Identity* (New York: Routledge, 1990).

16. Stoller, xv.

17. Bonnie Miller-McLemore, "Cognitive Neuroscience and the Question of Theological Method," *Journal of Pastoral Theology* 20(2) (2011): 64–92.

18. Shaun Gallager, *How the Body Shapes the Mind* (New York: Oxford University Press, 2005).

19. Raymond Gibbs, *Embodiment and Cognitive Science* (Cambridge: Cambridge University Press, 2005).

20. Bonnie Miller-McLemore, "Epistemology or Bust: Where are We Really Headed?" *Journal of Pastoral Theology* 2, (1992): 66–85; Bonnie Miller-McLemore, "Epistemology or Bust: A Maternal Feminist Knowledge of Knowing," *Journal of Religion* 72(2) (1992): 229–247; Bonnie Miller-McLemore, *Also a Mother: Work and Family as Theological Dilemma* (Nashville: Abingdon, 1994).

21. Similar books, such as Prokhovnik (1999), have continued to appear since the early 1990s.

22. Charles Taylor, *Philosophical Arguments* (Cambridge: Harvard University Press, 1995), 180.

23. Race, queer, and disability studies are among other prominent movements that have made significant contributions to this shift in attention to bodies. Much more could be said than space allows on the influence of such work on scholarship in religious and theological studies.

24. Jean Baker Miller, *Towards a New Psychology of Women* (Boston: Beacon Press, 1987), 24.

25. Maya R. Rivera, *Unsettling Bodies*, Fall 26.2 (2010): 119.

26. P. Fonagy and M. Target, "The Rooting of the Mind in the Body: New Links between Attachment Theory and Psychoanalytic Thought," *Journal of the American Psychoanalytic Association* 55 (2007): 411.

27. Naomi Goldenberg says the "body that Brown depicts is impossible to particularize, impossible to touch" (Goldenberg 1993, p. 33).

28. Ibid., 419.

29. M. Glaz & J. S. Moessner, eds., *Women in Travail and Transition: A New Pastoral Care* (Minneapolis: Fortress, 1991).

30. See Nancey Eisland, *The Disabled God: Toward a Liberatory Theology of Disability* (Nashville: Abingdon Press, 1994); Eizabeth Moltmann-Wendal, *I Am My Body: A Theology of Embodiment* (New York: Continuum, 1995); C. T. Gilkes, "The 'Loves' and 'Troubles' of African-American Women's Bodies," in Emilie Townes, ed., *A Troubling in My Soul: Womanist Perspectives on Evil and Suffering* (Orbis: Maryknoll, 1993); G. Ward, "On the Politics of Embodiment and the Mystery of All Flesh," in L. Isherwood and M. Althaus Reid, eds., *The Sexual Theologian: Essays on Sex, God, and Politics* (New York: T & T Clark, 2003); Anthony Pinn, "Sweaty Bodies in a Circle: Thoughts on the Subtle Dimensions of Black Religion as Protest," *Black Theology: An International Journal* 4(1) (2006): 11–26; Marcia Mount Shoop, *Let the Bones Dance: Embodiment and the Body of Christ* (Louisville: Westminster John Knox: 2006).

31. L. Wacquant, *Body and Soul: Notebooks of an Apprentice Boxer* (Oxford: Oxford University Press, 2004).

32. Dorothy Bass, *For Life Abundant: Practical Theology, Theological Education, and Christian Ministry* (Grand Rapids, MI: Eerdmans, 2008).

33. Shoop, 2.

34. S. R. Bales, *When I Was a Child: Children's Interpretations of First Communion* (Chapel Hill: University of North Caroline Press, 2005), 1.

35. Ibid., 101.

36. Ibid., 103.

37. Ibid., 6.

38. Don Saliers, *Worship as Theology: Foretaste of Glory Divine* (Nashville: Abingdon, 1994).

39. Ibid., 164.

40. Melvin Konner, *Evolution of Childhood: Relationships, Emotion, and Mind* (Cambridge: Harvard University Press, 2010), 78.

41. Ibid., 83.

42. Ibid., 732.

43. Ibid., 17.

44. Ibid., 600.

45. Ibid., 718.

46. Ibid., 5.

47. Ibid., 749.

48. Ibid., 4.

49. Ibid., 8.

50. Ibid., 77.

51. Ibid., 126.

52. Ibid., 129.

53. Ibid., 126.

54. Ibid., 129–130.

55. Ibid., 214.

56. Ibid., 382.

57. Ibid., 219.

58. Ibid., 217.

59. Ibid., 218.

60. Ibid., 207.

61. Ibid., 208.

62. Ibid., 212–213.

63. Ibid., 151–152.

64. Ibid., 152.

65. Havas, D. A., A. M. Glenberg, K. A. Gutowski, M. J. Lucarelli, and R. J. Davidson, "Cosmetic Use of Botulinum Toxin-A Affects Processing of Emotional Language." *Psychological Science* (2009), http://pss.sagepub.com/ content/21/7/895; accessed September 18, 2012.

66. Konner, 376.

67. Ibid., 380.

68. Ibid., 365.

69. J. Shulevitz, "Why Fathers Really Matter," *The New York Times*, September 18, 2012, http:// www.nytimes.com/2012/09/09/opinion/sunday/why-fathers-really-matter.html.

70. Konner, 470.

71. Ibid., 436.

72. Ibid., 431.

73. Ibid., 427.

74. Ibid., 442.

75. Ibid., 447.

76. Ibid., 678.

77. Ibid., 73.

78. Ibid., 623.

79. Ibid., 748.

80. Ibid., 73.

81. Ibid., 142.
82. Ibid., 447.
83. Ibid., 500.
84. Ibid., 545.
85. Ibid., 515.
86. Taylor, 11.
87. Ibid.
88. Ibid., 167.
89. Gill, 89.
90. Ibid., 81.
91. Ibid., 88.
92. Ibid., 89.
93. Ibid.
94. Taylor, 169.
95. Gill, 85–86.
96. Ibid., 90.
97. Ibid., 91.
98. W. J. Jennings, *The Christian Imagination: Theology and the Origins of Race* (New Haven: Yale University Press, 2010).
99. Mary Fulkerson, *Places of Redemption: Theology for a Worldly Church* (New York: Oxford University Press, 2007).

REFERENCES

Bales, S. R. *When I was a Child: Children's Interpretations of First Communion.* Chapel Hill: University of North Carolina Press, 2005.
Bass, Dorothy. *For Life Abundant: Practical Theology, Theological Education, and Christian Ministry.* Grand Rapids: Eerdmans, 2008.
Benjamin, M. "Jewish Thought, Feminist Ethics, and the Obligated Self." Paper presented at Stanford University, February 28, 2011.
Bordo, Susan. *Unbearable Weight: Feminism, Western Culture, and the Body.* Berkeley: University of California Press, 2003.
Bourdieu, Pierre. *Distinction: A Social Critique of the Judgment of Taste.* Translated by Richard Nice. Cambridge, MA: Harvard University Press, 1984.
Brown, N. O. *Life Against Death: The Psychoanalytical Meaning of History.* New York: Vintage Books, 1959.
Butler, Judith. *Gender Trouble: Feminism and the Subversion of Identity.* New York: Routledge, 1990.
de Certeau, M. *The Practice of Everyday Life.* Translated by Steven Rendall. Berkeley: University of California Press, 1984.
Eisland, Nancey. *The Disabled God: Toward a Liberatory Theology of Disability.* Nashville: Abingdon, 1994.
Farley, E. Theologia: *The Fragmentation and Unity of Theological Education.* Philadelphia: Fortress, 1983.
Fonagy, P., & Target, M. "The Rooting of the Mind in the Body: New Links Between Attachment Theory and Psychoanalytic Thought." *Journal of the American Psychoanalytic Association* 55 (2007): 411–456.
Fowler, James. W. *Stages of Faith: The Psychology of Human Development and the Quest for Meaning.* San Francisco: Harper & Row, 1981.
Fulkerson, M. M. *Places of Redemption: Theology for a Worldly Church.* New York: Oxford University Press, 2007.
Gallager, S. *How the Body Shapes the Mind.* New York: Oxford University Press, 2005.
Gibbs, R. W. *Embodiment and Cognitive Science.* Cambridge: Cambridge University Press, 2006.

Gilkes, C. T. "The 'Loves' and 'Troubles' of African-American Women's Bodies." In *A Troubling in My Soul: Womanist Perspectives on Evil and Suffering*. Edited by E. Townes. Orbis: Maryknoll, 1993.

Gill, S. "Embodied Theology." In *Religious Studies, Theology, and the University: Conflicting Maps, Changing Terrain*. Edited by L. E. Cady & D. Brown. New York: State University of New York Press, 2002.

Glaz, M., & Moessner, J. S., eds. *Women in Travail and Transition: A New Pastoral Care*. Minneapolis: Fortress Press, 1991.

Goldenberg, N. *Resurrecting the Body: Feminism, Religion, and Psychoanalysis*. New York: Crossroad, 1993.

Green, A. "Has Sexuality Anything to Do with Psychoanalysis?" *International Journal of Psychoanalysis* 76, (1995): 871–883.

Harding, Sandra. *The Science Question in Feminism*. Ithaca, NY: Cornell University Press, 1986.

Harding, Sandra. *Whose Science? Whose Knowledge? Thinking about Women's Lives*. Ithaca, NY: Cornell University Press, 1991.

Havas, D. A., A. M. Glenberg, K. A. Gutowski, M. J. Lucarelli, and R. J. Davidson. "Cosmetic Use of Botulinum Toxin-A Affects Processing of Emotional Language." *PsychologicalScience*. 2009.

Hrdy, S. B. *Mother Nature: A History of Mothers, Infants, and Natural Selection*. New York: Pantheon, 2000.

Hrdy, S. B. *Mothers and Others: The Evolutionary Origins of Mutual Understanding*. Cambridge, MA: Harvard University Press, 2011.

Jennings, W. J. *The Christian Imagination: Theology and the Origins of Race*. New Haven, CT: Yale University Press, 2010.

Keller, E. F. *Reflections on Gender and Science*. New Haven, CT: Yale University Press, 1985.

Kohlberg, Lawrence. *The Philosophy of Moral Development: Moral Stages and the Idea of Justice*. San Francisco: Harper & Row, 1981.

Konner, M. *Evolution of Childhood: Relationships, Emotion, and Mind*. Cambridge, MA: Harvard University Press, 2010.

LaMothe, K. L. "What Bodies Know about Religion and the Study of it." *Journal of the American Academy of Religion* 76(3) (2008): 573–601.

MacIntyre, A. *After Virtue*. Notre Dame University of Notre Dame Press, 1981.

May, M. A. *A Body Knows: A Theopoetics of Death and Resurrection*. New York: Continuum, 1995.

Miller, J. B. *Toward a New Psychology of Women*. Boston: Beacon, 1976.

Miller-McLemore, B. J. "Epistemology or Bust: Where are We Really Headed?" *Journal of Pastoral Theology* 2 (1992): 66–85.

Miller-McLemore, B. J. *Also a Mother: Work and Family as Theological Dilemma*. Nashville: Abingdon, 1994.

Miller-McLemore, B. J. "Cognitive Neuroscience and the Question of Theological Method. *Journal of Pastoral Theology* 20(2) (2011): 64–92.

Moltmann-Wendal, E. *I Am My Body: A Theology of Embodiment*. New York: Continuum, 1995.

Morrill, B. ed. *Bodies of Worship: Explorations in Theory and Practice*. Collegeville: Liturgical Press, 1999.

Nelson, James. B. *Embodiment: An Approach to Sexuality and Christian Theology*. Minneapolis: Augsburg, 1978.

Paulsell, Stephanie. *Honoring the Body: Meditations on a Christian Practice*. San Francisco: Jossey-Bass, 2002.

Pinn, Anthony B. "Sweaty Bodies in a Circle: Thoughts on the Subtle Dimensions of Black Religion as Protest." *Black Theology: An International Journal* 4(1), (2006): 11–26.

Prokhovnik, R. *Rational woman: A Feminist Critique of Dichotomy*. London: Routledge, 1999.

Rivera, M. R. *Unsettling Bodies*. Fall, 26(2) (2010): 119–123.

Ruddick, S. *Maternal Thinking: Towards a Politics of Peace*. Boston: Beacon, 1989.

Saliers, Don E. *Worship as Theology: Foretaste of Glory Divine*. Nashville: Abingdon, 1994.

Shoop, Marcia W. M. *Let the Bones Dance: Embodiment and the Body of Christ*. Louisville: Westminster John Knox, 2010.

Shulevitz, J. "Why Fathers Really Matter." The *New York Times*, September 18, 2012, http:// www.nytimes.com/2012/09/09/opinion/sunday/why-fathers-really-matter.html.

Stein, R. "The Enigmatic Dimensions of Sexual Experience: The "Otherness" of Sexuality and Primal Seduction." *Psychoanalytic Quarterly* 67 (1998): 594–625.

Stein, R. "The Poignant, the Excessive, and the Enigmatic in Sexuality." *International Journal of Psychoanalysis* 79 (1998): 253–268.

Stoller, P. *Sensuous Scholarship*. Philadelphia: University of Pennsylvania Press, 1997.

Taylor, C. *Philosophical Arguments*. Cambridge, MA: Harvard University Press, 1995.

Turner, B. S. "Recent Developments in the Theory of the Body." In *The Body: Social Process and Cultural Theory*. Edited by M. Featherstone, M. Hepworth, & B. S. Turner. San Francisco: Sage, 1991.

Underwood, R. L. "Hope in the Face of Chronic Pain and Mortality." *Pastoral Psychology* 58(5–6) (2009): 655–665.

Wacquant, L. *Body and Soul: Notebooks of an Apprentice Boxer*. Oxford University Press, 2004.

Ward, G. "On the politics of embodiment and the mystery of all flesh." In *The Sexual Theologian: Essays on Sex, God, and Politics*. Edited by L. Isherwood & M. Althaus Reid. New York: T & T Clark, 2004.

Part I

Exploring the Senses

ONE

Smelling Remembrance

Martha S. Jacobi

The smell, as well as the sight and images, of the *Yad Vashem*, Israel's Holocaust memorial site, is deeply etched into my neural circuits: musty, close, and the scent of the eternal fire burning in the center of the square of niches in which the ashes of a tiny fraction of the victims were placed. The memorial museum was dimly lit—yet just before the exit back into the fresh air outside, there was, when I was there, a plaque bearing the words of the Ba'al Shem Tov, "Forgetfulness leads to exile, while memory is the secret of redemption." Outside, I walked through the Garden of the Righteous, and smelled the trees planted in remembrance of those who died helping to save Europe's Jews. Never again would I forget the difference between the smell of death and the smell of life.

In an oddly familiar way, the Babylonian Talmud, echoing the prophet Isaiah, embraces this profound and primitive way of "knowing" by smelling as sacred, as it reports an ancient Sanhedrin ruling, that "In the case of the Messiah it is written that he smells a [person] and judges."[1] And so I cannot help but wonder—was that how Jesus knew who would betray him, there at the table that last night, in the midst of the aromatic bread and wine, smelling, eating, and drinking . . . *"in remembrance . . . "* as they had done so many times before.

SMELL AND REMEMBRANCE

"Mmmmm . . . . That smells good!" What comes to mind? Freshly baked bread? A morning cup of coffee? Earth and air after a soaking rain? A just-delivered bouquet of red roses? Burning candles and incense? Maybe. Or maybe not. Either way, the sense of smell is intimate and direct. It is, in fact, the sense most linked with emotions and with memory, with life and with death. For one person, the smell of flowers may associate to the joy of a wedding or Easter, for another, the association may be to the sadness of profound loss or a funeral. To one, the lingering scent of incense in the sanctuary evokes a sense of safety and/or holy mystery; to another, it activates the full-body panic of an inability to breath; to yet another, it is just a scent in the air until it is no longer noticed. Smell and remembrance go together.

SMELLING . . .

Technically known as olfaction, the human sense of smell eludes precise description. The sense of smell is a sense full of paradox. Awareness of scent can attract us to something or lead us to avoid it. We may respond to our unique perceptions of scent with pleasure, disgust, or neutrality. Sometimes we will perceive a scent to be familiar, yet remain unable to recognize or name it. Other times, awareness of a scent will evoke within us a feeling of curiosity or interest. But most of the time, we notice a new scent-in-the-air only until we become habituated to it, and then our brains move on by ignoring it and/or noticing another one—and most often this process happens outside of our conscious awareness. As every dog or cat owner knows well, scents are everywhere. Scents are in the air we breathe. The *sense* of smell, however, happens in the brain.

Olfaction is a central part of the human brain-body system for detecting and assessing danger and/or safety, yet its perceived role in that system is often marginalized in favor of vision, hearing, and touch. In the West, from Plato and Aristotle forward, olfaction has typically been labeled as an "animal sense," and until late in the twentieth century the sense of smell received little scholarly or popular attention.[2] Yet this evaluation of the status of olfaction is far from universal with regard to either time or place. Cultural and sensory anthropologists regularly observe that different cultures attend to, combine, and value the disparate sense perceptions in various ways, creating what are called "sense ratios."[3,4] Walter Ong refers to this phenomenon as "the shifting sensorium."[5] Theological and sensory anthropologist Ian Ritchie notes that smell is both "a means of knowing and . . . a metaphor for knowledge."[6] Naturalist Diane Ackerman describes olfaction as "the mute sense,"[7] a sense without words. We experience it directly, she observes, but can only describe the experience with metaphors, the descriptions of other odors, or by referring to another sensory perception, for example, textures determined by touch. Consider it: try to describe the smell wax-polished pews, or the difference in the sanctuary when the carpet has been replaced!

The distinctive nature of olfaction is even more apparent in its physiology. It is the only sense that is dependent on another bodily function, that of breathing. To breathe is to smell, Ackerman reminds us. From our first breath at birth to the last respiration of dying, we are smelling—something—and responding to it.[8] This is a lot of work for the cells of the organs related to breath and smell! To keep up with the challenge, the olfactory neurons replace themselves every twenty-eight to thirty days.[9] When we breathe in, the molecules of what we call "odors" rise up to the top of the nose, and travel from there to the olfactory mucous membrane, with its millions of sensory receptor cells. These receptor cells send signals to and through the olfactory bulb and from there, via the olfactory nerve, directly into the limbic system of the brain. It is in the limbic system that thick and deep neural associations are formed, and rapid assessments of danger or safety are made. Only then does neocortical, "top brain," conscious awareness of the scent emerge in the form of a recollection, the noticing of a felt sense in the body, or a perception of a shift in emotional feeling.[10] What this means is that the olfaction system processes the chemical composition of respirated air (and/or other substances) integratively with other sensory processing systems. In doing so, the complete sensory processing system signals relevant parts of the brain to develop neural networks for recognition of whatever we inhale—in particular places and at particular times. This subcortical, neurochemical brain activity is as spontaneous and organic as breathing itself. The olfactory system thus interacts with the other externally and internally activated sensory systems (sight, sound, touch, taste, interoception, and proprioception) as part of the nonconscious, nearly instantaneous neuroceptive and orienting processes occurring in the deepest structures of the brain[11] as they respond to any perception of newness or difference in the external environment.[12]

Olfaction is, however, a penultimate and imperfect system, and especially so in cultures in which smell holds a low position in the sense ratio. Some toxic or otherwise dangerous vapors, such as natural gas and carbon monoxide, are undetectable to human olfaction, so the limbic system's "danger alarm" (the amygdala) fails to signal any need or impetus for action. For people with food allergies, sometimes the odor of an allergen mismatches with the interoceptive experience of inhaled chemical sensitivity and/or ingested physical toxicity. This is also true of the various plants that are known to be toxic to human beings. Although foods, plants, and berries may be experienced as having a pleasing odor, consumption of some of them could prove fatal, or at the very least, unpleasant.

Conversely, we can experience chemical irritations and/or aversive physical and emotional responses from inhaling vapors related to a substance that may be quite benign, and sometimes just from recollecting having previously done so. (Think for a moment or two of peeling and dicing onions or hot peppers — or when a dog has just had a close encounter with a skunk — and see what happens!) When this occurs, the brain-body's internal sensory systems may become hyperactivated and overwhelmed, leading to a less-than-accurate neuroceptive process and assessment of the actual degree of bodily threat related to that particular vapor.

Additionally, respiratory infections (even common colds), blocked nasal passages, brain and nerve damage, numerous illnesses (such as Parkinson's, schizophrenia, and dementia), aging, and even some medications can result in a temporary or permanent loss of smell, known as anosmia. Anosmia is often accompanied by a loss of taste. Though not usually considered serious in itself, anosmia may contribute to unintentional weight loss and symptoms of depression, especially those focused around loss of interest and enjoyment in eating, social activities, loss of meaning, and a sense of spiritual malaise.[13]

Regardless of where it is placed in the sense-ratio, olfaction is of profound significance for how we live, and for how we live healthfully — and faithfully. With every breath, what we smell intimately links the brain-body system with memory, mood, and meaning.

OLFACTION AND MEMORY

There are two basic types of memory systems in the human brain-body system, often referred to as the *explicit* and *implicit* memory systems. The *explicit* memory system is what we commonly refer to as memory: the facts we know or can easily recollect, and the stories and narratives that we can, and do, tell about ourselves, others, and the world around us. The explicit memory system necessarily involves the "top-brain," the neocortex, in order to give sequential ordering, language, and meaning to our experiences. By contrast, the *implicit* memory system, as the name suggests, works behind the scenes, driven by the subcortical structures of the limbic system and brain stem. Emotional and physical memories are held as neural networks within these deep, nonconscious structures of the brain. The implicit memory system helps our brain-bodies "know what to do" in activities critical to survival, in ordinary daily living, and in other learned activities, such as walking, singing, dancing, lighting a candle, playing an instrument, riding a bicycle, or driving a car.

Both the explicit and the implicit memory systems, however, are rooted in the subcortical structures of the brain, the limbic system, and brainstem. In a well-functioning brain-body system, the subcortical activity links and flows smoothly up from there to the areas of the neocortex relevant for movement, reasoning, language, and imagination. Because the molecules of odor pass quickly and directly into the particular limbic structures that they do, the amygdala and the hippocampus, they become directly and indirectly associated with *both* explicit and implicit memory. In other words, the sense of smell leads to rapid and long-lasting associations (memories) with specific people, places, things, and events, and with the bodily sensations that we experience and have come to label as feelings, emotions, and/or moods.

This associational property of olfaction is strong and bidirectional. For example, when remembering a beautiful day at the beach, you might experience the "sense memory" of the smell of salty, moist air, or the smell of pine trees and dirt when remembering a walk in a park. When remembering a hot summer's day in a busy city, you might perceive the smells of the people or the garbage awaiting collection. It is common for firefighters, when remembering various calls, to smell the smoke from the scenes embedded within their memories.

Likewise, the smelling of odors in the environment has the power to bring up various memories from the past, positive and negative, that are associated with those smells. The smell of freshly cut grass is a legendary and familiar example of the associational quality of olfaction. The smell of certain woods or waxes can bring back memories of worship spaces as well as home furnishings. The smell of a perfume or cologne may revive the memory of a loved one. The smell of burning wood may bring up the memory of a campfire—or a house fire.

The associational property of olfaction with prior, and especially formative and/or unusual life experiences (both positive and negative) is clearly profound. The olfaction-related memory networks are among the earliest developed after birth, and in an undamaged olfactory system, they remain active until death. When adverse life events are incompletely processed, the smell of an odor related to the event is a potent activating mechanism for its implicit memory networks, resulting in responses ranging from an ephemeral, visceral felt sense of discomfort and emotional dis-ease, to a post-traumatic sensory re-living (flashback) of the event. The latter response has been a common experience among first-responders, relief workers, and residents and employees in lower Manhattan after the events of September 11, 2001.[14]

And yet, those same deep, long-lasting, implicit olfactory memory networks also have the power to bring the emotional valence of past positive experiences and relationships into the present. The common habit of keeping, holding, and smelling the garment of a loved one who has died is well known for its paradoxical evoking of relational memories and mood in the processing of grief. At the beginning of life, young children are notorious (at least to their parents) for rejecting blankets and stuffed animals offered as soothing "replacements" for those that have been lost or are unavailable—even if they appear identical—because the replacements "don't smell right." Only the *real* cuddly will do, transitional and representational object that it has become for the child, and s/he will know it when s/he smells it—and it better not have been washed!

For both children and adults, olfaction-in-the-present consists of chemical interactions and neurochemical responses that may or may not yet have developed neural networks for associational memory, explicit or implicit. Olfaction, thus, affects mood: to smell is to feel, as well as to breathe and to remember.

OLFACTION AND MOOD

From early childhood on, as was alluded to above, intentional experience with "how things smell" is a part of the way that we explore and relate to and with our immediate environment. Odors surround us. Those that are new and different catch our attention . . . then fade away as others take their place. Odors that are familiar may bring a smile or a grimace to our faces. The immediacy of olfaction in daily life shapes how we perceive ourselves and our world. The chemosensory responses that we experience may be pleasant or distasteful—and they may shift the mood-related processes in our brains, for better or for ill.

Intentional smelling is a feature of inhalant use in that certain vapors (associated with particular odors) are known to be physiology- and mood-altering. Bring to remembrance, for example, the smell and associated effects of eucalyptus, or peppermint—or *Vicks*. Then do the same for tobacco, or marijuana, glue, or (depending on your age!) freshly printed mimeograph ink, and school paste. In each of these instances the odors related to the vapors of certain substances have both chemical and memory-associational components. In this way, the odor of the vapor may attach to the chemosensory response. The chemosensory response, in turn, may include a change in mood as well as a neuroceptive memory association to the circumstances and/or environment in which the vapor is inhaled.

When the effect of the vapor is strongly pleasurable or numbing, the associated odor of the vapor connects with the neurophysiological mood altering effect of the vaporous substance, and the stage is set for potential inhalant misuse, abuse, and/or addiction. In this case, intentional smelling is "gone awry" and becomes confused with intentional inhaling of particular vapors *in order* to experience their effects. The chase of the mood-change effect overrides potential chemosensory irritation as well as recognition that a neurochemical dependence has begun.

Of greater relevance to this chapter, however, is intentional smelling "gone right," that is, the intentional inhalation of vapors, the intentional and discerning *smell* of their associated odors, and the role of smelled-inhaling in fostering healing and hope (positive mood) within the already-and-not-yet fullness of God's reign. Two such instances are considered here: 1—the direct effect of odor choices made in aromatherapy, and 2—the indirect effect of the intentional ritual use of incense in worship.[15]

Aromatherapy, the healing art and science of using scent—and there-fore the olfactory system—to alleviate suffering, cure various conditions, invoke the presence of deities, and/or mediate various kinds of spiritual experiences is indeed ancient, despite usually being considered today (at least by much of Western allopathic medicine) as a "complementary" or "alternative" approach to healing. Aromatherapy makes use of the essential oils derived from plants, trees, flowers, and herbs both through application on the skin for transdermal chemical response and/or energetic interaction, and from the release of the vapors of the oils into the environment. The latter may be strengthened or diffused with heat and circulation of the air.[16] Of course, where there are vapors to be inhaled or oils to be rubbed, there may also be odors to be smelled—and thus associated with the vapors, the oils, and their potential chemical effects.

Over millennia and across myriad cultures, particular plants and their scents became associated with the ability to bring relief to persons suffering from various particular physical maladies and emotional conditions. Although aromatherapy remains controversial within the allopathic medical community and among some pastoral caregivers, the tools of contemporary Western science are increasingly being employed to identify and validate the healing chemical interactions that may occur in the treatments. What seems unstudied and unclear, however, is the degree to which a positive relational attunement of the aromatherapy practitioner to the aromatherapy recipient (the "smeller") creates and/or enhances a positive, relational mood-association with the chemosensory effect of the particular odors used in the healing context, and vice versa.[17] Also unstudied, and not discussed in the literature of aromatherapy, is the degree to which subtle nonconscious brain-body to brain-body odor emanation and perception between the aromatherapist and her/his client may (or may not) impinge on the results of an aromatherapy intervention—or any other human (or human-divine) encounter.

Related to but distinct from aromatherapy is the use of incense in worship, a liturgical practice with equally deep roots, if with wide variation in practice, in the history of God's relationship with creation and in particular with God's people. The theology and history of this practice in Judaism and Christianity is rich indeed; of concern to the present chapter, however, is the olfactory experience of worshippers in the midst of the smoke and vapors of burning incense. For some, the properties of the vapors and/or the smoke are experienced as chemosensory irritants, and their physical experience becomes highly unpleasant, leading to the development of negative memory associations. For those without such adverse physical response, however, the liturgical use of incense, typically frankincense, may actually strengthen its pre-existing symbolic and spiritual associations.

In a recent study by a United States—Israeli team of researchers, the inhaled vapors of frankincense were discovered to be psychoactive. The resulting hypothesis of the researchers is that the olfactory experience of liturgical use of incense leads to a subjectively felt sense and emotional mood in which anxiety and depression are reduced, and feelings of warmth, calm, and peace are enhanced.[18] These findings, combined with the persistence and pervasiveness of the ritual/liturgical use of incense across religio-spiritual traditions, suggests the possibility of a positive chemosensory associational process related to incense (and other odors as well) that both mediates spiritual experiences and aids worshippers in remembering the texts, hymns, and rituals of their traditions.

OLFACTION AND MEANING

The interactional process of associational memory networks with freshly respirated chemicals of scent hints toward a theology of smell, toward the role of olfaction in lived religion as well as spiritual experience, and toward concerns of meaning in the context of smell. We are smelling-beings who can also be smelled by other smelling-beings. Yet olfaction is but one aspect of the human sensorium, and the sensorium is but one aspect of human embodiment. It is as fully human beings that we become, in Walter Brueggemann's schema and language,[19] "disoriented" from God, the world, and ourselves. Could it be that the sensorium's role, in which olfaction plays a crucial part in orienting and assessing physical danger/safety, in some way "mirrors" a deeper spiritual dynamic in the relationship between God and God's people? For what else is repentance than a reorienting of our embodied selves to God, the source of our life, our wholeness, our salvation? How then, might we "smell God" and live?

Smelling God! The very words seem to turn at least my Euro-descended American Lutheran theological imaginings and articulations inside out and upside down—*if* I forget either the deeply paradoxical nature of olfaction *or* the mystery of incarnation, of the Word made flesh in Jesus Christ. But the idea of "smelling God" suggests that there is something—someone—to be smelled, who can also smell me. "Smelling God," like all olfactory experience, is rich with imagery! The very idea of it shifts the sense ratio of any religio-spiritual experience away from the more describable senses of vision, hearing, touch, and even taste, to that which can only be articulated in terms of other senses, or in the language of metaphor, story, and imagination.

Sensory and theological anthropologist and Episcopal priest Ian Ritchie writes about collegial conversation and his direct experience of the primacy of olfaction in African religion in which, he reports, "one encounters 'Chief Sniffers' who sniff every participant at the entrance of the worship area in order to discern whether the person's intentions are good or evil."[20] Ritchie also reports that some Christian churches in Africa have incorporated an "Office of 'Chief Sniffer'" into their corporate life and worship assemblies.[21] With this powerful image in mind, Ritchie then turns his scholarly attention onto olfaction and scent within the biblical witness in a manner that is foundational to any consideration of theological meaning-making in relation to the sense of smell.

As noted toward the beginning of this chapter, Ritchie affirms "the role of smell as a means of knowing and as a metaphor of knowledge."[22] He traces and lifts up the power of Hebraic anthropomorphizing images *of* God and sensory experiences attributed *to* God. Ritchie notes that God's nose/nostrils are referenced seven times in the Hebrew Bible,[23] and that the Song of Songs sings openly and joyously of the scents of sexual love and union.[24] Citing the work of P. A. H. de Boer, Ritchie reminds his readers of the likelihood that "religions of the ancient Near East held that God or the gods had a fragrance, and . . . they thought of God as discerning through the senses of smell and taste just as much as through the oral and visual senses."[25]

But Ritchie's particular contribution lies in his understandings of the Hebrew text and pre-1900 English language translations of Isaiah 11.3 in which God's deliverer "'smells' in the fear of the Lord."[26] Ritchie observes a Reformation-era comfort with a higher valuation of olfaction in the sense ratio, and quotes John Calvin's commentary on Isaiah: "We ought to attend . . . to the metaphor in the verb *smell*, which means that Christ will be so shrewd that he will not need to learn from what he hears, or from what he sees; for by *smelling* alone he will perceive what would otherwise be unknown."[27] In other words, God's messiah will judge by smell, by the deeply embedded neurobiology of olfaction and its equally deeply incarnated associational and implicit memory.

Olfaction—whether human or divine—is thus an intimately relational sense. To smell is to know and remember deeply, intimately, honestly; to be smelled by God is to be known and remembered by God.

What, then, might happen today if olfaction's value in the sense ratio was greater in relation to embodied spirituality? A theological hermeneutic of olfaction rises by association . . .

. . . REMEMBRANCE (THE SCENT OF SACRED)

In Genesis 2 God breathes life into the earth creatures and makes of them living, *smelling*, and *smelly* beings. Thus anthropomorphized, God can smell them, and they can smell the scent of God. The divine act of creation is imbued with a scent through which both God and creation are intimately associated, intimately linked, in their respective innermost knowing. Throughout scripture, God *smells*—the odors of sacrifice, the fragrance of first fruits, the stench of injustice. God *remembers* God's own creative and liberating acts, as well as humanity's moments of faithfulness amidst the folly of disoriented forgetfulness. And God calls upon humanity, likewise, to *remember* the God who breathed life into them, the God who made them and sustained them. God calls upon humanity to *smell God,* and to *remember*.

In Jesus's incarnation the sensory metaphors merge with flesh and blood, with the very brain-body of the Word made flesh, living, dwelling, and *smelling* among us; exuding both human odor *and* the scent of God. Jesus smelled fish frying on an open fire, bread baking, desert sand, and fresh flowing water. Jesus smelled life: he smelled the odors of sweat and excrement. And Jesus smelled death: he smelled illness and decay, then the sweet spices laid out on bodies to cover the unmistakable stench of death. Jesus smelled the wine and unleavened bread of Passover, and he smelled the blood of the animals scarified at the Temple. Jesus smelled his own blood, his own sweat and excrement, his own imminent death, and the fear and grief of his mother and his friends.

Yet on the night before he died, Jesus took bread (freshly baked?), blessed it, broke it, and gave it for all gathered at table to eat. *"Do this [— smell this—] in remembrance of me."* And likewise with a cup of wine, fragrant, its scent associating it forever with Jesus, with his followers' relationships with one another and with God, with that moment, and every moment like it yet to come. It was the unmistakable *scent of sacred,* the scent of holy mystery, the scent of remembrance. And deep within it was, and is, the *Scent of God.*

A fanciful theological re-imagining? Perhaps. Yet when baby-smells (of all sorts!) co-mingle with the scents of water, oil, and candles in Baptism, God's people are *Sensing Sacred.* When the aroma of a loaf of bread and the bouquet of a cup of wine in Holy Communion become scent molecules processed by the olfactory system as well as the digestive system, God's people are *Sensing Sacred.* When God's people inhale the odors of those around them, at worship and on the street; when they attend to the distinctive odors of city and open country, of earth, stream, lake, and sea; when and wherever they *"smell remembrance"* of the creative and redeeming work of God in Jesus Christ, they are *Sensing Sacred.* In Ritchie's words, *"The Nose Knows."*[28] The nose knows and is known by God—even when human olfaction errs or fails. Even then, "the nose" knows and is known by God as neural networks reconfigure themselves and the sense ratio of the sensorium shifts its priorities with innermost knowledge that *Smelling Remembrance* is *Sensing Sacred.*

SMELLING REMEMBRANCE

It is worth noting that attending to any particular sense tends to shift its place within the sense ratio, at least for a time. This chapter thus concludes with a set of experiential exercises for engaging your own olfactory processes and religio-spiritual associations in contexts of corporate worship and in the course of daily living. Breathe, smell, and remember, even as you are smelled and remembered by the living God!

1. Let yourself become aware of a scent-memory that you *associate positively* with your religio-spiritual experience. Notice the felt sense of the scent-memory in your body; notice the emotional quality of the experience.
2. Let yourself become aware of a scent-memory that you *associate negatively* with your religio-spiritual experience. Notice the felt sense of the scent-memory in your body; notice the emotional quality of the experience. Then, let yourself become aware of a scent-memory that you *associate positively* with Spirit-presence, with God, or with a sense of grace. Notice the felt sense of this scent-memory in your body, notice the emotional quality of the experience. Notice the physical shift that takes place as you *smell remembrance* into your innermost being. Imagine God *smelling remembrance* of you in God's innermost being. Come back into the present and search for words to represent your unique experience.
3. Allow yourself to attend to your sense of smell, with intentionality, in worship, in your own personal religio-spiritual practice and/or devotion, as well as in daily life events. What do you notice? What associations come to mind in relation to what you smell? What associations, if any, are shifting as you attend to them differently? What happens when you *smell remembrance* of the *scent of Spirit* into your associations?

NOTES

1. *Sanhedrin* 93b, quoted in *The Talmud of Babylonia: American Translation*, trans. by J. Neusner (Chico, CA: Scholars Press, 1985), 110–11, cited in Ian D. Ritchie, "The Nose Knows: Bodily Knowing in Isaiah 11.3," *Journal for the Study of the Old Testament* 87 (2000), 66.
2. David Howes, ed., *The Varieties of Sensory Experience: A Sourcebook in the Anthropology of the Senses*, (Toronto: University of Toronto Press, 1991). The Isaiah text referenced is Isaiah 11:3.
3. Michael Lambek, "Foreword," in *The Varieties of Sensory Experience: A Sourcebook in the Anthropology of the Senses* (Toronto: University of Toronto Press, 1991), x.
4. Kenya J. Tuttle's "Have We Lost Our Taste? Caring for Black Bodies through Food," chapter 10 in the present volume, gives a compelling example of the power of selective, intentional, and cultural value shifts in the sense ratio, for good and for ill.
5. Walter J. Ong, "The Shifting Sensorium," in *The Varieties of Sensory Experience: A Sourcebook in the Anthropology of the Senses* (Toronto: University of Toronto Press, 1991), 25.
6. Ritchie, 59.
7. Diane Ackerman, *A Natural History of the Senses* (New York: Vintage Books, 1995), 5. Originally published New York: Random House, 1990.
8. Ibid., 6

9. Ibid., 10. See also Maria Lis-Balchin, *Aromatherapy Science: A Guide for Healthcare Professionals* (London/Chicago: Pharmaceutical Press, 2006), 60.

10. Lis-Balchin, 60.

11. These structures include the midbrain, periaqueductal gray area, and the insula. See Steven W. Porges, *The Polyvagal Theory: Neurophysiological Foundations of Emotions, Attachment, Communication, and Self-Regulation* (New York: W. W. Norton and Company, 2011). Porges coined the term "neuroception" to refer to the brain processes that determine whether a person, situation, and/or the external environment is safe, dangerous, or life-threatening (11).

12. Ibid.

13. Mayo Clinic. www.mayoclinic.org/symptoms/loss-of-smell/basics/causes/sym-20050804; www.mayoclinic.org/symptoms/loss-of-smell/basics/definition/sym-20050804 (both retrieved March 15, 2014).

14. Even fourteen years later, clients in my pastoral psychotherapy practice who are addressing post-traumatic stress symptoms related to 9/11 still report the smell of the devastated World Trade Center area as one of the most potent and symptom activators that they have experienced.

15. A more thorough treatment of aromatherapy and the use of incense in pastoral care, counseling, and liturgy is presented by Jennifer L. Baldwin in chapter 11 of the present volume: "Holy Transitional and Transcendent Smells: Aromatherapy as an Adjunctive Support for Trauma in Pastoral Care and Counseling."

16. Gregory A. Crawford, *The Medical Library Association Guide to Finding Out about Complementary and Alternative Medicine* (New York: Neal-Schuman Publishers, Inc., 2010).

17. Lis-Balchin, p. 72, raises the question of a placebo effect in aromatherapy. The question raised here regarding relational attunement and associational process in olfaction is my own.

18. Federation of American Societies for Experimental Biology (2008, May 20). Burning Incense Is Psychoactive: New Class Of Antidepressants Might Be Right Under Our Noses. *ScienceDaily*. Retrieved August 31, 2013, from http://www.sciencedaily.com/releases/2008/05/080520110415htm#.Twox2zy9vc.facebook

19. Walter Brueggemann, *Praying the Psalms* (Winona, MN: Saint Mary's Press, Christian Brothers Publications, 1986).

20. Ritchie, p. 64.

21. Ibid.

22. Ritchie, 61.

23. Ibid.

24. Ibid.

25. Ibid., 62 See also the cited work, P. A. H. deBoer, "An Aspect of Sacrifice: II. God's Fragrance," in *Studies in the Religion of Ancient Israel* (VTSup,23; Leiden: E.J. Brill, 1972), 37–43.

26. Ritchie, p. 68.

27. John Calvin, *Isaiah Commentary* (Edinburgh: Calvin Translation Society, 1850), p. 376, cited in Ritchie, p. 68.

28. Ritchie, p. 59.

REFERENCES

Ackerman, Diane. A Natural History of the Senses. New York: Vintage Books, 1995. Originally published New York: Random House, 1990.

Brueggemann, Walter. Praying the Psalms. Winona, MN: Saint Mary's Press, Christian Brothers Publications, 1986.

Calvin, John. Isaiah Commentary. Edinburgh: Calvin Translation Society, 1850. Cited in Ian D. Ritchie, "The Nose Knows: Bodily Knowing in Isaiah 11.3," in *Journal for the Study of the Old Testament* (2000): 59–73.

Crawford, Gregory A. *The Medical Library Association Guide to Finding Out About Complementary and Alternative Medicine*. New York: Neal-Schuman Publishers, Inc., 2010.

Federation of American Societies for Experimental Biology. "Burning Incense Is Psychoactive: New Class Of Antidepressants Might Be Right Under Our Noses." *ScienceDaily*, 2008, from http://www.sciencedaily.com/releases/2008/05/080520110415. Retrieved August 31, 2013.

Howes, David, ed. *The Varieties of Sensory Experience: A Sourcebook in the Anthropology of the Senses*. Toronto, Canada: University of Toronto Press, 1991.

Lambek, Michael. "Foreword." In *The Varieties of Sensory Experience: A Sourcebook in the Anthropology of the Senses*. Edited by David Howes. Toronto: University of Toronto Press, 1991, i-xi.

Lis-Balchin, Maria. Aromatherapy Science: A Guide for Healthcare Professionals. London/Chicago: Pharmaceutical Press, 2006.

Mayo Clinic. www.mayoclinic.org Accessed March 15, 2015.

Ong, Walter, J. "The Shifting Sensorium." In The Varieties of Sensory Experience: A Sourcebook in the Anthropology of the Senses. Edited by David Howes. Toronto: University of Toronto Press, 1991.

Porges, Steven W. The Polyvagal Theory: Neurophysiological Foundations of Emotions, Attachment, Communication, Self-Regulation. New York: W. W. Norton and Company, 2011.

Ritchie, Ian D. "The Nose Knows: Bodily Knowing in Isaiah 11.3." In Journal for the Study of the Old Testament 87, (2000).

TWO

Embodying Christ, Touching Others

Shirley S. Guider

TOUCH, THE LEAST OF THE SENSES?

Touch is powerful. I learned many years ago how powerful it can be. A young man had been admitted to the intensive care unit after being severely injured in an automobile accident. He was in a coma and, per hospital policy, every four hours a head-to-toe assessment was performed. The last assessment tests the Babinski reflex by running a blunt object up the outside of the bottom of the foot from heel toward the toes. A positive test (toes flaring) indicates the possibility of brain or spinal cord injury.[1] After performing the assessment, several of my colleagues and I got into the habit of tickling the bottom of his feet before covering them with a sheet. When he awoke from his coma, he told the staff that he knew he was not going to die. This was surprising; he had been severely injured and there were questions about whether he would survive. When asked how he knew he was not going to die, he said, "You wouldn't tickle the feet of a dying man." At some level the difference in the touch between the assessment and the tickling registered in his mind. He then interpreted the light, playful touch as a sign of hope and encouragement.

Some consider touch the least of the five senses. In fact, "a long tradition of Western philosophical reflection on the senses has identified touch as the lowest sense, the most animal, servile, and unconscious of the resources of the human sensorium."[2] I disagree. Rather, touch is an essential part of building relationships between human beings. A single touch can communicate love or hate, can bring with it pleasure or pain. We turn and embrace one another to share our joy, to provide comfort

41

when we are frightened or scared, to express our pain and sorrow. Touch or our failure to touch another also communicates what we feel about one another. We willingly embrace those to whom we feel close but tend to keep others at arm's length. The question of whom we touch, how often, and whom we fail to touch conveys important information about those relationships. The question a Christian should ask is, what do we communicate about the love of Christ when we refuse to touch the other? Who is "untouchable" to us? Those who had AIDS were "untouchable" until Princess Diana dared to embrace them. While one needs to be careful about one's motives when touching another, we also convey much about Christ's love and acceptance by our willingness to touch those deemed "untouchable" by society.

THE BIOLOGY OF TOUCH

Our skin is the largest organ of the body. The surface area of the skin has an enormous number of sensory receptors that can distinguish between hot, cold, touch, pressure, and pain. A piece of skin the size of a quarter (about one square inch) contains more than 3 million cells, 650 sweat glands, 77 feet of nerves with greater than one thousand nerve endings, and 20 feet of blood vessels.[3] Unlike our other senses (sight, smell, taste, and hearing) touch is not limited to one area of the body. Touch receptors exist wherever skin is, therefore the sensation of touch occurs over the entire body. The skin forms the boundary between the self and other, between an individual and the rest of the world. "More than any other sense, touch establishes our sentient border with the world."[4] Not only is skin the largest organ, but "the tactile system is the earliest sensory system to become functional in all species thus far studied—human, animal and bird."[5] Nearly all mammals respond to touch. Montague writes,

> The manner in which the young of all mammals snuggle up to and cuddle the body of the mother as well as the bodies of their siblings or of any other introduced animal strongly suggests that cutaneous stimulation is an important biological need, for both their physical and behavioral development. Almost every animal enjoys being stroked or otherwise having its skin pleasurably stimulated. Dogs appear to be insatiable in their appetite for stroking, cats will relish it and purr, as will innumerable other animals both domestic and wild, apparently enjoying the stroking at least as much as they do self-licking. The supreme note of confidence offered a human by a cat is to rub itself against your leg.[6]

The way we utilize the word "touch" in the English language reflects the importance of this sense. As Montague notes, we talk about how others either "rub us the wrong way," or "touch us deeply."[7] People have "abrasive" or "prickly" personalities and may need to be "handled with kid gloves" and "get under our skin."[8] Some individuals are "thin skinned" and oversensitive or easily "irritated."[9] When others behave irrationally, we say they are "out of touch with reality" or "have lost their grip."[10] Finally he writes, "a deeply felt emotional experience is described as 'touching.'"[11] We say of some people that they are "tactful," and of others that they are "tactless," that is, either one has or does not have a sense of what is fitting and proper in dealing with others.[12] Typing touch into the search engine on the website *Merriam-webster.com* elicits a long list of definitions using touch as a verb, noun, in verb phrases, or as idioms.[13] Touch, though, elicits more than a physical response. As Montague indicates, touch is perceived both physically and emotionally.

> Touching is defined as "the action, or an act, of feeling something with the hand, etc." The operative word is feeling. Although touch is not itself an emotion, its sensory elements induce those neural, glandular, muscular, and mental changes which in combination we call an emotion. Hence touch is not experienced as a simple physical modality, as sensation, but affectively, as emotion. When we speak of being touched, especially by some act of beauty or sympathy, it is the state of being emotionally moved that we wish to describe. And when we describe someone as being "touched to the quick," it is another kind of emotion that we have in mind.[14]

TOUCH: A BASIC HUMAN NEED

Research has shown that not only is touch one of our senses, it is a basic human need. Infants process most information through touch. As early as 1915, in a study of sensory-deprived orphans, researchers found that infants who were held and stroked thrived whereas those who were not were underweight and withdrawn.[15] In recent times, similar observations have been made about the children cared for in state-run institutions in Romania. Those who had been deprived of touch for long periods or only touched in order to change soiled linen "become depressed and apathetic, fail to gain weight, and, in extreme cases, die."[16] Not only is infant mortality high for those not held or cuddled, children who survive infancy in this environment exhibit many of the aberrant behaviors described in the literature: hyperactivity, disorganization, failure to thrive or attachment disorders.[17] Recognizing the need for touch, Phyllis Davis, among others, has expressed concern that the recent focus on sexual harassment in schools and workplaces has created a society where touch has become taboo, even in nursery and preschools. She warns, "The implications for children—our future—involve significant effects on their growth, development, and emotional well-being."[18]

In the 1950s, psychologist Harry Harlow experimented with rhesus monkeys and touch. In this well-known experiment on touch and nurture, infant monkeys were given the choice of a wire or terry cloth covered mother who dispensed nourishment. The young monkeys preferred the one covered in terry cloth. He then changed the experiment and only the wire surrogate dispensed milk. Even when the terry cloth covered surrogate did not dispense nourishment, the infant monkeys preferred to cling to them. He found that those who had the terry cloth mothers were better adjusted than those "raised" by the wire surrogates.[19]

TOUCH SHAPES OUR SOCIAL CONNECTIONS

Touch also shapes our social connections. "The power of touch lies in its capacity to establish relationships. Gestures of contact—handshake, kiss, or caress—define the nuances of our relationships, the subtle inflections of class, power, and familial bonds."[20] Touch communicates a human being's feelings toward and emotional connection to one another.[21] We also have the ability to convey many different emotions via a simple touch. Psychologist Matthew Hertenstein, in a 2009 study, showed that human beings can "decode emotions via touch alone."[22] The study attempted to show that human beings are able to decode the same emotions via touch alone as they can through voice and face. The researchers wondered whether the participants would be able "to communicate two classes of emotions via touch: (a) five emotions that have proven to be decoded in the face and voice in different cultures (anger, fear, happiness, sadness, and disgust), and (b) three prosocial emotions related to cooperation and altruism (love, gratitude, and sympathy)."[23] Even though we live in a touch-phobic society, he was able to find volunteers who attempted to communicate a list of emotions to a blindfolded stranger through touch alone. He affirmed his hypothesis that human beings can send emotions through touch alone. To Hertenstein's surprise eight emotions: anger, fear, disgust, love, gratitude, sympathy, happiness and sadness were communicated with an accuracy rate of 50 to 70 percent, an accuracy comparable to that of facial and vocal recognition.[24] It is difficult to lie with our touch. As Phyllis Davis writes,

> Touch is stronger than verbal or emotional contact. No other sense arouses us as touch does. It affects nearly everything we do. We've always known that; we just didn't know that it was biologically driven. If touch weren't so powerful, and didn't feel so darn good, there would be no human species, no parenthood, no survival. We touch and desire touch because it is our biological key to the door called "species survival."[25]

Despite all we know about the power and need for touch, in our society today we are often enjoined not to touch. Individuals in America go to great lengths not to touch one another, even accidently. Just watch the behavior of those in an elevator when it gets crowded. People jockey for position in order to avoid touching one another. In contrast to other cultures, most individuals in the United States prefer a personal space of at least eighteen inches. Americans generally do not hug or kiss another in greeting, unless the person is a relative or very close family friend. As an illustration, *The International Student Guide* has the following instructions in relating to Americans.

> The average personal distance varies from culture to culture. Americans tend to require more personal space than in other cultures. If you try to get too close to an American during your conversation, he or she will feel that you are "in their face" and will try to back away. Try to avoid physical contact while you are speaking, since this may lead to discomfort. *Touching is a bit too intimate for casual acquaintances. Don't put your arm around their shoulder, touch their face, or hold their hand.* Shaking hands when you initially meet or part is acceptable, but this is only momentary.[26]

The perception of others is that those in the United States are adverse to touch, except in a clearly defined set of circumstances. In fact Davis indicates that, in our society, we have relegated touch to five symbolic areas: rituals—handshakes, dancing, pats on the back; hostility—fighting discipline and contact sports; vicarious touching—we sit in front of television or go to a movie and watch others touch; professional touching—the intent of the person touching is to perform a service (e.g., a hairdresser, chiropractor, or massage therapist); and grooming—touching is performed under the guise of grooming the other. (People brush or stroke or push wayward hairs back into place. We straighten each other's collars and hems, tuck in blouses and skirts, pick cat hairs off clothing, and remove price tags for people.)[27]

More and more, those who live in America rely on verbal skills and less on touch and nonverbal communication. In 1989 Montague perhaps prophetically wrote,

> With our increasing sophistication and disengagement from each other, we have come to rely excessively on verbal communication, to the extent of virtually excluding the universe of nonverbal communication from our experience—to our great impoverishment. The language of the senses, in which all of us can be socialized, are capable of enlarging our appreciation and of deepening our understanding of each other and the world in which we live. Chief among these languages is touching. The communications we transmit through touch constitute the most powerful means of establishing human relationships, the foundation of experience.[28]

In our world today, with the ubiquitous presence of Facebook, Twitter, and e-mail we have come to rely more on words alone to communicate with one another. While this can be helpful for a quick connection, can we truly "touch" one another through these mediums? If you are hurting and you need someone to touch you, to provide comfort, to hold you when you grieve and in times of distress, can this be done via e-mail?

WHY ARE WE ADVERSE TO TOUCH?

Why do Americans regulate touch to symbolic areas? The move away from touch has deep roots in our Judeo-Christian narrative. The injunction not to touch occurs numerous times in the Bible. As an example, the woman, in replying to the serpent in the Garden of Eden says, "But God said, 'You shall not eat of the fruit of the tree that is in the middle of the garden, nor shall you touch it, or you shall die.'"[29] God, however, had only commanded that human beings not eat of the tree of knowledge of good and evil. The reality is that disobeying God by a deliberate action, eating that which was forbidden, is what spells death. The woman has taken God's caution about not eating of the tree one step farther, if you even touch the tree you will die. Now, a simple touch of the tree spells death for human beings in the mind of the woman. The equation touch equals death is taken a step farther in the book of Exodus. In Exodus 19:12 the Israelites are warned not to go up Mt. Sinai or even to touch the edge of the mountain. Anyone who touches it shall be put to death. A different twist on the dangers of touch can be found in Leviticus. The people are warned over and over not to touch that which is unclean: the carcass of unclean livestock, water that touches that which is unclean, a menstruating/bleeding woman. This sanction against touching that which is deemed "unclean" permeates American society.

Those who provide pastoral care have been taught that maintaining appropriate boundaries is an important aspect of this care. Some pastoral theologians teaching in seminaries have been trained in the psychodynamic, psychoanalytical school. Those who have been trained in this school of thought often embrace an understanding that touching a client is inappropriate in the therapeutic setting. Carmel Harrison et. al note that "the psychodynamic therapist believes that therapeutic transference would be exacerbated through touch; thus its exclusion was considered necessary to ensure psychoanalytical, boundaried and effective interventions."[30] This understanding of the danger of touch permeates the practice of pastoral care. Pamela Cooper-White, writing to pastors and pastoral counselors, recognizes that giving hugs in a parish setting is often an expected part of the role. However, she maintains that touch "never means just one thing"[31] and cautions both counselors and pastors to examine the underlying dynamics present in the relationship.[32] Karen McClintock, writing in response to sexual harassment in the church, recommends asking permission before one touches a parishioner. She notes that asking may seem awkward at first, but easily becomes the norm. She writes, "If the idea of turning down a hug is hard for you to imagine, try it a few times and see how it works. The harder it is to do, the more you will become aware of the pressure people feel when someone is crossing a physical or sexual boundary with them."[33]

We have been conditioned by both our culture and education in seminaries not to touch. What do we say pastorally and theologically when we fail to "reach out and touch someone?" Do we, both figuratively and literally, embrace those who are dying? We are, as Elaine Graham has written, embodied. As she notes, "The pastoral encounter itself is always necessarily and variously embodied: the touch, be it informal or as a ritual of anointing or healing; or the reassurance of eye contact, the one-to-one conversation."[34] Perhaps her understanding of embodiment can help define the ways in which touch can and should be used to convey the presence of Christ.

EMBODIMENT

Elaine Graham posits that embodiment is more than just a current fad that excites our passion; rather, it points us to the incarnational nature of all theology and all practice of pastoral care. She argues that "bodily practice is the agent and vehicle of divine disclosure; the faithful practices of the Body of Christ are 'sacraments' of suffering and redemption."[35] Because embodied practice and the incarnation of Jesus as male has been the means through which God has been revealed, she contends that feminist theory and politics have inherited an ambivalence toward the body. "'Liberal' feminists prefer to reclaim women's rationality and to strive to exhibit intellectual equality with men, regarding embodiment as a barrier to emancipation."[36] I agree with Graham, but would push this disregard of the body further. While many women may regard embodiment as a block to freedom or full equality with men, many men also disregard the embodied nature of our lives. If this were not so, people, both men and women, would take better care of their bodies and their environment. They would listen when the body screams to touch and be touched, to be embraced and to embrace. As much as we would wish to conceive of ourselves as composed primarily by our intellect, we are incarnate in the world just as Christ was. We long for intimacy, to be held in both the loving embrace of another as well as the caring arms of our gracious God.

The postmodern perspective and its claim about the particularity of life may be helpful here. Postmodernity asserts that each person is born into a particular time, place, space, class, country, etcetera. Thus, the incarnation of God as the second person of the Trinity took place in a particular time, two thousand years ago, in a particular place, in the man known as Jesus. No one, try as they might, can escape their embodied existence. In addition, the church describes itself as the body of Christ. Therefore, each Christian is called, through their baptism, to embody

Christ to the world.[37] As Graham notes, the mechanism of divine disclosure is through the body of Christ in its teaching, preaching—in word and in sacrament.[38]

Graham sounds a call for an embodied practice of care to start by listening to people's experience of embodiment and enjoins them to pay attention especially to those places where appearances and reality seem out of step.[39] She reminds us that those who give and receive pastoral care are constantly confronting the effects that illness and aging, as well as the effect that poverty, with its concomitant lack of proper nutrition and preventative care, have on our bodies and well-being.[40]

The heart of Christian faith, for Graham, is what was confessed as truth at Chalcedon that Jesus Christ is the Son of God, Emmanuel, God with us. The mystery of the incarnation: that our God chose to put aside God's divinity and share our human existence in the form of the person of Jesus is the foundation of Christian faith. As she notes,

> Christians acknowledge the reality of God's self-revelation in the form of a human life; but a practical theology that tells stories of embodiments can really examine what it might meant for God to be revealed in a human *body*, broken and suffering, whose resurrection proclaims that Love is stronger than death.[41]

Bodies, for Graham, are where "nature and culture, construction and agency"[42] meet. Our bodies are not simply receptacles for mind and soul, or as she writes "fleshly husks in which the 'real' self is trapped, nor simply the repositories or objects of cultural forces."[43] Rather, it is through our bodies that human beings exist, function, and have the capacity to act and affect the world in which we live. It is because we are embodied, incarnated in flesh and blood, that we have the ability not only to create relationships with one another but also to build human communities. In other words, our embodied interactions with one another create our human relationships and our social world, for good or ill.[44]

> A practical theology of the body/our bodies is therefore never merely the statement of principles; more the cultivation of the *habitus* of the body whereby the words of suffering and redemption may become flesh. If theological values have any substance, they will exist in primary form as bodily practices—clinical, liturgical, kerygmatic, prophetic—and only derivatively as doctrines and concepts.[45]

WE EMBODY CHRIST

In Lutheran circles, one speaks about the means of grace. This is defined as the time and place when we know that Christ, our Emmanuel, God with us, is present. One of the means of grace is the "mutual conversation and consolation of the brethren."[46] For me, this means that Christ is present through us when we provide care in Christ's name. Thus, when one assumes the role of caregiver one becomes, as one congregation noted in the bulletin, ministers of God. As one visits the sick and embraces them with loving care, our touch "transcends being simply an activity or gesture . . . it becomes a manifestation of ourselves."[47] I would add that not only is it a manifestation of ourselves but it is also sign of Christ's presence. When one visits the sick and feeds the hungry, one embodies the love of Christ to the other. Thus, as Phyllis Davis writes, "in touching each other with love, we are really touching God, and it is only when we are touching God that we are truly whole!"[48]

Rather than set firm boundaries that prohibit touch in our pastoral care, one needs to recognize that there are times when touch is needed to convey the presence of Christ in our lives. The model for touch is also present in the Bible in the pastoral care of Christ. Jesus willingly broke the boundaries of his time and touched those who were untouchable. The gospels abound with examples of how Jesus used touch to communicate God's love and care.

Every gospel has stories of Jesus touching those who were untouchable, unclean, or who were separated from God because of illness or disability. In the gospel of Matthew, immediately after delivering the Sermon on the Mount, Jesus is confronted by a leper, one deemed ritually unclean by the ordinances in Leviticus. Jesus reaches out his hand, touches him and he is made clean (Matthew 8:1–4). Later in the same chapter, Jesus touches the hand of a woman (Peter's mother-in-law) and her fever leaves her. In John, Jesus touches the eyes of the man born blind anointing them with a paste (John, chapter 9). Not only does Jesus touch this man, he spits on the ground and uses the mud created by this act combined with the physical touch of his hand as well as the waters of the pool of Siloam to give the man sight.[49] In Mark, one who is deaf and has a speech impediment is brought to Jesus. Jesus takes the man aside, touches him before putting his fingers in the man's ears and spitting then touching the man's tongue that he might hear and speak (Mark 7:32–35). In Luke he sees a funeral procession where a young man, the widowed mother's only son, has died. He touches the bier (again something that has been designated as unclean because it touches a dead body), commands the young man to rise, and, to the surprise of all, he does (Luke 7:9–19). *The Interpreters Dictionary of the Bible* states that the verb touch as used in these instances "implies a touch which tends to hold and even sometimes to cling."[50] Thus the author notes that Jesus "really held the leper . . . he gripped the fevered hand of Peter's mother-in-law."[51] These are not casual touches; rather Jesus reaches out and holds those who come to him.

Not only did Jesus touch others in care and healing, he allowed others to touch him. One story, told in all three synoptic gospels (Mark 5:25–34, Matthew 9:20–26, Luke 8:43–48), is the story of the hemorrhaging woman. We are told she has suffered much at the hands of physicians as they attempt to cure her bleeding that has lasted twelve years. One can speculate that her suffering was compounded by her inability to be touched. Since a bleeding woman was considered unclean, no one could touch her without becoming unclean himself or herself. Jesus senses her touch and rather than chastise her, he proclaims that her faith has cured her. In Luke it is a woman of the streets, a sinner who, to the consternation of the Pharisees, touches Jesus. She washes his feet with her tears, dries them with her hair, kisses his feet and anoints them with perfume (Luke 7:36–43). In the gospel of John, it is Mary, Lazarus's sister, who performs this act of touching and anointing, foreshadowing Christ's crucifixion and death. "Her action corresponds to the costliness of Jesus's dangerous and subversive act in raising her brother to life (11:45–57). Mary's unconventional touch of Jesus's feet articulates the reciprocity of love in this Gospel. But it also foreshadows the footwashing, where Jesus touches the feet of his disciples at the Last Supper, and symbolic expression of union in his death, indicating both intimacy and service (13:8)."[52]

We need to carefully consider the boundaries that we have drawn in our community, the church. As Phyllis Davis writes,

> The greatest healer I know, Jesus the Christ, said, "When two or more are gathered in my name, then so shall I be." And that love, power, and energy is required for true healing. Without that divine touch, we are incomplete in our search for intimacy, healing, health, and well-being. Without that divine touch, we are incomplete in our search for love.[53]

Based on a practical theology of embodiment and Christ's actions of embracing the other, pastoral caregivers need to consider ways to make touch part of our practice in our churches. Modeling Jesus's touch, holding the other, gripping them tight, expressing the love of God in Jesus Christ embodied in the caregiver is essential for the well-being of the community. This can be done in a variety of ways. One way is by ritualizing touch—healing services, laying on of hands, services of blessing, and so on. In this setting touch is not only public and ritualized but also occurs with the consent of the individual who comes forward.

The Lutheran order for a service of healing includes prayers that remind the body of Christ that God desires the health of all people and came that we might have life abundantly. The prayers include not only those who are sick or injured, but also those in broken relationships or in emotional distress, and a prayer to restore to wholeness whatever is "broken in our lives, in the nation and in the world."[54] In this context the officiant lays his/her hands on the head of each person who comes forward and says, "I lay my hands upon you in the name of our Lord and Savior Jesus Christ beseeching him to uphold you and fill you with his grace that you may know the healing power of his love."[55]

The prayers end with the following entreaty to God that one might come to know the healing presence of Christ.

> Gracious God, in baptism you anointed us with the oil of salvation, and joined us to the death and resurrection of your Son. Bless all who seek your healing presence in their lives. In their suffering draw them more deeply into the mystery of your love, that following Christ in the way of the cross they may know the power of his resurrection; who lives and reigns forever and ever.[56]

By coincidence, a service of the word for healing was scheduled for my last Sunday as a pastor in a congregation I served. Nearly everyone present came forward for the laying on of hands. As I laid my hands upon each person for the last time as their pastor, I was profoundly moved. As I looked into each person's face and pronounced the blessing, I felt the presence of Christ blessing the relationship we had shared, promising grace and hope for the future.

Another time and place where touching might be incorporated is during the distribution of the bread during the Eucharist. I was taught that when receiving the host/bread one does so with the hands cupped so that this precious gift of the body of our Lord is received with reverence and care. After placing the bread in the recipient's hand, simply hold his/her cupped hands as one reminds the communicant that this is the body of our Lord, given for them.

Finally, though one should question whether touching or hugging a parishioner meets their need or one's own need, there are times when it is appropriate to touch. As one ages, the number of individuals that one can go to and ask for a hug decreases. As Tiffany Fields notes, "Ironically, the older some people get, the more they want to be touched, but the opportunity to be touched by friends and family gets markedly reduced because many people do not like touching older people."[57] Holding hands in prayer when visiting those who are shut-in, accepting their hugs may be other times where touch is appropriate.

Though trained to question the meaning of touch, there were several times in my ministry when the choice was between following the "rules" or embodying Christ and touching the other in an intimate caring fashion. The first was when I visited a friend dying of AIDS in a hospice. This was at a time when many were still wearing gowns and gloves when simply in the presence of an individual with AIDS. We had known each other for several years; we both knew that he was dying. He had been a priest at one time and had just gifted me with his daily missal.[58] Rather than sit in the chair next to the bed, at his urging, I sat next to him on the bed. We embraced each other, as together we read from his missal. I am still profoundly moved by the memory of his touch for I know that God was present with us as we prayed the hours. The second was when I was called to the bedside of a parishioner who was dying of cancer. She had

had a rocky relationship with the previous pastor and initially refused my attempts to visit her. When she finally allowed a pastoral visit it lasted several hours. Over the next few months she began to lose her battle with cancer. Her son, who was taking care of her, called and asked if I could stay with her since he did not want to leave her alone while he ran some errands. As we sat talking, she asked if I could hold her. I climbed into the big bed with her, sitting with my back on the headboard and wrapped my arms around her. As she laid her head on my shoulder she began to talk about dying, her hopes and fears, and her trust in God. As she said, "We have not known each other long, but we have known each other deep." The deeply knowing was embodied in the ability to hold and be held not only in the arms of a pastor but also in the arms of a loving God. Being held enabled her to face her future with faith and trust in a God who holds us in the palm of his hands.

Touch is a powerful way to communicate the love of God in Christ Jesus. Used carefully and with thought, touch can strengthen the ties that one has to each other and to God in the fellowship we call the church, the body of Christ.

NOTES

1. The Babinski test is performed by running a blunt instrument up the outside of the foot from the heel and curving toward the toes. For infants and young children (usually under two) the toes will flare. Once an individual begins walking, the toes curl. If the toes flare in an adult it may be indicative of a spinal cord or brain injury. In the intensive care unit it is part of the assessment performed by nurses.

2. David Chidester, "Haptics of the Heart: The Sense of Touch in American Religion and Culture," *Culture and Religion: An Interdisciplinary Journal* 1, no. 1 (2000): 63. He notes that Aristotle considered touch to be both metaphysically and morally inferior to the others senses. Elizabeth Harvey in "The Portal of Touch" also notes that while Plato saw touch as fundamental to the experience of the body, "his ambivalence about its importance is registered through his refusal to name it, an elision that necessarily works as a kind of erasure" (Elizabeth D. Harvey, "The Portal of Touch," *American Historical Review* 116, no. 2 [2011]: 387). See also Bonnie Miller-McLemore's reference to a "new kind of Platonism" when discussing Sam Gill's work in the introduction. She notes that too often "the body itself, its literal physicality, almost drops out of the picture" (page 9 of the introduction).

3. Naomi E. Balaban and James Bobick, *The Handy Anatomy Answer Book* (Canton, MI: Visible Ink Press, 2008), 41.

4. Elizabeth D. Harvey, "The Portal of Touch," *American Historical Review* 116, no. 2 (2011): 385.

5. Ashley Montague, *Touching: The Human Significance of the Skin*, 3rd ed. (New York: Harper & Row Publishers, 1986), 4.

6. Ibid., 26.

7. Ibid., 10.

8. Ibid.

9. Ibid.

10. Ibid.

11. Ibid., 11.

12. Ibid., 6.

13. "Touch," merriam-webster.com. http://www.merriam-webster.com/dictionary/touch, accessed January 10, 2016.

14. Montague, *Touching*, 2nd ed., 103.

15. Sara Wuthnow, "Healing Touch Controversies," *Journal of Religion and Health* 36, no. 3 (Fall 1997): 221.

16. Patricia L. Blackwell, "The Influence of Touch on Child Development: Implications for Intervention," *Infants and Young Children* 13, no. 1 (2000): 28–29. See her discussion of the historical accounts of deprivation of touch. A comparison of two types of institutions, one a foundling home and the other a nursery, demonstrated the importance of touch in the growth and social development of infants and young children. The foundation of her research is attachment theory which states that for normal social development to occur, an infant must form secure, consistent attachments with an adult. She found that "data from animal and human research on touch and development reveal a complex interaction between tactile stimulation and child development" (35).

17. Ibid.

18. Phyllis Davis, *The Power of Touch: The Basis for Survival, Health, Intimacy, and Emotional Well-Being* (Carlsbad, CA: Hay House, 1999), Kindle edition, Location 290.

19. Harry F. Harlow, "Monkey Love Experiments," *The Adoption History Project*, accessed May 21, 2014, http://darkwing.uoregon.edu/~adoption/studies/HarlowM-LE.html. When the experimental subjects were frightened by strange, loud objects, such as teddy bears beating drums, monkeys raised by terry cloth surrogates made bodily contact with their mothers, rubbed against them, and eventually calmed down. Harlow theorized that they used their mothers as a "psychological base of operations," allowing them to remain playful and inquisitive after the initial fright had subsided. In contrast, monkeys raised by wire mesh surrogates did not retreat to their mothers when scared. Instead, they threw themselves on the floor, clutched themselves, rocked back and forth, and screamed in terror. These activities closely resembled the behaviors of autistic and deprived children frequently observed in institutions as well as the pathological behavior of adults confined to mental institutions, Harlow noted. The awesome power of attachment and loss over mental health and illness could hardly have been performed more dramatically.

20. Harvey, 386.

21. Christina Davis, in chapter 9, discusses the effect of harmful touch. She indicates that survivors of sexual abuse often view the body, the recipient of abuse, as vehicle of evil. If the negative, hate-filled emotions of the abuser have been communicated to the survivor, then, as she notes, rituals of healing touch, where positive messages are received, might be one way in which survivors of abuse can begin to heal.

22. Rick Chillot, "Louder Than Words," *Psychology Today* (March/April, 2013): 54.

23. Matthew J. Hertenstein, Rachel Holmes, and Margaret McCullough, "The Communication of Emotion via Touch," *Emotion* 9, no. 4 (2009): 567.

24. Ibid., 569. He expected that the accuracy would be closer to 25 percent.

25. Phyllis Davis, *The Power of Touch*, Location 290.

26. International Student Guide to the United States of America, accessed June 3, 2014, http://www.internationalstudentguidetotheusa.com/articles/understanding-american-culture.html. The italics are mine.

27. Davis, 90–93. She notes that some children need touching so much that they will deliberately provoke parents or teachers.

28. Montague, xv.

29. Genesis 3:3, New Revised Standard. All scripture quoted is from the NRSV.

30. Carmel Harrison, Robert S. P. Jones, and Jaci C. Huws, "We're people who don't touch: Exploring clinical psychologists' perspective on their use of touch in therapy," *Counseling Psychology Quarterly* 25, no. 3 (September, 2012): 277. They indicate that 30 percent of humanistic therapists believe that touch could be therapeutic, while only 6 percent of psychodynamic therapists believe that touch can be beneficial to a client's progress. Psychodymanic therapists, per the authors, believe that the risk of the touch

being misinterpreted is high enough to exclude touching in therapy. It is important to note that most clinical psychology programs are not as wedded to this psychodynamic/psychoanalytical school of thought.

31. Pamela Cooper-White, *Many Voices: Pastoral Psychotherapy in Relational and Theological Perspective* (Minneapolis: Augsburg Fortress, 2007), 171.

32. Ibid. See also her discussion of the case study of "Miranda" and "Sara" and how the touch of the therapist "Sara," who was trying to empathize with "Miranda," actually derailed the therapy session in *Shared Wisdom: Use of Self in Pastoral Care and Counseling* (Minneapolis: Augsburg Fortress, 2004), 132–155. She contends that pastors need to ask themselves, "Whose need is being met by touching?"

33. Karen A. McClintock, *Preventing Sexual Abuse in Congregations* (Herndon, VA: Alban Institute, 2004), 41. I do not disagree with either Cooper-White or McClintock and have recently asked a distressed young woman if she needed a hug. I simply wonder if the discussion around the meaning of touch inhibits pastoral caregivers from touching. As Christina Davis notes, this focus on avoiding inappropriate touch may make pastoral caregivers feel ill equipped to respond to those who have been harmed by sexual violence.

34. Elaine Graham, "Words Made Flesh: Women, Embodiment, and Practical Theology," *Feminist Theology*, no. 21 (May 1999): 113.

35. Ibid., 109.

36. Ibid., 112.

37. See also Christina Davis's discussion, in chapter 9, of the body is anointed by the Holy Spirit in baptism.

38. Ibid., 113.

39. Ibid.

40. Ibid.

41. Ibid., 114.

42. Ibid., 115.

43. Ibid.

44. Ibid., 114–115. See her discussion on "Where's the Body?" She asserts that such disembodied concepts such as power and truth are always embodied.

45. Ibid., 120.

46. Theodore G. Tappert, ed. "The Smalcald Articles," *The Book of Concord* (Philadelphia: Fortress Press, 1959), 310. Article IV on "The Gospel" notes that this is based on Matthew 18:20, understanding that where two or three are gathered in his name, Christ is present.

47. Suzanne M. Peolquin, "Helping through Touch: The Embodiment of Caring," *Journal of Religion and Health* 28, no. 4 (Winter, 1989): 303.

48. Davis, 14.

49. Dorothy Lee, "The Gospel of John and the Five Senses," *Journal of Biblical Literature* 129, no. 1 (2010): 124. Lee notes that Christ's touch, in this instance, "expresses the intimacy of love."

50. N. Turner, "Touch," *The Interpreter's Dictionary of the Bible* (Nashville: Abingdon Press, 1986), 675.

51. Ibid.

52. Lee, 124.

53. Davis, 145.

54. *Occasional Services: A Companion to the Lutheran Book of Worship* (Minneapolis: Augsburg Fortress, 1982), see prayers on pp. 91–93.

55. Ibid., 94.

56. "The Service of Healing," *Life Passages: Marriage, Healing, Funeral* (Minneapolis: Augsburg Fortress, 2002).

57. Tiffany Field, *Touch* (Cambridge, MA: MIT Press, 2001), Kindle edition, Locations 437–438.

58. The missal was from his own liturgical book that has instructions on celebrating the Roman Catholic Mass throughout the year as well as how to pray the different "hours" of the day, morning, noon, evening, and so forth.

REFERENCES

Balaban, Naomi E. and James Bobick. The Handy Anatomy Answer Book. Canton, MI: Visible Ink Press, 2008.

Blackwell, Patricia L. "The Influence of Touch on Child Development: Implications for Intervention." Infants and Young Children 13, no. 1 (2000): 25–39.

Chidester, David. "Haptics of the Heart: the Sense of Touch in American Religion and Culture." Culture and Religion: An Interdisciplinary Journal 1, no. 1 (2000): 61–84.

Chillot, Rick. "Louder Than Words," Psychology Today, (March/April 2013): 52–61.

Cooper-White, Pamela. Many Voices: Pastoral Psychotherapy in Relational and Theological Perspective. Minneapolis: Augsburg Fortress, 2007.

———. Shared Wisdom: Use of Self in Pastoral Care and Counseling. Minneapolis: Augsburg Fortress, 2004.

Davis, Phyllis. The Power of Touch: The Basis for Survival, Health, Intimacy, and Emotional Well-Being. Carlsbad, CA: Hay House, 1999. Kindle edition.

Evangelical Lutheran Church in America. "The Service of Healing," Life Passages: Marriage, Healing, Funeral. Minneapolis: Augsburg Fortress, 2002.

Field, Tiffany. Touch. Cambridge, MA: MIT Press, 2001. Kindle edition.

Graham, Elaine. "Words Made Flesh: Women, Embodiment, and Practical Theology." Feminist Theology 7, no. 21 (May 1999): 109–121.

Harlow, Harry F. "Monkey Love Experiments," The Adoption History Project. Accessed May 21, 2014. http://darkwing.uoregon.edu/~adoption/studies/HarlowMLE.html.

Harrison, Carmel, Robert S. P. Jones, and Jaci C. Huws. "We're people who don't touch: Exploring clinical psychologists' perspective on their use of touch in therapy." Counseling Psychology Quarterly 25, no. 3 (2012): 277–287.

Harvey, Elizabeth D. "The Portal of Touch." American Historical Review 116, no 2 (2011): 385–400.

Hertenstein, Matthew J., Rachel Holmes, and Margaret McCullough. "The Communication of Emotion via Touch." Emotion 9, no. 4 (2009): 566–573.

International Student Guide to the United States of America. Accessed June 3, 2014. http://www.internationalstudentguidetotheusa.com/articles/understanding-american-culture.html.

Lee, Dorothy. "The Gospel of John and the Five Senses." Journal of Biblical Literature 129, no. 1 (2010): 115–127.

Lutheran Church in America. Occasional Services: A Companion to the Lutheran Book of Worship. Minneapolis: Augsburg Fortress, 1982.

McClintock, Karen A. Preventing Sexual Abuse in Congregations. Herndon, Virginia: Alban Institute, 2004.

Merriam-Webster.com. "Touch." Accessed January 10, 2016. http://www.merriam-webster.com/dictionary/touch.

Montague, Ashley. Touching: The Human Significance of the Skin. 2nd ed. New York: Harper & Row Publishers, 1978.

———. Touching: The Human Significance of the Skin. 3rd ed. New York: Harper & Row Publishers, 1986.

Peolquin, Suzanne M. "Helping thorough Touch: The Embodiment of Caring." Journal of Religion and Health 28 no. 4 (1989): 299–322.

Tappert, Theodore G., ed., The Book of Concord. Philadelphia: Fortress Press, 1959.

Turner, N. "Touch." The Interpreter's Dictionary of the Bible. Nashville: Abingdon Press, 1986.

Wuthnow, Sara. "Healing Touch Controversies." Journal of Religion and Health 36, no. 3 (1997): 221–230.

THREE

Savoring Taste as Religious Praxis

Where Individual and Social Intimacy Converge

Stephanie N. Arel

"Oh taste and see that the Lord is good," Psalm 34:8 declares, expressing intense exultation in knowing the Spirit.[1] In a like manner, in the Bhaga-vad-Gita Krishna declares, "I am the taste of water," at once revealing how the joint material and spiritual energies of the Lord are made known through taste.[2] For centuries, taste has served as a sensual component of divine perception or worship across cultural and religious divides. Both Catholic and Protestant Christians experience taste at the sacraments of communion; in the Jewish religion, after the blessing at the Passover Seder, participants consume among many foods *charoset*, which symbolizes the mortar slaves of Egypt used to make bricks. Followers of Islam ingest a sweet date to break the fast during Ramadan, while ghee is both medicinal and sacred in the rites of the Hindus. All of these religious practices have something in common: corporeality, through taste, integrates the prosaic and the extraordinary, just as it simultaneously conjoins the intimate individual act of eating with the social engagement related to food in religious customs. This chapter explores how the extraordinary merges with the quotidian in the somatic experience of taste, examining further how the intimate act of eating connects people to each other via taste, and then, by extension reveals some aspect of the divine.

Although taste has been an important part of religious practice for centuries, the Cartesian dualistic body-mind construction turned critical theory away from theories of embodiment, especially those situated around sensual experience. Studies of religion similarly de-emphasize taste despite the fact that taste and food abounds in religious textual traditions, practices, and aesthetics. However, recent scholarship theorizing the body in the humanities and social sciences challenges the inheritance of the Cartesian system encouraging scholarly attention to carnal knowledge. In *Making Sense of Taste,* Carolyn Korsmeyer models the turn to bodies and taste as objects of analysis, disputing philosophy's relegation of taste as a subjective category that provides little to no information about the outside world. Instead, she claims that food and taste provide sensory data to the body, which engage with cognitive capacities and assist in meaning making.[3] Thus, sensual experiences via taste work as important indicators often demarcating religious communities and ratifying divine presence.

Korsmeyer and other feminist theorists have long supported the body as a source of knowledge, validating the theorization of the centrality of the somatic in all aspects of human experience. Informed by the work of feminist theorists, including Korsmeyer, Susan Bordo, Gail Weiss, and Susan Hackman, who provide methods of approach to the body, I turn attention to the body via taste in an effort to undermine epistemological dualisms that seek to separate the body from the mind, or the rational from the somatic and intuitive. This approach recognizes that body, as Bordo asserts, no longer serves "as an obstacle to knowledge," as interpreted by Cartesian dualism, but instead the body prevails as a "vehicle of human making and remaking of the world, constantly shifting location, capable of revealing endlessly new points of view."[4] The body reveals multiplicity in experience and is a valuable site for analysis.[5]

Recently, the dual sensibility embracing the centrality of the body in experience and in knowledge production has emerged in affect theory, both in its philosophical and psychological conceptions. Affect theorists' renewed interest in the "biological portion of emotion"[6] places emphasis on bodily experiences and recognizes the relationship of an affect to its object.[7] Affects are understood to be participating in an "ongoing process" that enlarges experience contributing to self-formation.[8] In her work, Patricia Clough recognizes an "affective turn" in humanities scholarship which, she states, "invites a transdisciplinary approach to theory and method" necessary to theorizing the social, blurring the lines between the organic and the inorganic, and inserting the technical into the body's capacity to "affect and be affected."[9] In affect, no category of being is delimited; the body and what is organic comes into contact with other matter or material, and the experience of every meeting contributes to how a person comes to understand the world. Affect theorists' commitment to explicating the interchange between the material and human life impels a study of the senses, supporting how food and bodies intertwine to expose a new way of understanding. Through the lens of affect theory and feminist critique, I consider taste, traditionally relegated to lower senses, but here approached as an embodied encounter with the world that familiarizes and informs the self about that world. Taste, like sight, is at its basest a mode of apprehension similar to the sense of sight in the phrase, "I see." Taste enables knowing, particularly knowing about religious communities and the divine.

In my investigation regarding how religion and experiences of divinity become known when the intimate and social converge at the corporeal location of the mouth in taste, I situate taste biologically, incorporated with the body and epistemologically sound. Thus, I present taste as a physiological, somatic sensory impression, asserting where taste links experience and comprehension at the intersection of the physical and the cognitive. This assertion compels my approach of taste as an affective experience, which makes claims upon the body. Next, I trace taste as an epistemological source that leads to recollection, connecting to the past, while bringing the body into the present in a unique way. Taste, thus, represents at least one way that the body knows. At the core of this essay, and where taste in this analysis leads, is the integration of the prosaic and the extraordinary through taste manifested in the body's "knowing" the divine. Thus, finally I consider taste as praxis within religious communities and as religious experience that illuminates an aspect of God in any particular religion. I cite from many religions, yet focus most in depth on the Abrahamic religions, not to compare them methodologically, but to show how via taste the body figures in religious matters. Ultimately, I show the validity of taste in perceiving the divine and as an important aspect of religious praxis, illustrating the body as an epistemological category.

PROUST'S PRELUDE TO TASTE

To frame the study of corporeality through taste, I refer to the well-known and widely quoted passage about the madeleine from Marcel Proust's *A la recherché du temps perdu*. This selection draws attention to the experience of taste as a phenomenon that begins as an intensely personal experience. The corporeal event of eating expands time and space, while impressing upon Proust's narrator (also named Marcel) something distinctly physical: taste, both somatically and affectively charged, reaches back to assist recollection, while rendering Marcel completely and immediately present. For Marcel, eating the madeleine registers, all at once, a sensory phenomenon, an intimate encounter, an affective interruption, and a memory linked to something pleasurable. That taste means something to his understanding of the world is supported by how often the piece is quoted; people read Proust's madeleine episode and recognize their own personal experiences within it.

> No sooner had the warm liquid mixed with the crumbs touched my
> palate than a shudder ran through me and I stopped, intent upon the

extraordinary thing that was happening to me. An exquisite pleasure
had invaded my senses, something isolated, detached, with no suggestion of its origin. And at once the vicissitudes of life had become indif-
ferent to me, its disasters innocuous, its brevity illusory– this new sensation having had on me the effect which love has of filling me with a
precious essence; or rather this essence was not in me it was me. . . .
Whence did it come? What did it mean? How could I seize and appre-
hend it? . . . And suddenly the memory revealed itself. The taste was
that of the little piece of madeleine which on Sunday mornings at Combray (because on those mornings I did not go out before mass), when I
went to say good morning to her in her bedroom, my aunt Léonie used
to give me, dipping it first in her own cup of tea or tisane. The sight of
the little madeleine had recalled nothing to my mind before I tasted
it.[10]

Proust's narrator Marcel engages taste viscerally recognizing it as "extraordinary." Tasting the madeleine provides him "exquisite pleasure"
and fills him with a precious essence, which his being and body become.
Proust's literary expression of taste offers a foundation from which the
corporeal experience of taste can be fruitfully explored. Here, taste
emerges as an epistemological category used to ratify the inexplicable
while directing the individual to what is somatically and symbolically
central. In Marcel's tasting the madeleine the physiological, individual,
and cultural aspects of taste emerge and converge illustrating what Korsmeyer calls a phenomenology of taste.[11] Furthermore, as Kenya J. Tuttle's essay notes regarding the experience of taste in this volume, taste
becomes internalized for Marcel, informed simultaneously by culture
and his own physical, yet psychic experience.

BIOLOGY

Negotiating taste first as a biological event elucidates its status as an
intimate personal experience—eating functions as the action evident of
this penetratingly personal encounter. While eating food centralizes taste,
"to concentrate on taste to the exclusion of other senses means to fail to
recognize that the experience of eating is also dependent on the haptic
sensitivity of tongues and mouths, on our olfactory abilities, and on sight
and sound."[12] Taste thus encompasses an entire corporeality, prevailing
in bodies and involving multiple physical mechanisms.

The major organ of taste is the tongue. At the site of the tongue, the
sensory endings of the papillae perceive particular tastes of which there
are five: sweet, sour, bitter, salty, and umami or savory.[13] These basic
tastes combined with olfactory input permit the perception of a large
variety of flavors. In Marcel's experience, this synthesis of the senses
involves peripheral input modulated by affects, physiological and metabolic states, and social or cultural cues that surface as a memory.[14] Fur-

ther, taste receptors control what may or may not be consumed; on an evolutionary basis they warn organisms about what is detrimental to consume,[15] while they also play a role in homeostasis, seeking to assist bodies find balance in neurological, physiological, and psychological life.

Affects are spontaneous muscular glandular responses located throughout the body and triggered at subcortical centers that influence homeostasis.[16] In affective experience, the connections between body and mind happen so rapidly that visceral phenomena frequently evade conscious processes; thus, the experience of taste immediately produces somatic changes. In addition, affects are spontaneous and intractable but also malleable through taste. Take the pleasure of consuming something sweet. Due to the stimulation of particular cells on the tongue, the brain perceives sweet, and the body (if the two can be disassociated) experiences positive affect.[17] Positive affective charges can be enhanced or decreased in intensity based on what has been consumed prior to the sweet sensation; pleasing or pleasurable images present during consumption also increase positive affect.[18] While sweet tastes produce enjoyment, bad or bitter tastes often provoke disgust. Disgust lets bodies know what should be rejected, but it translates to an entire meaning system about what qualifies as good or bad, worthy or unworthy.[19] Food thus elicits affect via taste, and taste, in turn, communicates value as taste "gets under your skin and into your bones."[20]

In Proust's example, Marcel experiences a convergence of affects through the sweet taste of the madeleine, emerging in his expression as "love." This love, enunciated as "exquisite pleasure," begins as an individual phenomenon initiated as the objects of taste actually enter the body.[21] Then, the affective response, as Marcel notes, seizes him and arrests his body bringing it into the present while connecting him to the past, or the world outside of himself in Combray.

While Proust reveals affects as a result of taste in fiction, Ayurvedic medicine, a system of Hindu traditional healing in India, directly relates emotions, or affective constellations (affects that modulate, combine, or control each other), to taste in a religious system.[22] In fact, Ayurveda holds that taste and emotions are "identical forces on different planes of existence," such that "taste is to the body what emotion is to the mind."[23] In affective terms, taste evokes the visceral experience of affects that become translated through cognition into emotions. Particular tastes interpreted as felt experiences describe a particular individual's energetic state. For instance, in Ayurveda, sweet tastes equate to satisfaction or greed; sour tastes reveal interest or envy; salty indicates excitement or overindulgence and pungency to extroversion or anger; bitter tastes divulge distress or anguish, and astringent tastes point to shame and fear.[24] Affects, personality traits, and taste converge in this system grounding emotional inclinations and making these nearly indistinguishable from the experience of the body.[25]

Taste and personality also converge in the idea of taste as a preference resulting from socialization and conditioning,[26] constituting taste's role as forming the very basis of culture. In his work *Distinction: A Social Critique of the Judgment of Taste*, Pierre Bourdieu recognizes taste as preference, which designates social states, but he resists distinguishing this aspect of taste from its role as a sense or sensory experience. Desire to divorce taste as corporeal from taste as a social predilection thereby relegating sensory taste as "crude" is, to Bourdieu, a fallacy. As Bourdieu states, "the archetype of all taste" including that which precedes food ingestion and corporeality "refers back to the oldest and deepest experiences, those which determine and over-determine the primitive oppositions—bitter/sweet, flavourful/insipid, hot/cold, course/delicate, austere/bright—which are essential to gastronomic commentary as to the refined appreciation of aesthetes."[27] Thus, Bourdieu conflates sense and preference, merging the taste for what he calls "refined objects" with the taste of flavor for foods. This integration exposes taste as a factor in aesthetics. Like art, taste has an ability to "express and manifest a reality different than that of an accepted social consciousness."[28] Taste alters this consciousness from the root of the body, connecting the quotidian and biological need for the consumption of food to the interpretation of beauty. Thus, taste promotes a way of knowing that is "intuitive, affective, contemplative," while it is also characterized by "surrender, mystery, imagination, experience, surprise, and passion."[29]

PERCEPTION

The biological, evolutionary, and affective modes of taste, even in its alliance to preference, inform the body about some state of being. Taste satisfied physiologically emerges as homeostasis; affectively, balance equates to regulation. But taste, as indicated, does more than signal to the body a physical state; it also involves cognition, processing the outside world even as food is consumed; food, as Ben Highmore writes, "is the sine qua non of taste's affective function."[30] Taste indicates an affective reality. Despite the negligence of taste in scholarship, religions and religious practices have understood the persuasiveness of the senses to influence affects and have utilized the senses to convey religious values and meaning. In fact, taste as both the actual act of eating food and taste as a metaphor function as powerful ways to connect with or perceive the divine.

In the Qur'an, taste occupies a status that enables the sensual experience to indicate something important about a particular relationship with God. That is, taste informs faithful Muslims something about their relationship to the divine. Generally, the experience of taste reflects either an understanding of the mercy of the Lord,[31] or the evil that ensues if someone refuses to follow Allah. Situated as an indicator of the struggle between good and evil, taste substantiates the position of the believer in relationship to Allah. In the first case, taste ratifies paradise where "the rivers of wine [are] delicious to those that drink" and "rivers of clarified honey," illustrating forgiveness and mercy.[32] However, the Qur'an declares to and threatens unbelievers, "Taste you the torment of the Fire which you used to deny."[33] In lieu of tasting mercy, in this case, those who reject Allah taste punishment.[34] In either case, via taste, corporeality in Muslim life informs practitioners about the status of their relationships with God.

The Judaic and Christian traditions also position taste between the battle of good and evil so that the visceral and religious merge. The experience of tasting death emerges in Matthew 16:28, while the taste of suffering infiltrates Job's story. In Judaism and Christianity, perhaps the most familiar example of knowing aligned with taste surfaces in the Hebrew Bible when Adam and Eve eat from the tree of knowledge. Seduced by the devil, Genesis 3: 7–8 recounts, "the woman saw that the tree was good for food, and that it was a delight to the eyes, and that the tree was to be desired to make one wise, she took of its fruit and ate; and she also gave some to her husband, who was with her, and he ate. Then the eyes of both were opened, and they knew that they were naked." Through sweet fruit they come to know not only that they are naked but also that evil exists in the world, apart from God, whereas prior to eating from the tree, they knew only of good. The Bible points to the precise point that taste provides knowledge not only about the everyday but also about the extraordinary, in this case, good and evil.

Although taste indicates Adam and Eve's suffering and encounter with evil in the Bible, taste also ratifies delight in the divine encounter. In Christianity, taste substantiates the goodness of the divine; "Oh taste and see that the Lord is good," Psalm 34:8 celebrates. Particularly in reference to taste, Bonaventure states that the "senses [take] delight in an object perceived" aligned with God.[35] Such delight, or knowing delight, brings affect to the fore in taste and represents somatic knowing in relationship to God. For Bonaventure, taste is critical and having a renewed sense of taste constitutes being restored in God, as when the soul "embraces in love the Word incarnate, receiving delight from him and passing over into him through ecstatic love;" when this happens, through Christ, the Christian self "recovers its sense of taste and touch. Having recovered these senses, when it sees its Spouse and hears, smells, tastes and embraces him, the soul can sing like the bride the Canticle of Canticles."[36] Similarly, the medieval mystic Hadewijck speaks of tasting and masticating the sweetness of the Lord, where the love ingested provides a source of feeding.[37] In this instance, food is tantamount to love that nurtures the Christian self.

In these Christian examples, food functions metaphorically to convey a relationship to the divine, but food also plays an important role in binding religious members to each other and to particular religious narratives. In Christian practice, uniting the community together happens through the celebration of the Eucharist, but communal connection through food also occurs outside of the pulpit in family homes, as well as in other traditions. A fruitful example of the imbrication of religious history and personal life emerges in the celebration of the Seder meal. During Jewish Passover, this meal commemorates the exodus of the Jews from slavery in Egypt. The food rituals critical to the Seder symbolize this exodus not only in food presentation but also in the tastes each particular food provides. In this way, the Seder exemplifies in a religious ritual the convergence of the metaphoric and physical aspects of taste, centralizing the experience of bodies, especially as enslaved and marginalized, during the event. Each element of the Passover meal reminds participants of a complicated and embodied history. For instance, the Lamb shank visually recalls the sacrifice of the paschal lamb and alludes to the fact that God passed over the homes of the Jews slaughtering only the Egyptian's first born during Passover. The bitter herbs signify bondage and sorrow, epitomized in their sharp taste, while the roasted egg marks the possibility for renewal. The *charoset*, a mix of fruit and nuts, replicates through food the bricks or mortar the Jews used as slaves to build Egyptian buildings and is generally eaten with bitter herbs so that its sweetness does not deceive the consumer. A dish of salt water "chemically replicates" the tears shed in captivity, in which the parsley or chervil is dipped to mark a renewal. Every element of the Passover meal serves an aesthetic function visually, metaphorically, and affectively via the body and taste, illustrating how taste and bodies add dimensions to religious rituals helping participants connect with others, the past, and to the divine. Furthermore, as one of the five senses, taste participates in the stages of memory, evident during a Seder, to remind those in attendance of their individual connection to a communal event. As a result of perceived experiences, taste assists in the formation of this memory. As Korsmeyer asserts, in this case taste emphasizes "the immediacy and vivacity of the recollection," which takes the form of bodily experience virtually reenacted.[38]

TASTE AS PRAXIS

In religious events generally, as in the Seder, taste has symbolic significance as a particular sensual experience but also as particular taste of foods. Evident in Judaism, Christianity, and Islam, manna and the taste of manna permeate religious texts as evidence of God while also being a major form of sustenance. In the Hebrew Bible, manna from heaven blesses the Israelites in the desert. It appears at first to assuage hunger in the escape from Egypt and is described as either "a fine flaky substance, as fine as frost on the ground"[39] or as made of coriander seed having the taste of "wafers made with honey"[40] and the "color of gum resin."[41] In Islam, presented by Moses and Allah, manna rains down from the clouds, a gummy substance similar to the consistency described in the Hebrew Bible, acquired without any effort. For Muslims, manna tastes sweet and has healing properties.[42] In the New Testament, in John 6, Jesus declares that manna came from God as bread from heaven feeding the multitudes, but it also converts from its earthy, physical substance to become the Word, or Christ's body. In each of these religions, actual manna needed for persistence, in the desert for instance, not only comes from God and therefore indicates God's presence but also sensually provides a sweet taste eliciting pleasure. Manna prevails as a religious symbol in which the quotidian and extraordinary merge. As bread from heaven, Peter Williams's hymn beseeches of manna, "feed me til I want no more."[43]

The confluence of everyday and extraordinary in manna finds its apex in the Christian description of the Last Supper adopted in the sacrament of Eucharist. The scene of the last supper represents a powerful recollection of taste in a religious narrative. With the twelve apostles surrounding him, Jesus announces that through consummation of his body in the form of bread and wine, sins will be forgiven. Matthew 26:25–28 recounts Jesus's words: "While they were eating, Jesus took a loaf of bread, and after blessing it he broke it, gave it to the disciples, and said, 'Take, eat; this is my body.' Then he took a cup, and after giving thanks he gave it to them, saying, 'Drink from it, all of you; for this is my blood of the covenant, which is poured out for many for the forgiveness of sins.'

John 6: 54–59 enumerates a similar lesson, including the implication that manna itself ascends when converted to the form of flesh. Jesus tells the Jews that the manna came from God not Moses. Then Jesus says to them:

> Very truly, I tell you, unless you eat the flesh of the Son of Man and drink his blood, you have no life in you. Those who eat my flesh and drink my blood have eternal life, and I will raise them up on the last day; for my flesh is true food and my blood is true drink. Those who eat my flesh and drink my blood abide in me, and I in them. Just as the living Father sent me, and I live because of the Father, so whoever eats me will live because of me. This is the bread that came down from heaven, not like that which your ancestors ate, and they died. But the one who eats this bread will live forever.[44]

In this biblical verse, literal consumption of bread now interpreted as Christ's flesh and the divine all transpire. Manna as sustenance from God becomes flesh metaphorically embodied in Jesus Christ sent from God. If one believes in this aspect of the Christian tradition, defined within the

Catholic Church as transubstantiation—where the bread and wine used at the sacrament of the Eucharist becomes the actual body of Christ— then those believers "actually become those substances. In which case the body and blood are literally re-presented: presented again to the congregation."[45] This communion occurs as an ecclesial practice and joins the faithful one to another, incorporating them into the body of the Church; it functions as a communion through taste of Christ's body by the individual's body. The Eucharist interpreted in this way represents the indispensible and essential action of taste in somatically conjoining the religious or the divine with the individual human body in community.

BONDING THROUGH TASTE

According to Julia Kristeva, the communal feast or communion among Christians constitutes agape,[46] reflected biblically when Jesus feeds the multitudes, welcoming the sinners without judgment, and eating with them. Taste in this case expands beyond the intimate act of sensual incorporation into the body of some other substance, binding the individual to the social, while validating physical, visceral, everyday sensual experiences as ways of knowing the divine. The intimate nature of taste relies not only on the individual idea of food consumption but also on what Korsmeyer calls the "social intimacy of eating."[47] As Korsmeyer asserts, "One of the most significant roles of food is social: eating is part of rituals, ceremonies, and practices that knit together communities."[48]

When food and God meet at the intersection of the private, intimate act of eating and the communal participation in something sacred, taste plays a role. While not necessarily articulated, taste is not only implicated in the act of eating itself but also in particular food prescriptions. For instance, numerous food taboos and edicts appear in the Hebrew Bible, in the Bhagavad-Gita, and in the Qur'an. Taste, as a somatic experience, frequently lies embedded within food rituals but often goes unnoticed or is taken for granted. In addition, other prevailing factors overshadow the religious meaning or significance of particular rituals. Take the luau for instance. In Hawaii, this celebration around food currently functions less like a religious event and more like a tourist attraction and income generator for hotels and service industries in Hawaii. Although Hawaiians participate in luaus, most often for children's birthdays or graduations, this ancient feast bears import prior to the Christian occupation of the island, embodying the Polynesian value of hospitality. The Hawaiian Luau presents a deeply encoded religious ceremony structured around the *kapu* system of native Hawaii.[49] Presenting prohibitions and restrictions, *kapu* is an adjective employed to describe something both divine and dangerous, evident in luaus as presented to kings but symbolically considered feasts to god(s). The foods prepared for the coming of the god's presence in the luau included *kūlolo* (a Hawaiian dessert), bread-fruit pudding, poi, bananas, fish, and `awa.[50] A medicinal plant, the `awa, known as kava, holds particular significance as sacred and used in prayer; bitter in taste, it is generally mixed with something sweet and used in conjunction with a prayer of gratitude to open up communication channels between people and the divine.[51]

In Hawaiian mythology, food used for offerings to gods is also given to people, or animals, that represent God. For instance, in some cases, the king assumes the role or figure of a god in the shape of a shark. The shark as a symbol could represent a dead relative transfigured into a shark guardian god, an `aumakua, or the chief, interpreted as a "shark that traveled on land."[52] In either case, the shark, a protective figure, is fed the same food that the chief receives. The ceremony involved pouring the `awa, pig, bananas, and other offerings into the shark's mouth.[53]

Human bodies serving as personification of a god or gods receive food offerings also emerge in the traditions of the Nyoro Kingdom, today commonly known as Uganda. In Nyoro culture, a person serves as the medium of a god during séances. During the course of this ritual, a spirit "climbs into the head" of the medium, the person who presumably assumes a dissociated state, and communicates with the people in attendance. Food is also necessarily present.

> A sacrificial meal has been prepared, and the *Cwezi* spirit eats of this (through the person of its medium), and distributes some of the food, usually millet porridge (*oburo*) but sometimes meat and certain vegetable dishes, to those present. This it may do by moulding little pellets of porridge in its fingers, spitting lightly on them to convey its blessing, and putting them in the mouths of anyone who is near. Feeding another person by putting pieces of food in his or her mouth in this manner is called *kubegera*, and, as a kind of epitome of commensality, it signifies a very close attachment.[54]

Like mother to child, the spirit communicates to others by feeding him or her. This example simultaneously highlights the act of taste during a sacrificial meal, within which millet is offered; a grain that has religious significance related to ritual cultivation of crops and physical nourishment, the millet signifies the presence of the sacred on earth and, often presented at shrines for gods, is known for its essence or force.[55]

CONCLUSION

Food and taste are important aspects of religious culture. The sensual experience of taste and the intimate act of eating take place individually, but as shown, bind the faithful to one another and their particular God. The examples from the ancient religious beliefs in India, Hawaii, and Africa help to expand beyond the Abrahamic religions to show how taste takes a primary role in religious experiences across geographical, cultural, and social divides. Touching on taste in these cultures reveals the universal interpretation of food as symbolic, physical, and linked to the divine in some meaningful way. All of these religious practices have something in common: corporeality, through taste, integrates the prosaic and the extraordinary, while conjoining the intimate individual act of eating with social engagement.

This imbrication via taste happens through bodies: *charoset* assumes, in memory, the properties of bricks and mortar; manna consumed by the multitudes transposes into Christ's body; the Hawaiian king takes on the body of a shark. These transmogrifications begin at the site of the tongue. And taste as a visceral phenomenon triggers affects helping to contribute to emotional states that support religious beliefs and practices. Taste's immediacy points to what is central to the body and the experience of taste itself, but it also helps bodies understand value of food and of what particular foods symbolize in the everyday and in the encounter with God. Taste, aligned with religious rituals or used in religious texts, indicates the divine in some way. Ultimately, the body comes to know where the prosaic and extraordinary meet in religious communities and events where the intimate and social converge in taste.

NOTES

1. Scripture quotations are from the *New Revised Standard Version of the Bible*, The Division of Christian Education of the National Council of the Churches of Christ in the U.S.A., 1989.

2. *The Bhagavad-Gita*, trans. Barbara Stoler Miller (New York: Bantam Dell, 2004), 7.8:74.

3. Carolyn Korsmeyer, *Making Sense of Taste: Food and Philosophy* (Ithaca: Cornell University Press, 1999), 68 and 115.

4. Susan Bordo, *Unbearable Weight: Feminism, Western Culture, and the Body* (Berkeley: University of California Press, 2003), 227.

5. This body is also, as Bonnie Miller-McLemore asserts in the introduction of the volume, "not simply a physical entity; it is always already shaped by culture" (10). As such, the body and its experience of taste are imbricated both with the personal and with the social or cultural.

6. Donald L. Nathanson, *Shame and Pride: Affect, Sex, and the Birth of the Self* (New York: W. W. Norton & Company, 1992), 49.

7. Eve Kosofsky Sedgwick, *Touching Feeling: Affect, Pedagogy, Performativity* (Durham, NC: Duke University Press, 2004), 99–101; Sedgwick differentiates drives in psychoanalytic theory from affects. Either a drive is operating or it is not; affects allow for more possibilities than "on and off."

8. Melissa Gregg and Gregory J. Seigworth, eds., *The Affect Theory Reader* (Durham: Duke University Press, 2010), 5.

9. Patricia Ticineto Clough and Jean Halley, eds., *The Affective Turn: Theorizing the Social* (Durham: Duke University Press, 2007), 2–3.

10. Marcel Proust, *In Search of Lost Time: Swann's Way*, Vol. 1, trans. C. K. Scott Moncrieff and Terence Kilmartin (New York: Modern Library Paperback Edition, 2003), 60.

11. Korsmeyer, 6.

12. Ben Highmore, "Bitter after Taste: Affect, Food, and Social Aesthetics," in *The Affect Theory Reader*, ed. Melissa Gregg and Gregory J. Seigworth (Durham: Duke University Press, 2010), 120.

13. Stephen A. Gravina, Gregory L. Yep, and Mehmood Khan, "Human Biology of Taste," *Annals of Saudi Medicine* 33, no. 3 (2013): 217.

14. Ibid., 221.

15. Silvan Tomkins, *Affect, Imagery, Consciousness*, 4 Vols., (1962; reprint, New York: Springer Publishing Company, 2008), 39, 414.

16. Ibid., 135.

17. Nak-Eon Choi and Jung H. Han, *How Flavor Works* (West Sussex, UK: John Wiley & Sons, Ltd., 2015), 185.

18. Ibid.

19. For an extensive treatment of disgust see Martha Nussbaum, *Hiding from Humanity* (Princeton, NJ: Princeton University Press, 2006).

20. Highmore, 126.

21. Korsmeyer, 29.

22. Tomkins, 76.

23. Robert E. Svoboda, *Prakriti: Your Ayurvedic Constitution* (Twin Lakes, WI: Lotus Press, 1989), 23.

24. Ibid., 23.

25. Furthermore, as Jennifer Baldwin points out in her chapter on hearing in this volume, such "somatic attunement," here embodied in the experience of taste, fosters awareness and compassion toward the self and the other (109).

26. Tomkins, 367.

27. Pierre Bourdieu, *Distinction: A Social Critique of the Judgment of Taste*, trans. Richard Nice (Cambridge: Harvard University Press, 1984), 72–73.

28. John Dykstra Eusden and John H. Westerhoff, *Sensing Beauty: Aesthetics, the Human Spirit, and the Church* (Cleveland: United Church Press, 1998), 3.

29. Ibid., 4.

30. Highmore, 126.

31. Dr. Muhannad Taqî-ud-Dîn Al-Hilâlî and Dr. Muhammad Muhsin Khân, *Translation of the Meaning of the Nobel Qu'ran in the English Language* (Madinah, K. S. A.: King Fahd Complex for the Printing of the Holy Qur'an), 545.

32. Ibid., 689.

33. Ibid., 557.

34. Ibid., 707.

35. Saint Bonaventure, *The Journey of the Mind to God*, trans. Philotheus Bohner, O. F. M. (1956; reprint, Indianapolis: Hackett Publishing Company, 1990), 71.

36. Ibid., 89.

37. Caroline Walker Bynum, *Holy Feast and Holy Fast: The Religious Significance of Food to Medieval Women* (Berkeley: University of California Press, 1988), 156–157.

38. Korsmeyer, 221.

39. Exodus 16:14.

40. Exodus 16:31.

41. Numbers 11:7.

42. Taqî-ud-Dîn Al-Hilâlî and Muhsin Khân, *Translation of the Meaning of the Nobel Qur'an in the English Language*, 12.

43. Rosewell Dwight Hitchcock, Zachary Eddy, and Philip Schaff, eds. *Hymns and Songs of Praise for Social and Sabbath Worship* (New York: A. S. Barnes & Company, 1875), 160.

44. John 6:54–59, *New Revised Standard Version of the Bible*, The Division of Christian Education of the National Council of the Churches of Christ in the U.S.A., 1989.

45. Korsmeyer, 139.

46. Julia Kristeva, *Tales of Love*, trans. Leon S. Roudiez (New York: Columbia University Press, 1987), 149.

47. Korsmeyer, 202.

48. Ibid., 9.
49. Ralph Simpson Kuykendall, *The Hawaiian Kingdom*, Vol. 1 (Honolulu: University of Hawaii Press, 1938), 8.
50. Samuel Manaiakalani Kamakau, *Ka Po'e Kahiko: The People of Old*, trans. Mary Kawena Pukui and ed. Dorothy B. Barrère (Honolulu: Bishop Museum Press, 1964), 51.
51. Canoe Plants of Ancient Hawaii, http://www.canoeplants.com/awa.html, accessed March 30, 2015.
52. Kamakau, 143.
53. Ibid., 76–77.
54. John Beattie, "Group Aspects of the Nyoro Spirit Mediumship Cult," *Rhodes-Livingstone Journal* 30 (1961), 15–16.
55. John Beattie, *Other Cultures: Aims, Methods and Achievements in Social Anthropology* (1964; reprint, Abingdon: Routledge, 2004), 235.

REFERENCES

Al-Hilâlî, Dr. Muhannad Taqî-ud-Dîn and Dr. Muhammad Muhsin Khân. *Translation of the Meaning of the Nobel Qu'ran in the English Language.* Madinah, K. S. A.: King Fahd Complex for the Printing of the Holy Qur'an.

Beattie, John. "Group Aspects Of The Nyoro Spirit Mediumship Cult." *Rhodes-Livingstone Journal* 30 (1961): 11–38.

———. *Other Cultures: Aims, Methods and Achievements in Social Anthropology.* 1964. Reprint, Abingdon: Routledge, 2004.

The Bhagavad-Gita. Translated by Barbara Stoler Miller. New York: Bantam Dell, 2004.

Bordo, Susan. *Unbearable Weight: Feminism, Western Culture, and the Body* (Berkeley: University of California Press, 2003.

Bourdieu, Pierre. *Distinction: A Social Critique of the Judgment of Taste.* Translated by Richard Nice. Cambridge, MA: Harvard University Press, 1984.

Canoe Plants of Ancient Hawaii. Last accessed March 30, 2015. http://www.canoeplants.com/awa.html.

Choi, Nak—Eon and Jung H. Han. *How Flavor Works.* West Sussex, UK: John Wiley & Sons, Ltd., 2015.

Clough, Patricia Ticineto and Jean Halley, eds. *The Affective Turn: Theorizing the Social.* Durham, NC: Duke University Press, 2007.

Eusden, John Dykstra and John H. Westerhoff. *Sensing Beauty: Aesthetics, the Human Spirit, and the Church.* Cleveland, OH: United Church Press, 1998.

Gravina, Stephen A., Gregory L. Yep, and Mehmood Khan. "Human Biology of Taste." *Annals of Saudi Medicine* 33, no. 3 (2013): 217–222.

Gregg, Melissa, and Gregory J. Seigworth, eds. *The Affect Theory Reader.* Durham, NC: Duke University Press, 2010.

Highmore, Ben. "Bitter after Taste: Affect, Food, and Social Aesthetics." In *The Affect Theory Reader*, edited by Melissa Gregg and Gregory J. Seigworth, 118-137. Durham, NC: Duke University Press, 2010, 120.

Hitchcock, Rosewell Dwight, Zachary Eddy, and Philip Schaff, eds. *Hymns and Songs of Praise for Social and Sabbath Worship.* New York: A. S. Barnes & Company, 1875.

Kamakau, Samuel Manaiakalani. *Ka Po'e Kahiko: The People of Old.* Translated by Mary Kawena Pukui. Edited by Dorothy B. Barrère. Honolulu: Bishop Museum Press, 1964.

Korsmeyer, Carolyn. *Making Sense of Taste: Food and Philosophy.* Ithaca: Cornell University Press, 1999.

Kristeva, Julia. *Tales of Love.* Translated by Leon S. Roudiez. New York: Columbia University Press, 1987.

Kuykendall, Ralph Simpson. *The Hawaiian Kingdom*, vol. 1. Honolulu: University of Hawai'i Press, 1938.

Nathanson, Donald L. *Shame and Pride: Affect, Sex, and the Birth of the Self.* New York: W. W. Norton & Company, 1992.

New Revised Standard Version of the Bible, The Division of Christian Education of the National Council of the Churches of Christ in the U.S.A., 1989

Nussbaum, Martha. *Hiding from Humanity.* Princeton, NJ: Princeton University Press, 2006.

Proust, Marcel. *In Search of Lost Time: Swann's Way,* vol. 1. Translated by C. K. Scott Moncrieff and Terence Kilmartin. New York: Modern Library Paperback Edition, 2003.

Saint Bonaventure. *The Journey of the Mind to God.* Translated by Philotheus Bohner, O. F. M. 1956. Reprint, Indianapolis: Hackett Publishing Company, 1990.

Sedgwick, Eve Kosofsky. *Touching Feeling: Affect, Pedagogy, Performativity.* Durham, NC: Duke University Press, 2004.

Svoboda, Robert E. *Prakriti: Your Ayurvedic Constitution.* Twin Lakes, WI: Lotus Press, 1989.

Tomkins, Silvan. *Affect, Imagery, Consciousness,* 4 Vols. 1962. Reprint, New York: Springer Publishing Company, 2008.

Walker Bynum, Caroline. *Holy Feast and Holy Fast: The Religious Significance of Food to Medieval Women.* Berkeley: University of California Press, 1988.

FOUR

Akroatic, Embodied Hearing and Presence as Spiritual Practice

Jennifer Baldwin

How often in today's world do we truly feel heard and seen by another? How often, especially in larger cities, do we go about our daily lives largely unaware of the others in our midst? How many times a day do we say "Hey. How are you?" as we continue to walk past one another barely remaining within earshot to catch the customary "fine," "good," or "busy" response? How frequently do we find that even in the midst of conversation we have missed entire segments of what the other has said either from getting distracted by our own thoughts or by the sounds of our surroundings? For all of the available ways to communicate (phone, text, skype, social media, email, in person, etc.) there persists a challenge in truly and fully connecting or "tuning in" with others. How do we "hear" those things that are unsaid (and unseen in our visual communication)? Moreover, if we struggle to uncover the focus and openness to connect to the others in our midst who may actively be soliciting our attention, how do we even begin to create the space to truly listen and connect to our self or the divine? Truly, how do we fully attune and attentively hear?

This chapter will offer the sense of hearing as a fully embodied, open, and active means of attunement to self, others, and the divine. As such, akroatic (harmonic and rhythmic attunement) embodied hearing and presence, I will argue, is a spiritual practice that opens up new ways to being and thinking about religious, secular, and personal interaction. What is akroatic embodied hearing? Akroatic listening is a term employed by Lisbeth Lipari[1] that she derives from interdisciplinary study of sound and the action of listening. Most simply, she discusses akroatic as attunement to harmony and rhythm. She argues that listening is not simply a matter of attention or of the mechanism of sound reception and interpretation; rather listening is a fully somatic engagement in which one attends to the multidimensionality of communication. Akroatic embodied hearing and presence is receptive to the flow of emotional energy, aware of one's own internal somatic life, and inviting of the many non-verbal means of being present with self, others, and/or the divine. This chapter will trace embodied, akroatic hearing as a nonlinear spiraling journey of communication and presence that moves through reception, interpretation, response to return to a novel reception, interpretation, response, and so on.

RECEPTION: HEARING WITH THE WHOLE BODY

Since at least the time of the Enlightenment, the human sense of sight has received privileged attention as the primary sensory vehicle for rational thought (with hearing as a distant second due to its utility for receiving information via academic lectures) while attention to the senses of taste, touch, and smell have been banished. Banishment of taste, touch, and smell from "proper" historical discourse is largely due to the "messy" intimacy that these later senses require. While it is possible to see or hear in a "rational" way without intimate engagement with the object of sight or hearing, it is quite difficult to smell without participation and impossible to taste or touch without direct interaction. In the divide between sight and hearing on one side and smell, touch, and taste on the other, the line of separation between the two groups is drawn on the body. Sight and hearing as means of acquiring intellectual or rational data can be imaged to be dis-embodied while smell, taste, and touch are body-centered and invoke a sensuality that is anathema to the intention of the thinking and ordered orientation of modernity. Sight and hearing can be co-opted to support the philosophical tradition of separating the mind from the body, rationality from affect or sensation, order from chaos, the masculine from the feminine, active from passive, initiation from reception.[2] These dichotomous poles are invoked in an effort to control, order, and master the natural and social world. The first term in each of the pairs represents the desired way of being, while the latter term threatens the domain of the former. With regard to the human senses, in order to retain the "purity" of the sense of hearing as a vehicle of rationality, it had to become, in as much as it is possible, dis-embodied and cast as the silent partner of the more important speech whether written or verbal. However, this rendering of the sense of hearing from the body is fundamentally inaccurate. Hearing, like all of the other senses (including sight), *requires* participation of the body with the world. It is in fact impossible to hear, see, taste, touch, or smell without viscerally encountering the vibrations, if not the actual flesh, of the other.

While the practices of divide and conquer leading to the binary categories that include mind and body have been quite effective in reinforcing institutions of power and schools of philosophical discourse, it has also successfully and disastrously cut people off from their self, body, and from one another. Rational thought as the ultimate goal of education is no longer sufficient. Descartes's famous epistemological and existential confession "I think therefore I am" is incomplete. Human beings, as well as other species of life, are not solely a floating brain complete unto itself. Brains, as the habitat of the mind (perhaps), are physical and require interaction among neurons as well as new experiences with the internal and external environment. Without the physical interactions between the organism and its environment (where organism can be interpreted as the brain or as the full-bodied entity) there is nothing available "to think." Our environment matters. Our interactions with the others who share our environment matter. Our sensations of the physical and energetic beings of the others matter. Our bodies are essential to thinking and being.

Because our bodies, the environment, and our sensual encounters with our internal and external contexts matter, the mind and "rational" thought cannot truly be separated from the messiness of bodily lived experience. The dissection of knowledge, of humanity from self and community and the corresponding disavowal of the body is losing its authority as provider of universal reason and meaning. Increasingly, scientific disciplines are considering the body and mind not as two components or elements that can be hierarchically ranked but are inextricably linked. The reconnection of body and mind into "mindbody"[3] is a helpful step forward in providing awareness of how individuals may live more holistically, authentically, and integratively with somatic wisdom. Somatic wisdom is a full-bodied reception of all forms of energetic, relational, and content-oriented information though all dimensions of sensation. It is the "knowing" that comes from wise intuition that may be formed prior to the analytical frames offered by rational thought. In many ways, somatic wisdom can be identified as the "bodymind."

Somatic wisdom has historically been neglected at best and overtly discounted at worst. The separation of mind/reason/rationality from bodily awareness and knowing is both unhealthy and hamstrings fullness of understanding. The folly of this separation and assertion of the positive inclusion of the body is noted in Nietzsche's *Thus Spoke Zarathusta* at the conclusion of the nineteenth century. He warns,

> I want to speak to the despisers of the body. I would not have them learn and teach differently, but merely say farewell to their own bodies—and thus become silent. . . . But the awakened and knowing say:

body am I entirely, and nothing else; and soul is only a word for something about the body. . . . The body is a great reason, a plurality with
one sense, a war and a peace, a herd and a shepherd. An instrument of
your body is also your little reason . . . which you call "spirit"—a little
instrument and toy of your great reason. . . . Behind your thoughts and
feelings . . . there stands a might ruler, an unknown sage—whose name
is self. In your body he [*sic*] dwells; he [*sic*] is your body. There is more
reason in your body than in your best wisdom.[4]

Nietzsche's prophetic reclamation of body wisdom contra exclusive dependency on reason highlights the essential resource of the body as more
than your "best wisdom" or knowledge. If we accept Nietzsche's offering
of the body as who I fully am, then we must also re-engage the bodily
senses with full acceptance. It is not only touch, taste, or smell that is
messily embodied, it is also sight and hearing that must be embraced as
embodied sensation.

Lipari illuminates the full bodied-ness of the sense of hearing most
directly. She notes that listening requires interactions with the vibrations
of sound that in turn transform our entire body as a "resonating cham-
ber." She writes, "[A]s listeners, we are in fact participators of sound
because we actually touch the sound."[5] Thus, the physics of sound, music, and sonar tell us something important about listening: not only are
our ears incredibly sensitive to vibration, but so are our bodies and the
bodies of all beings and forms of matter on the planet."[6]

Organisms receive sound vibrations though the entire body, including
but not limited to the ear. The vibrations we receive include far more than
intellectual data for rational thinking. The reception of intellectual content is not in and of itself authentic listening/hearing. Full, attentive presence to another who is seeking to communicate involves attending to the
content, affect, and patterns of the verbal content while also attending to
the nonverbal communication offered by movement and relational energy. Reception of the communication offered by self, others, and the divine requires open attention to the multiplicity of sensory, energetic, verbal, and relational dynamics at play within and among individuals.

With regard to "listening" versus "hearing," Lipari offers the following distinction: "Etymologically, 'listening' comes from a root that emphasizes attention and giving to others, while 'hearing' comes from a root
that emphasizes perception and receiving from others. Indeed, the ideas
of 'gaining' and 'possessing' evoked by the word 'hearing' tend to fore-
ground the self's experience while the ideas of attention and obedience
resonating in the word 'listening' tend to focus on the other."[7] The primary distinction between the etymological characteristics of "listening"
and "hearing" is the dynamics of the flow of energy between communing
parties. "Listening" requires an active forward participation or an energetic "leaning in/forward," while "hearing" harkens toward a more open,
patient presence with another. The energetic dynamics of "listening" and

"hearing" are distinct; however, it is important to recognize that both ways of being present are required to fully and dynamically engage with self, an other, or the divine.

In order to authentically receive another (whether that other is a part of one's own self, another subject, or the divine) in a manner that is respectful of the similarities and differences, we must "listen" *and* "hear." Akroatic (harmonic and rhythmic attunement) embodied presence must actively "turn on" the multiple ways of receiving communication (verbal content, nonverbal expression and movement, and relational and affect energy), "tune in" to the particular other in our midst rather than the plurality of internal and environmental sounds that also beckon our attention, and openly hold relational space for authentic encounters that can facilitate deeper communication and understanding. Akroatic embodied presence dynamically balances between the active engagement of "listening" and the perceptive receiving of "hearing." Without an akroatic embodied presence, interactions with others devolve into interactions in which each party is so invested in "being heard" that no one is listening or hearing. Without akroatic embodied presence, individuals become so caught up in the unending demands of doing that we rarely, if ever, welcome the space to know our selves more fully. And without akroatic embodied presence, we become deaf to the "still small voice" of the divine that speaks to and lovingly guides our intuition.

Akroatic embodied presence facilitates authentic interaction with parts of self, others, and divine, responsively fluctuates between the active stance of "listening" and the receptive posture of "hearing," and is necessarily a body-centered practice. This form of dynamically receptive communicative presence is, at its essence, a spiritual practice that fosters correspondence among body sensation, energetic resonance, interpersonal connection, and transpersonal, attuned openness.

INTERPRETATION: EMBRACING ALTERITY AND THE HERMENEUTICS OF EMPATHY AND MULTIPLICITY

While akroatic embodied presence is universally available, it is highly countercultural and potentially antithetical to the aims of Western, commercialized societies that proliferate by separation of body, sensation, mind, and interpersonal connections and profit via distractions, fleeting satisfactions, and disposable desires. The predominant values and norms that foster economic boons, proliferation of popular cultural fame, isolated communities, and consumer disposability are constructed on epistemologies of power, profit, and mastery rather than attunement and relationality. Western society's obsession with profit and mastery are the natural products of philosophies that encourage separation or atomization of an organism in order to learn about the components as more important or interesting than the whole.

While making important gains in health and learning, the atomization of the environment initiated during the Enlightenment and Modern era has also wrought significant damage to society and the environment through systemic oppression of persons and creatures who are "other" and require domination. This perspective, laden with male and Eurocentric privilege, is evidenced in much of the philosophy of science from the seventeenth century forward. For instance, even the title of Francis Bacon's fragment *The Masculine Birth of Time* co-opts the notion of birth as a biological function of female bodies into a male production of rational and controlled time. This repression or violation of the body (cast as feminine and nature) is also noted by Archbishop Antje Jackelén. She writes, "This sounds like what has been described as the spirit of the English Royal Society: the male scientist subdues female nature, penetrates her and forces her to reveal her secrets. Or, more poetically expressed in Thomas Sprat's History of the Royal Society: 'The Beautiful Bosom of *Nature* will be Expos'd to our view: we shall enter into its *Garden*, and tast [sic] of its *Fruits*, and satisfy our selves with its *plenty.*'" [8] The conflation of nature, feminine, and body in contrast to joining of science, masculinity, and rationality create a relational, disciplinary, philosophical dynamic in which the natural, feminine, and embodied are abused and traumatically dissociated from the scientific, masculine, and rational. This traumatic dissociation of nature, feminine, body, and holistic relationality cede centers of authority to the scientific, masculine, rational, and segmented dissection of knowledge.

The process of how one gathers information is important; though, often times, how one interprets data is more telling of the values and aims of the individual or community. Much has been written, said, and discussed about "postmodernity" among scholars across disciplines for decades. While there is little agreement about dates for the onset of the era, definitions of the term, or whether or not postmodernity "exists" as a distinct era from the modern era, most scholars and individuals will note that there seems to be a shift in dominant narratives and which groups are permitted to set those narratives. Gone are the days of unilateral trust in institutions of power and the stories they tell to mold the world. The predominant gains of modernity through a trust in scientific methods to foster unending progress largely blew away in a mushroom cloud, faith in governmental and religious powers to herald in utopian societies burned to ash in chimneys, and hope in technology to lead us to a Jetsonian society has become lost in a sea of social media, cravings for the latest iphone, and entertainment while neglecting serious social needs.

As institutions of authority are no longer trusted to provide a stable center for life and community, people begin to wonder where to turn for stabilization and security in the world? Do we turn to cable news? Buzzfeed? Youtubers offering plenty of how-to's? For many individuals there is a gnawing need for true, yet person-specific, connection. However, many of us are so bombarded with local and tribal voices seeking to fill the void left by institutions of authority that it is difficult to hear anything. So we turn on our ipods, fix our eternal gaze on Facebook, and wonder why we feel so alone. In the wake of modernity and scientific rationality's failures to midwife the birth of a new (and perfect) society, there is a return to prior wisdoms. The embracing of wisdoms from a "simpler," healthier by-gone era are found in popular cultural trends of everything from paleo diets ("eat like your caveman ancestors") to genetic testing ("discover who you really are by learning about your ancestral roots"), from the rise of yoga in gyms across the United States, to the ever-growing population of people who identify their religious affiliation as "spiritual, not religious." It is ironically interesting that the modern attempt to acquire universal truth through detailed dissection of the world has transitioned into the postmodern recognition that only through recognizing difference and context are we able to access holistic life. The desire for a holistic and rich life and understanding must embrace the body and the wisdom of receptive sensuality as an epistemological resource and provide a hermeneutical structure that attunes to the harmony of contextualized multiplicity.

Akroatic embodied hearing and presence as a spiritual practice that infuses and informs all dimensions of inter- and intrapersonal relationality requires an open and informed awareness of alterity. One of the dominant and overarching assumptions of the modern era of enlightenment is that all human experience is consonant and can be expressed in universal terms. As postmodernity has rightly challenged, this appeal to universal human experience is fundamentally flawed in its misappropriation of the experience of persons with significant social power onto all persons. The beautiful and challenging variations of human experience are whitewashed when a drive toward universal and unitary expression trumps the multitude of diverse, intersectional, and contextual realities. Attention to the great variety of experience necessitates an honoring of the "other-ness" in self and in relationship. Recognition of alterity is not merely a philosophical trope. Recognition of alterity is imperative in creating just societies and communities and is rooted in an awareness of the alterity within each individual.

Recognition of alterity begins with somatic attunement to our own bodies and the connections among proprioceptive sensation, affect, and parts of oneself. In our current cultural epoch of distraction and bodily dissociation, very few people are truly aware of themselves. When one attunes to body, emotion, thoughts, and beliefs, one begins to become more aware of the variety and multitude within each of us. Walt Whitman's well-known poem "Song of Myself" includes the lines "Do I contradict myself? / Very well then I contradict myself, / (I am large, I contain multitudes.)"[9] Whitman poetically highlights the natural human internal multiplicity that emerges from healthy psychological development. The internal multiplicity that undergirds each of us permits us to adapt to a variety of relational and environment encounters and is manifest in body sensations. If one takes a moment to recall a life event that elicited a strong emotion, we may find that the emotion of fear connects with a tightening of the core muscles, a sensation of nausea in the stomach, and a belief that we are not safe. Likewise, once we attend to the fear enough that that part of us is soothed, we may also be aware of the emotion of sadness coupled with a heaviness in the heart area and a belief that we are always alone. And if we can attend to that part of us, we may become aware of an inner strength that allows us a feeling of calm compassionate curiosity and a belief that people did the best they could and, while that may still not be good enough, we can survive and be ok. The parts of us (in this example) that resonate with fear and sadness are distinct somatic, emotional, and cognitive entities and make up some of who we are and facilitate our capabilities. The dimension of the self that is grounded, calm, compassionate, centered, curious, creative, courageous, and connected sustains the multiplicity generated by individual and contextual experiences.[10] Recognition and honoring of the alterity within is the essential foundation of healthy recognition of alterity in others.

The honoring of alterity is a foundational element in akroatic embodied hearing and presence. It is, in many regards, a precondition for interpretation. If the interpretation of somatically received information isn't automatically provided by societal authority and social conditioning (which it shouldn't be), how then do we make sense of our experiences and the information gifted to us by others. By valuing and granting alterity importance and significance, akroatic embodied hearing and presence must proceed via a hermeneutics of multiplicity and empathy.

A hermeneutic of multiplicity takes seriously the presence and perspective of otherness that is highlighted through alterity. As we somatically attune to our body and the presence of others, we become increasingly aware of our own internal multiplicity; and by acknowledging and internally caring for our own multiplicity, we gain the lenses to respectfully attend to the multiplicity of persons in community and the multiplicity within persons in community. Antje Jackelén insightfully connects alterity and interpretation via plurality. She writes, "By this development [aiming to grasp meaning that points toward a possible world, about its reference to new worlds or new 'modes-of-being-in-the-world'], the notion of *otherness* entered the discourse of interpretation. When otherness is taken seriously, it encourages a plurality of readings and acknowledges the otherness within the interpreter."[11] "Otherness within the interpreter" is a given of internal and relational multiplicity within discourses of understanding, meaning, as well as within divine, communal, and personal identity. Full-bodied attention to the variety of external and relational shifts that healthfully occur in the presence of listening/hearing is built on the foundation and mirrors how one negotiates their internal multiplicity.

A hermeneutics of multiplicity is not only vitally important for intra- and interpersonal encounters; it is of great import for theological reflection and faithful confession of the divine. Theologian Laurel Schneider offers the concept of "the One" as the established though significantly limited dominant trope of divinity, which, she argues, influences the history of culture and society in which systems of unilateral power and agency are reinforced to the oppression of alterity and multiplicity. She writes,

> Oneness and unity, like all abstractions (including the abstraction of divine multiplicity) are vulnerable to the fallacy of misplaced concreteness. Their usefulness makes it easy to forget that they are concepts placed upon reality to sort its ontological multiplicity. No matter how many times we may wish to lift our gaze from the cacophony of embodied existence toward the serenity of unifying concepts in the hope of bringing closure to the world's actual unruly shiftiness, the attempt to construct a summary "after all" fails. . . . Without the multiplicity of matter, unity slips into ideology and begins to dream—noisily—of reductions, closures, and totality. . . . Although unity (even more than oneness) is an ingredient of sanity for human beings, neither idea is adequate to conceptualize divinity, or world. It is out of the logic of the One that Hell's eternity was made, to squash the real multiplicity of divinity and world into a basement closet of ice, and so to pretend that it is 'in charge of the world'. . . . This dream of the One is a denial of incarnation and a serious error in theological thinking.[12]

Schneider correctly names multiplicity as not only a hermeneutic but an ontological reality while also distinguishing "unity" from "singularity." In all cases of conceptual abstraction, there is a risk of losing connection with the reality that the concept is attempting to embrace. Leading with a conception of normative singularity of identity, persons, communities, animals, or apples miss out on the vast array of what is present in existing matter. Moreover, it removes us from "the cacophony of embodied existence" in which resides the messiness of the actual world. With regard for akroatic embodied hearing and presence as a spiritual practice that opens up connection to the divine, singularity promotes acknowledgment of one strategy for engaging the world as the total and sole option which necessarily diminishes the varieties of relational and responsive strategies that each person possesses. When individuals are locked into a hermeneutics of "the One" (whether "the One" is a rigid divine monotheism, singularity of personality in which what I experience in this moment is regarded as the totality of who I am, or a universalizing of human experience), the options for interpreting our awareness and sensations become highly curtailed and inflexibly devolve into the binary of either right or wrong. Multiplicity, as a hermeneutical and ontological option, is all around us and offers resources for living from a position of in/corporeal cohesion. Cohesion of multiple parts/components, rather than integration,[13] honors the wise presence and graceful compassion that can emerge from embracing multiplicity as identity, hermeneutic, and ontology.

Observance, recognition, and an honoring of alterity is a precondition for akroatic embodied hearing and presence. The act of hearing and presence involves relationality. When one openly receives the alterity within, among, and surrounding, a hermeneutic of multiplicity is the natural lens through which one begins to interpret all interactions. The relationship formed, nourished, and sustained by akroatic embodied presence involves, at minimum, two distinct parties. While one of the parties may be the individual, part of an individual, or self of the individual, the other party must be, in some measure, distinct. If I am unaware of the multiplicity and alterity within myself, I may lose awareness of resources for coping, connection, or empathy that are present within and from that loss may not be capable of being fully present, resonant, and connected with the other before me or with the divine. Connecting awareness among body sensation, affect, beliefs, and parts within myself facilitates the capacity to utilize the energetic resonance between people as a means of presence.

Human beings (and many other mammals) utilize "mirror neurons" which activate when an individual performs an action and when that individual observes another performing the action. The "mirroring" of an "others" movement (large and nuanced) forms the basis of empathy. For instance, when I see a person seated with their shoulders shrugged forward, legs bent with feet on the floor, and knees at chest level and with their arms hugging their legs and head bent down with their forehead on their knees, my mirror neurons activate reminding my body of the experience of sitting in that posture. If I am aware of the connections between body sensation, proprioception, affect, beliefs, and parts, I can gently intuit that the person before me is likely experiencing sadness, despair, exhaustion, abandonment, and may believe that they aren't good enough, worthwhile, or something similar. If my own parts who hold the somatic, affective, and cognitive dimensions that match this posture get activated without my ability to recognize the multiplicity within myself, I may be so attuned and resonated with the person before me that I am unable to provide a stable and compassionate presence. However, if I am aware and attendant to the alterity within myself, I retain an ability to be fully present without projecting my experiences with this posture onto the other's current experience.

The compassionate and curious opening of interpretation then becomes the source of a hermeneutic of empathy. Empathy, as distinct from sympathy as a "feeling with," centers on a "feeling or sensing into" the experience of another. While sympathy includes a joining with the other in a more complete way than empathy, the recognition of the experience of the other while retaining one's own experience is the strength of empathetic response. It is akin to saying that one has aware compassion for the struggle while still retaining enough self-distinction to provide balanced assistance. Empathy begins with an assumption of shared, yet distinctly individualized, human affective response and meaning making. While each person has their own distinct history of interpersonal interactions, learned schema for ordering new experiences, and internal narratives, empathy is what allows us to put ourselves "in another person's shoes" with the intention of compassionate understanding rather than "fixing."

If hermeneutics provides the lens or fore-structure through which we interpret and understand, then a hermeneutic of empathy is what allows us to attend to the needs of internal and external others without becoming overwhelmed by their experience. In a ministry of pastoral care, if the caregiver becomes fully involved in the emotional content of the care receiver, then the caregiver can no longer offer the kind of stable care that is required by the care receiver. The balance point between feeling into while remaining distinct is a challenge for many individuals; however, the challenge is more easily met with an honoring of alterity and an awareness of multiplicity. A hermeneutic of empathy offers the lenses of understanding, contextualization, and compassion in the process of akroatic embodied hearing and presence. It is the somatic resonance between self and others that provides the connection for empathy, and it is a commitment to empathy as an interpretative lens that facilitates compassionate and appropriate response.

RESPONSE: REVERSING TRADITIONAL DESIGNATIONS OF RELATIONAL POWER

Akroatic embodied hearing and presence is not limited to the reception and interpretation of somatic, affective, energetic, movement, and content. Fully engaged somatic presence must also include a response and how we respond is a matter of ethics. Lipari discusses, in reference to akroatic listening, an "ethics of attunement." [14] She offers "akroatic thinking as a 'thinking listening.'" She writes, "*thinking listening as a way of being* [emphasis hers] creates the possibility of an ethics driven neither by rules and obligations nor by outcomes and consequences, but rather, one that is drawn towards an ethics of attunement—an awareness of and attention to the harmonic interconnectivity of all beings and objects." [15] Lipari's ethics of attunement echoes H. Richard Niebuhr's classic text of Christian ethics, *The Responsible Self.* [16] Through this text Niebuhr offers three categories for ethical decision making: the teleological, deontonlogical, and responsible with associated symbols of man-the-maker, man-the citizen, and man-the-responder, respectively. For Niebuhr, the ultimate aim of ethics is to "know thyself" and "to seek guidance for our activity as we decide, choose, commit ourselves, and otherwise bear the burden of our necessary human freedom."[17] He offers man[sic]-the-responder as a more authentic means of acting in the world. Rather than making choices in relation in order to achieve a desired goal or because an external authority deems such behavior as "right," Niebuhr argues that ethical action is response/able. Responsibility, for Niebuhr, has four elements: response, interpretation, accountability, and social solidarity.[18] These four elements highlight the relationality implicit in "responding" to another, the inescapability of the process of interpreting the "actions" of others and self, the necessity of thoughtfully claiming one's own responsive affect, energy, movement, and language, and the call for responses that are contextual and attuned to the larger social surroundings and needs. Translated into the current discussion, responding ethical action is attuned to the needs of self and others through a harmonizing of somatic resonance of body, affect, energy, motion,[19] and context.

Inherent within all relationships, internal and external, is a flow of power. While it is common to hear about economic power, political power, or physical power, it is less common to attend to the dynamics of power that exist within and among all relationships. Tracing relational power is at the same time imminently available and elusively complex. When limiting the scope of awareness, relational power is fairly easy to "tune in to." For instance, think about who holds the predominance of power between a police officer and a driver who is pulled over and issued a speeding ticket. Think of who brokers the upper hand of power between a parent and a child (at least most of the time). How about the power relationship between a physician and nurse or physician and patient? These examples are fairly clear-cut: the former most often wields more power than the latter. To complicate matters, think about who makes the decisions in your relationship with your best friend or partner. My hope is in these relationships the balance of power is fairly neutral with an alteration of who holds "the upper hand" depending on the situation or context. Relational power, theologically and psychologically, boils down to an individual's or group's ability to advocate for their own well-being and the agency to move toward flourishing fulfillment. Power is not an all-or-nothing enterprise; it is fluid and present in every living creature (or internal part). Relational power employed well and with mutuality will contribute to the overall health, security, and development of all relational parties. When misused and/or used unilaterally, relational power can become destructive toward all participants.

An awareness and attention to relational power is essential in how one authentically practices akroatic embodied hearing and presence. Reception of the other is the first component to akroatic embodied hearing and presence and requires awareness of the multitude of ways in which human beings receive parts of self, external others, and the divine. In receiving the internal, external, or divine other, we are granted the opportunity to discern the flow of relational power between self and another. The discernment of relational power requires somatic awareness, a calming of our internal system in order to gauge the dynamics of the relational encounter, and embracing of the opportunity to connect with another part, person, or divine presence. Akroatic embodied interpretation is the second component and necessitates an openness to alterity, multiplicity, and empathy. With regard to relational power, the somatic resonance that fuels our interpretation has the potential to foster or impede further connection. If I encounter another and interpret the encounter in such a way as to activate defensive parts of myself, I will access my available power and respond in a manner to disconnect and push the other away; however, if I encounter another and interpret the resonance between us as nonthreatening or as engaging, I will utilize my relational power to enhance the connection between us. As Niebuhr, and others, rightly recognize, all actions are based as much, if not more, on our interpretation of an encounter as the quality of the encounter itself. Response is the third dimension of akroatic embodied hearing and presence. Given an authentic and centered reception, attuned and empathic interpretation of our encounter with alterity, how then shall we respond with a healthy use of relational power?

Akroatic embodied response recognizes a great variety of means of responsiveness including but not limited to the many ways in which we receive: verbal, emotional, energetic, movement, or physical touch. Verbal responsiveness is the most common and includes conversation. While dialogue (or some forms of monologue) can be attuned and responsive to the internal and relational context, it very seldom takes this quality in ordinary lived experience. As such, this is the form of response that is most likely to occur and is most likely to miss the mark of an attentive and authentic engagement. While I have the option to respond to another being or part verbally, there are a great variety of other responses that rarely are granted academic attention but can be far more attentively effective. I can attend to the somatic shifts and associated affect occurring in my own body and allow the other to witness and receive my experience. I can offer an energetic exchange either through conscious breathing or imagery. I can also move my body to mirror the other or engage in compassionate, consensual touch to express care and presence.[20] Responsive offerings can come in a variety of forms; the essential element is that the response is attuned and emerges from a centered, fully embodied place of resonance that is sensitive to the flow of relational power and the present state of power.

Most of the time when we attend to and analyze relational power, we perceive the party with the upper hand of power as being the active agent who speaks, acts, and establishes the relational norms. Correspondingly, the listening, attending party is identified as the party with less relational power. However, this equation of action and power is not always accurate; especially in the case of the practice of akroatic embodied hearing and presence. At its most basic, akroatic embodied hearing and presence, particularly as a spiritual practice connecting the practitioner to the divine, is a practice of "truly attentive listen[ing]." Through her research on the power of listening, Lipari notes, "In general, truly attentive listeners not only elicit more information from speakers, but they also facilitate the speaker's long-term memory."[21] Lipari's statement supports the claim that the "passive" act of attentive listening is quite powerful in creating a relational dynamic that allows the "active" speaker to share more deeply and with greater retention of their speech. It truly embodies theologian Nelle Morton's phrase "hearing to speech."[22] Through akroatic embodied hearing and practice, the "hearer" is more often the holder of more relational power, while the "speaker" holds comparatively less. This reversal makes a lot of sense when applied to the practice of psychotherapy or pastoral care. The "hearer" is often caregiver and the "speaker" is the care receiver.

It is helpfully important to identify this dynamic and how it extends beyond the realm of therapy or pastoral counseling and into many other domains of relational life. For example, in many Eurocentric churches the act of homiletics is a created action of the pastor and the congregation is generally considered a more-or-less passive audience. In this relational dynamic, the pastor's voice is the one dominating the space; however, the congregation members can either dismiss this show of power or, through attentive listening, facilitate a deepening of connection between leader, congregation, and God. Akroatic embodied hearing and presence occurs in services of ritual when all participants, regardless of spoken roles, are fully present and attendant to the variety of relational communication. The sharing of the relational power of reception, interpretation, and response generates a co-creation of meaning. For example, African-American congregations in the United States demonstrate a rich tradition of active and, at times, full-bodied participation in worship in which the congregants play an active verbal role in homiletics by encouraging and co-creating the sermon itself. This co-creation of meaning is requisite in the formation of healthy communal relationality. "Meaning is co-created in a way not necessarily attributable to either of the interaction partners. Mutual incorporation opens up potential new domains of sense-making; that is, domains of sense-making that were not available to me as an individual."[23] When communities of individuals share in the co-creation of life, we are joining with the creative energy of the divine.

THE ETERNAL SPIRAL FROM RESPONSE TO RECEPTION AND INTERPRETATION AND BACK AGAIN

Akroatic embodied hearing and presence is ultimately a spiritual practice in which we attune to the divine: transcendent, immanent, relational, and internal. This form of presence "requires an awareness of our habitual categories and a willingness to go beyond them. One suggestion is to listen from a space of emptiness and unknowing, to be strong enough to relinquish our perceived mastery, control, and foreknowledge while remaining attentive and aware."[24] The habitual categories that impede our individual and communal fulfillment of our true being are woefully inadequate and function to reinforce systems of domination in which the tremendous power and wisdom of the "quiet" is dismissed in favor of the brash and loud. While Christian scriptures describe the divine as both "whirlwind" and "still small voice,"[25] in our current society in which stillness and quiet are hard to come by and a symphony of distractions beckon us, it is with an openness to the multiple dimensions of relational reception and through the recognition of alterity, multiplicity, and empathy that we are best equipped to respond to our selves and others, human, animal, and environmental, with appropriate compassion and relational power.

The relational dynamic supported by a spiritual practice of akroatic embodied hearing is an eternal spiral in which response issues an invitation for another to receive via akroatic embodied hearing and presence. When participants can foster this form of relational attention and attunement, deeper and more meaningful connections become possible, internally, externally, globally, and universally, as each participant grows in self-understanding, harmony, and awareness to the divine presence in and with all.

NOTES

1. Lisbeth Lipari, *Listening, Thinking, Being: Toward an Ethics of Attunement* (University Park: Penn State University Press, 2014).

2. Feminist scholars across disciplines have long problematized dualisms and highlighted how dualist thinking strengthens social and cultural structures of power and oppression. For an example of this critique within Christian theology, see Sallie McFague, *Super, Natural Christians: How We Should Love Nature* (Minneapolis: Fortress Press, 1997).

3. While I appreciate the joining of "mind" and "body" in the term "mindbody," this unitary term does retain the privilege of mind first and body second. I wonder about the shift in awareness and attention if instead body was granted privilege. How would thinking and being differ if it emerged from the "bodymind"?

4. Friedrich Nietzsche, *Thus Spoke Zarathustra*, trans. by Walter Kaufmann (New York: The Modern Library, 1995), 34.

5. Lipari, 31.

6. Ibid., 43.

7. Ibid., 50.

8. Antje Jackelén, *The Dialogue between Religion and Science: Challenges and Future Directions* (Kitchener: Pandora Press, 2004), 37.

9. Walt Whitman, *Leaves of Grass* (Dover Publications; Original 1855 edition).

10. The Internal Family Systems model of psychotherapy provides the most robust exploration of the parts of persons, the internal dynamics within each person, and the role of Self as the source of spirituality and connection to the divine. See www.selfleadership.orgfor more information.

11. Jackelén, 20.

12. Laurel Schneider, *Beyond Monotheism: A Theology of Multiplicity* (New York: Routledge Press, 2008), 200.

13. "Integration" as a psychological term and as a religion-and-science methodology are problematic in that they tend toward the development of a singularity rather than a unity of multiplicity. While I believe that "integration" could provide a fruitful image for trauma-sensitive theology at some point in the future, it first requires some intentional rehabilitation from its current usage that has functioned to shame trauma survivors in the awareness and experience of internal multiplicity.

14. Lipari, 2–3.

15. Ibid.

16. H. Richard Niebuhr, *The Responsible Self: An Essay in Christian Moral Philosophy* (New York: Harper and Row Publishers, 1963).

17. Ibid., 48.

18. Ibid., 61–65.

19. Embodied and mindful movement is a key resource in full presence. Emmanuel Lartey's chapter in this volume expounds on the role of the sense of proprioception in religious practices of healing and spirituality.

20. Please refer to chapters 2 and 9 authored by Shirley Guider and Christina Davis respectively for further assessment on the healthful and harmful dimensions of the use of touch in Christian practice and care.

21. Lipari, 90.

22. Nelle Morton, *The Journey Is Home* (Boston: Beacon Press, 1985).

23. Lipari, 131.

24. Ibid., 99.

25. In consideration of the Christian narratives of creation, particularly Genesis 1, I am creatively intrigued by the idea of a reversal of power in which creation practices akroatic embodied hearing that hears God into speech and permits the divine to know Godself fuller and with more longevity.

REFERENCES

Jackelén, Antje. *The Dialogue Between Religion and Science: Challenges and Future Directions*. Kitchener: Pandora Press, 2004.

Lipari, Lisbeth. *Listening, Thinking, Being: Toward an Ethics of Attunement*. University Park: Penn State University Press, 2014.

McFague, Sallie. *Super, Natural Christians: How We Should Love Nature*. Minneapolis: Fortress Press, 1997.

Morton, Nelle. *The Journey is Home*. Boston: Beacon Press, 1985.

Niebuhr, H. Richard. *The Responsible Self: An Essay in Christian Moral Philosophy*. New York: Harper and Row Publishers, 1963.

Nietzsche, Friedrich. *Thus Spoke Zarathustra*. Translated. by Walter Kaufmann. New York: The Modern Library, 1995.

Schneider, Laurel. *Beyond Monotheism: A Theology of Multiplicity*. New York: Routledge Press, 2008.

Whitman, Walt. *Leaves of Grass*. Dover Publications: 1855.

FIVE

Devotional Looking and the Possibilities of Free Associative Sight

Sonia Waters

Sight is often imagined as a unidirectional sense that registers information from a passively available world.[1] But sight is better understood as a
reciprocal process between eye and object, between the thoughts or emotions of the viewer and the social information embedded in the objects
that we see. Every individual eye is already social, and every social object
rich with personal associations. Similarly, religious eyes looking at religious objects combine the viewer's life history with the context of her faith
tradition evoked by the image.[2] Our religious visual culture—statues,
images, prayer cards, powerpoint slides, or framed scripture verses—
become laden with personal meanings. They also influence the direction
of our theology, acting as sources of teaching or inspiration on what the
community believes about the Divine.

In this chapter, I focus on devotional looking as one particular visual
experience that can be cultivated for its pastoral possibilities. In times of
suffering or loss, when we are no longer sure how to articulate the connections between life experience and the teachings of our faith, we can
use the nonverbal process of devotional time with images to "look into"
these connections in new and creative ways. The process of sustained
devotional time looking at religious images can act as a kind of experiential free association, helping a person of faith think through the life difficulties that bump up against belief. It can inspire a visual theological
thinking that draws from both personal history and religious context into
new insights to one's faith.

I am defining devotional looking as a process of free associative thought, where an individual spends meditative time with an image that is derived from her religious tradition. The viewer cultivates a dreamlike engagement with the image, imaginatively interacting with its characters, allowing her thoughts and feelings to arise without censure, and making connections between the form and content of the image and one's personal questions or concerns. To describe this process of looking, I draw from psychoanalyst Christopher Bollas's theory of experiential free association. I then turn to visual studies theorist David Morgan's concept of *sacred gaze* to describe the social eye: how we look through the received traditions and expectations of religious community. I draw on examples from art historian James Elkins to return to the claim that concentrated time looking at images changes our thought life. I conclude with a case study of a man in the midst of grief and transition who used devotional looking to think through a condensed field of associations relating to aging, death, and the afterlife.

SIGHT AS PERSONAL INSIGHT

As we look throughout our days, we attach our own history, problems, and interests to the things we see in the world. This is the beginning of a visual free association. We continue to experientially free associate as we let our minds wander, attaching thought to vision, vision to emotion, emotion to thought and back to vision, creating a chain of associations that are actually a manner of thinking through areas of interest in our lives. Bollas draws on Sigmund Freud's claim that free association is like riding on a train while describing to someone else the changing views you see out the window. For instance, we see an airport, a canal, and a low hill graced with vineyards. The airport reminds us of our summer plans, past life-changing trips, the expansion of airports, the oddity of flight, and "innumerable part-thoughts that almost enter consciousness but don't quite make it."[3] Crossing the canal we think of a longed-for trip on a canal boat yet to be accomplished. We think of a relative's house, which was by a canal. We might also think of the dentist and a root canal. And, says Bollas, "so it goes for the other 'objects' passed along this journey," as the mind develops a meshwork of thoughts related to the sights in the window's frame.[4]

As the viewer's eye moves across her field of vision, her unconscious continues to make associations, knitting together lines of thought that combine and grow toward insight, much like the verbal practice of free associating in therapy.[5] This process can be emotionally rich, but it is also a form of thought. When an image or object evokes a moment of intense psychic interest, the unconscious brings disparate ideas together in new ways, connecting "constellations of thought, feeling and self-states" relat-

ed to that experience.[6] Bollas calls this process *condensation*. The viewer
continues to wander through her day associating to other objects and
images toward which she is drawn, breaking the original psychic interest
into new chains of associations. Bollas calls this process *dissemination*.
Thus the interaction between eye and object contribute to the infinite
combinations of associations in our evolving thought life, condensing
new connections and breaking up old constellations into new chains of
thought.

Objects in the world serve as a point of projection for personal content
but also provide a source of knowledge that enters new information into
the web of the viewer's growing mental life. Bollas explains that there are
two shafts of interest created by the objects we see, "one purely internal,
arising out of desire or affect, the other consisting of actual things we
encounter in the real."[7] Their material qualities, personal, and cultural
meanings contribute to the viewer's developing thought. The unconscious mind culls and combines from the world of things into the meshwork of the unconscious, generating the rich mental content that feeds a
creative and generative thought life.

Concentrated time looking at an image can cultivate these connections. From an artist's perspective, James Elkins gives the example of
observing his students at the Chicago Museum of Art, as they copy a
painting for hours every week. At first, they have a hard time looking at
one image hour after hour, week after week. According to Elkins the
paintings tangle into their daily lives, "recurring like hallucinations when
they are trying to eat or watch television."[8] Aspects of the painting condense with other experiences in their thought life. Over time they find
that "the paintings have surprised and bored them, chastised them in
their daydreams, scared them in nightmares, and eventually seduced
them."[9] The image has become an intimate part of their growing mental
life. Images thus require concentrated time to find a permanent place in
the viewer's imagination. He says, "A picture will leave me unmoved if I
don't take time with it, but if I stop, and let myself get a little lost, there's
no telling what might happen."[10]

This contemporary experience of concentrated looking is related to
the long history of Western Christian devotional practices. For instance,
Elkins comments on Medieval Christian practices at the height of devotional looking, claiming that time spent with images was meant to evoke
an intense visceral reaction that would change how the viewer experienced her faith.[11] The viewer was encouraged to identify with Jesus or
Mary bodily, and "to try to think of [oneself] as Jesus or the Mother of
God" over a long time of contemplation and prayer.[12] Elkins is clear that
this experience before art is more than a conjuring of emotion. It is an
empathic infiltration of the mind of the viewer into the mind and body of
the person depicted. The viewer would look at such an image steadily,
sometimes for hours or days on end, entering more and more deeply into

the mind of Jesus and Mary until "finally you would come to feel what they had felt, and you would see the world, at least in some small part, through their eyes." [13] This new insight through the sacred image would change how the viewer understood the doctrine represented in the painting, or how she saw herself in relation to God.

LOOKING THROUGH THE SOCIAL LENS

Religious images are particular objects that stimulate free association, and they do so through the communal experiences and messages of the faith. Visual studies theorist David Morgan calls religious looking *sacred gaze*. Sacred gaze is "the manner in which a way of seeing invests an image, a viewer, or the act of viewing with spiritual significance." [14] The viewer sees from a certain subject position that has internalized the expectations of context and community, including what to think or feel before an image. We are trained by our religious and social contexts toward seeing certain objects and images as sacred or as communications of theological or scriptural truth. These objects in turn aid in forming our religious subjectivity and sense of self.

This sacred gaze is situated within a range of communal practices the faithful enact upon seeing an image, which Morgan calls *visual piety*. Along with explicit catechetical training in the faith, religious objects convey implicit theological knowledge through how the object is bodily experienced in community. For instance, religious art is experienced within communal rituals, including actions such as processions, theatrical spectacle, commemoration of the dead, or teaching of the faith. [15] The image might collaborate with other meaning-laden aesthetic experiences such as dance, music, or architecture. [16] It also communicates broader social messages perpetuated through our faith traditions, such as raced or gendered discourses. The viewer's response to the object or image is further set within a range of expected worship practices or devotional expressions to the image. Embodied practices with objects or images combine with catechetical knowledge to help create, maintain, or transform the social and religious worldview of the viewer. What the viewer becomes through these repeated encounters is a religious subjectivity formed to a certain embodied knowledge of her faith.

Morgan thus focuses on the culturally constituted aspect of looking in a religious context. Through a combination of images, objects, and rituals, the religious eye is formed into a particular way of seeing the faith, "which structures social relations, self-concept, and experience of the sacred." [17] For example, a viewer might be trained over many years of worship in her faith tradition to see images of the Madonna and Child as sacred. When she sees a certain picture of a woman and child together, she is able to identify it as a Madonna and Child image through the expectations of her faith tradition. She feels a sense of humility or devotion. She might interact with the image by kneeling or lighting a candle, as she has seen others do since she was a child. Perhaps the soft, gentle gestures of Mary reinforce discourses around gender and motherhood that the viewer considers sacred for women. The expectation of a particular emotional response to seeing, the accompanying actions that feel appropriate, the thoughts that come to mind, or the sense of sacredness derived from the image are received from her social and theological context. In this way, seeing is never solely personal. It relies on a complex of "assumptions and inclinations, habits and routines, historical associations and cultural practices" that encourage our sense of the sacred.[18]

If the reception of religious images is culturally conditioned, how does the viewer come to individual insight through devotional looking? On the one hand, the objects and images of religion do express and maintain social and religious norms. Morgan calls this effect *the politics of things*, or how aesthetic objects are embedded within social fields of meaning. But there is also *the poetics of things*, "their capacity to act upon us, to assert agency, to make rather than to only be made."[19] This returns us to free association, and the power of images to feed our thought life. Morgan claims that images generate meaning, stimulate associations, and suggest new interpretations for making sense of the viewer's individual and communal life.[20] Looking engages the mind associatively, connecting the religious traditions and social expectations communicated through the image to the daily contingencies of the viewer's personal life. The image asserts agency upon the viewer by adding new possibilities and connections to the associative meshwork of the unconscious.

Elkins offers an example of concentrated time spent looking at a religious image, which illustrates the dialectic between personal and social looking. He reflects on the Russian Orthodox image, *Icon with the Fiery Eye*.[21] He imagines a viewer looking at the icon and seeing a very different image depending on her own physical or emotional state at the point of looking. The image could appear at one moment troubled, the next ancient, the next uncomfortable or peaceful, as the viewer keeps looking. But Elkins clarifies that the viewer's social and religious context would also influence the effects of looking over time. The viewer would see the icon differently if she was an Eastern Orthodox believer or from another culture or religion entirely. It would affect the viewer differently if she had just been to worship, or was feeling guilty for not attending at all. Elkins claims that over time, "when you have seen it enough and it is time to move on, the image will be quite complex—a kaleidoscope of thoughts and images that coalesce from all the individual moments that you spent thinking and looking."[22]

In sum, free association is continuously at work, stimulating the self's psychic interests and feeding our thought life "through engagement in the world of things."[23] It can be cultivated, as concentrated time with images further internalizes their effects. When we focus this time on images from our faith tradition, it becomes devotional, as we meet the theology, heritage, and practices of our faith in the image. As the viewer looks, she is able to consider anew the problems or questions troubling her mind, or create new syntheses between life experience and the social and cultural messages that inform her life, including those of her faith tradition.

CASE STUDY: GREG[24] AND GOYA'S *TRANSITION OF ST. JOSEPH*

To illustrate how visual free association can lead to theological reflection, I focus on the story of one participant in a small group project assigned to the task of looking at a religious image of their choice.[25] Greg was sixty-nine years of age, and newly retired from a career in finance. He had been a regular churchgoer for the last thirty years. His theological concerns were related to mortality, death, and the afterlife.[26] His father had died two years earlier. He chose a sketch of a painting by Francisco Goya (1746–1828) that he titled *The Transition of Saint Joseph.*[27] In it, Joseph is lying in a bed and looks sick and worn. Jesus is sitting next to him in a chair on the left, holding his hand and leaning over him. Joseph seems to be straining to look Jesus in the face. Mary is to the right of Joseph with arms open as if in prayer. Angels gather behind them, framing the composition of figures into a triangle. There are no walls to the room, only what appears to be clouds and light.

In the first session, Greg described his picture as Jesus at the bedside as Joseph is getting ready to die. He said he was very involved in it for the whole of the session. As he looked at the picture, he made up three or four different stories about it. He was trying to figure out what they were saying to each other, and wondering if Joseph was still alive or had already died. Greg said that he was attracted to the image because he saw another version at an exhibit of Spanish art. He had remembered it again when his father died. He looked for the image to use for our art project because the image still attracted him. He called it "so very involved, so very interesting."

In the second session, Greg agreed that the picture was partly about his father's death, but also about death in general. He said, "I'm starting to look ahead to friends dying, to me dying too, you know, other people dying and trying to figure out how that is all going to work." He gestured to his picture and concluded that this was a good way to think about all that. He had imagined them praying the Lord's Prayer together, because it was easy to imagine them praying together, or Joseph asking Jesus to help him pray. He said that they then moved on into broader discussions, and then "by the time I got to the end of the half hour they were all singing together." He commented on how Mary looked "out of it." He wondered what she was doing back there. Mary is sketchily drawn and her face is blurred in the background.

For the third session, Greg claimed, "they are still my friends." He had continued to play with entering into the picture, saying, "Sometimes I'm the old man and sometimes I'm the comforter." He still appeared to be concerned about Mary. He seemed uncomfortable that the focus was only on the men. He acknowledged that it was a sketch, so maybe that was why Mary was only barely drawn. Even Jesus is sketched. He admitted that the most powerfully drawn is the old man as he dies. Jesus is helping him through, or maybe talking to his mother and to his "father on earth." He then said that, because he volunteers for a chaplaincy organization, he thought Jesus was like a chaplain: "The Great Chaplain. He's also the Good Shepherd." Greg began another sentence, but then stopped. He turned to the question of why, if Jesus had raised people from the dead, he didn't raise Joseph. He concluded that Joseph "looks like he is very ill so that is probably why." He changed the subject, commenting on how his time with the picture was a good stimulus to the imagination and to prayer.

In the next session, when I asked if there were themes emerging for the participants, Greg replied that his remained the same: the father, and the old man dying. He added, "Sometimes I'm the old man, sometimes my father is." I confirmed that the issue was death. He replied that he is the oldest one now. I confirmed that it is his death as well. He replied in his understated way, "It'll be along. When it comes." Then he added that it would be nice to have a comforter there. His wife, who also participated in the group, broke in to say that she would recite a poem at his deathbed.[28] Greg laughed, but returned to his point. "I'll try to invite Jesus to be there too."

For our last session, Greg continued his imaginative engagement with the image. He told the group that he had entered his time of looking by saying "a little prayer" asking for help. Then he mentioned the title of the picture, *The Transition of St. Joseph*. He said that he had started taking the idea of transition seriously, and imagined the moment of death as a time of transition. He mentioned that there were no walls in the background, just light and angels. Greg thought that this also explained why Mary seemed so blurred and distant. He said, "It's as if the wall had come down and the heaven and earth are beginning to kind of just meet right there." Greg decided that this was a pretty interesting way of thinking about death and dying. He continued:

> We've really been thinking of our friend's death and then thinking about our relatives' deaths, we've been thinking about death a lot. And uh, we are both now the oldest I guess in our, in our lines. Which is a little scary, so—. Um, and we are not working full time any more so we have more time to think. (Chuckles) For better or for worse. So it was, it was, it was um, it was different this time, and it was very interesting.

It was also important for Greg to come to terms with the religious implications of his father's death. According to Greg, the idea of God had
never crossed his father's mind. That had worried Greg. He concluded
that *The Transition of St. Joseph* was very consoling for him. I confirmed
that he found the picture particularly consoling about his father's death.
He replied, "Yes, somehow yeah . . . Jesus is right there with him, holding
his hand."

CONCLUSION

Greg's time looking at his image utilized practices of visual piety learned
from his religious context, such as the Lord's Prayer, hymn singing, and
devotional contemplation. He further approached his picture from a particular sacred gaze. He found the subject matter spiritually meaningful
due to Christian theological teachings around the afterlife, salvation, and
the forgiveness of Jesus, well known to Greg after thirty years of church
attendance. Greg also was able to play with the subject matter of *The
Transition* because he was familiar with the history of Christian discourse
surrounding Joseph.[29] The Roman Catholic Church taught that Joseph
was a much older man, married to the young Mary.[30] Joseph disappears
early in the Gospel story, yet tradition believes he was a holy man with a
close relationship to Jesus. This theological tradition allowed Greg to
associate personally with the image. He was also an eldest son, and now
identified as an old man. Drawing from this received tradition, the depic-
tion of love between a father and son evoked a sacred feeling of intimacy.
It also allowed Greg to associate himself to Joseph as an old Christian
man.

    Greg viewed his picture from a Christian perspective that taught him
to hope in the afterlife. But recent personal changes had left him ambivalent about what death and heaven might mean for himself, his friends,
and his late father. Goya's manner of depicting this legend—the position-
ing of the characters and the lightly sketched horizon—led to associations
that knit together Greg's theology with recent personal experiences. He
connected the intimacy of the gaze between Jesus and the dying man to
Jesus's role as chaplain, comforter, and Good Shepherd. He struggled
with the lightly sketched Mary in the background. He considered what it
was like to feel "old" in light of his recent retirement and his new position as the eldest surviving male of his line. He interacted imaginatively
with the characters as if he was at the edge of his own death. Over time,
he articulated a theology of death and afterlife as a kind of transition. At
that moment, the world would fall away and the focus would be on
himself and Jesus. The dying old man would not fade, but become more
clearly and powerfully drawn as he moved toward heaven.

As Greg meditated with the picture, his associations to each character created a kaleidoscope of thoughts and images that coalesced from his time spent thinking and looking. Unconscious thoughts condense and disseminate into new creative combinations because the unconscious does not think in an ordered linear progression. As Freud said, there is "no negation, no dubiety, no varying degree of certainty" in our unconscious mental life.[31] Thus Greg's picture was about his father, but also his own death. It was about Jesus with his father, Jesus beside his own death-bed, and Greg's own role in comforting others. I imagine, as he troubled over Mary, that it was also about his wife and who would die first between them. It was about personal content, but also about theological questions. How did Jesus save at the moment of death? How was his presence felt? Was salvation in Jesus found at the other side of the transition or coextensive through the whole process of death? How does one invite Jesus to be present in moments of doubt and fear? Greg also came to his picture thinking about what it meant theologically for his father to die. He feared that his father had not known a relationship with Jesus. The picture allowed him to imagine that Jesus would be with every human being as they made this transition from life to death. If Jesus had been at his father's bedside when he died, "right there with him," then there was hope for salvation in this moment of presence and grace.

Thus, for religious eyes like Greg's looking at religious objects like Goya, sight combines the context of one's faith tradition with the associations that arise from personal and spiritual histories. Over a time of interacting with the image in a devotional and imaginative manner, Greg drew from both personal history and religious context into new insight regarding his faith. He was able to address some of his individual fears about aging and mortality. He was able to meditate on the social and religious messages of the image: what it communicated about the afterlife, the role of Mary as mother and wife, and the role of the old Christian man at death. He was able to articulate heaven in a way that combined the influence of the image with the teachings of his Christian faith. Like any thought, this is not the end of his efforts to trouble through how theology touches his personal life. But as he keeps looking, he will keep feeding these ever-growing chains of thought into new associations, making for a faith moving always to new insight.

NOTES

1. James Elkins, *The Object Stares Back: On the Nature of Seeing* (New York: Simon & Schuster Inc., 1996).
2. I am defining *religion* as historic, institutional expressions of faith that transmit a broad stream of tradition and practice from generation to generation through identifiable communities of worship, and *religious object* as a material object that finds its

meaning through its place within a particular religious tradition or religious community.

3. Christopher Bollas, *The Evocative Object World* (New York: Routledge, 2008), 5.

4. Ibid.

5. See Martha Jacobi, chapter 1, in this volume. The associative capacity of the senses also holds true for smells, as we "explore and relate to and with our immediate environment" through our olfaction.

6. Christopher Bollas, *The Infinite Question* (New York: Routledge, 2008), 53.

7. Bollas, *The Evocative Object World*, 92.

8. Ibid.

9. Elkins, *The Object Stares Back*, 42.

10. James Elkins, *Pictures and Tears: A History of People Who Have Cried in Front of Paintings* (New York: Routledge, 2004), 54.

11. Art historian Hans Belting claims that devotional practices with images were brought to the average layman by the Franciscan and Dominican orders. Through this new devotion, "the layman develops a private prayer life for which new kinds of texts and new kinds of images are produced. In this private life of prayers, the mysteries of faith are felt more than analyzed." See Hans Belting, *The Image and Its Public in the Middle Ages: Form and Function of Early Paintings of the Passion* (New Rochelle: Aristide D. Caratzas Publisher, 1990), 57.

12. Elkins, *Pictures and Tears*, 155.

13. Ibid.

14. David Morgan, *The Sacred Gaze: Religious Visual Culture in Theory and Practice* (Berkeley: University of California Press, 2005), 3.

15. Ibid., 53.

16. I am particularly fascinated with Emmanuel Lartey's description of Yvonne Daniel's work on dance practices in the African-American community in chapter 6 of this volume. The visual is one part of the multi-sensory experience of dance as a source of deep, layered communication—social and religious, affective and embodied— that feeds meaning-making.

17. Morgan, *The Sacred Gaze*, 68.

18. Ibid., 3.

19. David Morgan, "Introduction: The Matter of Belief," in *Religion and Material Culture: The Matter of Belief*, ed. David Morgan (New York: Routledge, 2010), 8.

20. David Morgan, "Introduction," in *The Visual Culture of American Religions*, ed. David Morgan and Sally Promey (Berkeley: University of California Press, 2001), 12.

21. For an example of a similar icon, see "Christ of the Fiery Eye" in Auburn University online, *Russian Icons Index*, accessed November 28, 2012, http://www.auburn.edu/~mitrege/russian/icons/christ-fiery-eye.html.

22. Elkins, *The Object Stares Back*, 38.

23. Bollas, *The Evocative Object World*, 63.

24. "Greg" is a pseudonym.

25. Each member of the group identified as Christian and attended the same church. They were instructed to choose a piece of religious art related to the Christian faith. This could also include images that reflected Hebrew Scriptures. The group gathered in the large sanctuary of their church once a week for four weeks and spent a half an hour looking at their chosen religious image. After a half hour of private looking, we then gathered together as a group in the side chapel to reflect on the difficulties or rewards of contemplating art, how we approached the practice of looking, and whether or not the art spoke to the viewer in particular ways.

26. Greg did not consciously enter into the process of looking to explore questions about death or the afterlife. He knew the picture appealed to him because of his recent losses. His questions were articulated more clearly as he spent time with his picture.

27. Francisco Goya, *Sketch for the Death of St. Joseph*, ca. 1787, oil on canvas, 54.9 x 46.4 cm, Flint Institute of Arts, United States. Greg confused the title of his painting with another rendition of the subject by Goya.

28. Greg's wife was referring to the Joyce Kilmer poem, *I think that I shall never see a poem as lovely as a tree,* that she recited to her mother while her mother was dying of cancer. She was laughing when she said it to Greg, as if to make fun of herself. At the time, I assumed that she was trying to lighten the intensity of how she had felt when she had talked about the poem and its relation to her mother's sickness and death.

29. David Morgan claims that this archive "plays a special role in the recognition of the sacred by linking the viewer to tradition, which the image updates or brings to life." See *The Embodied Eye: Religious Visual Culture and the Social Life of Feeling* (Berkeley: University of California Press, 2012), 60.

30. This tradition began with the infancy narratives in the *Protoevangelium of James* from approximately 150 CE. See Bob Hock, ed., *The Infancy Gospels of James and Thomas* (Santa Rosa: Polebridge Press, 1996).

31. Sigmund Freud, "The Unconscious," in *General Psychological Theory,* ed. Philip Rieff (1915; repr., New York: Touchstone Books, 1997), 134.

REFERENCES

Auburn University. "Christ of the Fiery Eye" in *Russian Icons Index*. Accessed November 28, 2012. http://www.auburn.edu/~mitrege/russian/icons/christ-fiery-eye.html.

Belting, Hans. *The Image and Its Public in the Middle Ages: Form and Function of Early Paintings of the Passion*. New Rochelle: Aristide D. Caratzas Publisher, 1990.

Bollas, Christopher. *The Evocative Object World*. New York: Routledge, 2008.

———. *The Infinite Question*. New York: Routledge, 2008.

Elkins, James, *The Object Stares Back: On the Nature of Seeing*. New York: Simon & Schuster Inc., 1996.

———. *Pictures and Tears: A History of People Who Have Cried in Front of Paintings*. New York: Routledge, 2004.

Freud, Sigmund. "The Unconscious." In *General Psychological Theory*. Edited by Philip Rieff, New York: Touchstone Books, 1997.

Goya, Francisco. Sketch for the Death of St Joseph, ca. 1787, oil on canvas, 54.9 x 46.4 cm, Flint Institute of Arts, United States.

Hock, Bob, ed., *The Infancy Gospels of James and Thomas*. Santa Rosa: Polebridge Press, 1996.

Morgan, David. *The Embodied Eye: Religious Visual Culture and the Social Life of Feeling*. Berkeley: University of California Press, 2012.

———. *The Sacred Gaze: Religious Visual Culture in Theory and Practice*. Berkeley: University of California Press, 2005.

———. "Introduction: The Matter of Belief" in *Religion and Material Culture: The Matter of Belief,* ed. David Morgan. New York: Routledge, 2010.

———. "Introduction" in *The Visual Culture of American Religions,* edited by David Morgan and Sally Promey. Berkeley: University of California Press, 2001.

SIX

Knowing through Moving

African Embodied Epistemologies

Emmanuel Y. Lartey

Over the past decade I have been engaged in a study of the spirituality and practices of some African traditional healers located in Ghana and in the African diaspora in the Americas. The questions that have inspired my study are the following: What do they actually do in the quest to bring healing to their clients? What do they know and how do they know it? How do they diagnose or recognize the nature of the illnesses they treat? By what means do they come to a diagnosis? How is this different from classic Western means of diagnosis and treatment? What are their forms of understanding and knowledge? How do they engage their patients in healing? What treatments do they offer and why? How do they know what is wrong and what to do about it? I am interested in the priest-healers' ways of knowing, and basically how they know what they know. I am researching what they know, their means of determining what is worth knowing. I wish to know how they evaluate and come to a judgment of what is needed and then how they use this knowledge. In a word, I have been researching the traditional healer's epistemology. Though there is a fairly extensive literature especially from the field of anthropology in this area, I have sought to give greater priority to the voice of practitioners than that of theorists. This chapter represents a relatively short account of a particular dimension of, a brief reflexive engagement with, and a reflection from a practical theological perspective upon the epistemology of African religious practitioners on the continent of Africa and in the African Diaspora in the Americas.

In traditional African society, though, there are variations on this theme; the healer is also a priest or priestess. Conversely, no one is a priest/ess who is not also a healer. One is considered to be spiritually adept and a "great priest/ess" only if one brings, out of one's spiritual exercises, specific benefits for the living community. Moreover, one attains the honored status of ancestorhood following one's death by virtue of the good one has done for the living community during one's earthy sojourn. This study has brought me to the heart of African religion and spirituality—a central understanding of which is that the well-being of the human person and community is the focus and purpose of spiritual or religious activities. For African religious practitioners, the spiritual and the material are fused. The unseen and the seen realms are related. The natural and the divine are in constant interaction. African religious practitioners' theology, spirituality, discernment, and practice are all of one piece. As a pastoral counselor deeply interested in theological and spiritual practices of care and therapy, I am intrigued at how Divine-human communication is so central and spirituality so essential in African traditional practices of healing and health promotion. As I have listened intensely and participated in the rituals and practices of African religious practitioners, what has been most fascinating for me is that instead of a logo-centric, word-based theory from which is derived particular practices, African priest-healers seem to know through a different means, a means more bodily, more incarnational, and especially more kinesthetic. Their knowledge seemed to be through bodies-in-motion. *Proprioception,* the term used to describe the sensory information that contributes to the sense of position of self and movement, seems to mark the key to human ontology and epistemology in African traditional and diasporan religious practice. I am struck by the centrality of rhythmic bodily movement in their rituals of discernment, diagnosis, and healing. This is the case not only in the continental practice of African Religious Traditions (ARTs) but intriguingly also prominently in the African diaspora in the "New World" of the Americas and the Caribbean. As such it is upon proprioception, especially rhythmic body movement in the practice of African sacred ritual that I wish to focus in this chapter.

The presence of the divine is signaled by particular forms of expressive movement within the bodies of priests, priestesses, diviners, or on occasion ordinary participants of a ritual. Although I have much familiarity with what anthropologists have long referred to as "possession," or what psychologists have dubbed "trance-states," and have consulted many texts that seek to throw light on this highly observable feature of African religious life, I was drawn to and paid attention to these phenomena because of the closeness of these forms of manifestation to the diagnostic and therapeutic activities of African practitioners of healing. What is of significance for me is how rhythmic bodily movement becomes a means by which the sacred healers come to some knowledge of what is at stake in the rituals of healing.

Anthropologist Katherine Geurts engaged in ethnographic study among the Anlo-Ewe people of South-East Ghana for twelve years. In her *Culture and the Senses: Bodily Ways of Knowing in an African Community,* she writes of becoming aware of what she describes as a "sixth sense" which the Ewe people appeared to recognize and develop. This "sense" was a way of knowing through and in the body. Whilst trying to capture what she was becoming aware of as a sensing or sense, Geurts came to realize that one discrete lexical term for "the senses" did not seem to exist in the Anlo-Ewe language.[1] Rather, what appeared to be used most frequently by her informants "was the very complicated and polysemous term, *seselelame*."[2] "*Seselelame*" (which can be translated loosely as "feeling in the body"), Geurts claims, "is best understood in reference to what Thomas Csordas has called 'somatic modes of attention.'"[3] Difficult if not impossible to translate into English, *seselelame*, Geurts continues "is an ideal illustration of a culturally elaborated way in which many Anlo-speaking people attend to and read their own bodies while simultaneously orienting themselves to objects, to the environment, and to the bodies of those around them."[4] Geurts comes to understand that *seselelame* refers to various kinds of sensory embodiment that do not fit neatly into Euro-American categories.

> On the one hand, it seems to refer to a specific sense or kind of physical sensation that we might call tingling in the skin (sometimes a symptom of impending illness), but in other instances it is used to describe sexual arousal, heartache, or even passion. In other contexts it refers to a kind of inspiration (to dance or to speak), but it can also be used to describe something akin to intuition (when unsure of exactly how you are coming by some information). Finally, people used it to refer to a generalized (almost synesthetic) *feeling in or through the body*, and it was proposed by some as a possible translation for the English term *sense*.[5]

The Anlo-Ewe term *seselelame*, then, conveys "hearing or feeling within the body, flesh or skin" —a way of experiencing and receiving knowledge through in-the-body sensation.[6] Geurts reports on the basis of her careful and intensive ethnographic investigation that *seselelame* was sometimes used to refer to experiences that were bodily based and that corresponded to the English concept of proprioception. But at other times it seemed akin to 'intuition' or even what might be termed "extra-sensory perception." She writes,

> Anlo-speaking people often described sensations for this kind of *seselelame* as uncanny feelings or messages they received that turned out to be a premonition. Examples include *seselelame* as a source of motivation to visit a relative right before he died or as confirming the presence of an ancestor at a specific communal event. A "message" was usually

associated with these kinds of *seselelame* experiences, and for that reason people often linked it to the English term for "hearing." They spoke
of hearing a message or hearing information not through their ears but
throughout their entire being; they somehow "knew something" but
could not really account for how they knew it. This kind of *seselelame*
was considered deeper and more mysterious than specific bodily sensations and was not necessarily attributed to them.[7]

AGBAGBADODO

Another Anlo-Ewe term that Geurts discusses is *Agbagbadodo*, which essentially denotes balancing a load, and a sense of balance in the Anlo-
Ewe language.[8] The verb *do agbagba* means "to carry something on the
head without touching it with the hands." A second usage of this expression has to do with "a baby's act of raising up on two feet and not falling
over," for example, to balance their body on two legs.[9] This skill, acquired in infancy, is so important that to never learn how to do it rele-
gates an individual to the level of an animal—crawling on four legs—and
not that of a human being. For the Anlo-Ewe, therefore, *agbagbadodo*
(roughly translated as balancing) is an essential feature of their definition
of being human. Only humans have this capacity, and it is a means of
distinguishing humans from other sentient beings. Now this brings to
mind the very obvious and evident oft-depicted view of West African
peoples in particular seen balancing objects on top of their heads while
walking through a market or down a street; a basket filled with mangoes,
a bucket of water, a bundle of firewood, a tray of carefully stacked
oranges, etcetera. For the Anlo-Ewe people, standing upright, balancing,
being able to balance things on one's head without the use of one's hands
whilst walking, are distinguishing skills of the human. Proprioception,
therefore, for the Anlo-Ewe people is an ontological and anthropological-
ly defining characteristic.

AZƆLIZƆZƆ

The English term *kinesthesia* comes from the Greek words *kinein*, which
means "to move," and *aesthesis*, which means "perception." Kinesthesia is
therefore etymologically "perception through movement;" in other
words, knowledge through movement. This is a commonly understood
and discussed phenomenon among dancers, about which more will be
said later in this chapter. Like dancers, many Anlo-speaking people
Geurts found "valued movement and believed that much could be perceived and understood by and about a person through his or her carriage
or walk."[10] The Ewe term *zɔ* refers to movement first and foremost and is
applied to various forms of movement. Anlo-Ewe speakers associate the

term *zɔ* with the phenomena of generalized movement of living bodies, essentially meaning to walk, to travel, to move. Westermann's dictionary of Ewe translates *azɔlizɔzɔ* as "walking, marching or gait." Geurts observes:

> In fact, walking (*azɔlizɔzɔ* or *azɔlinu*) carried such significance that the Anlo-Ewe language contained dozens of ways symbolically essentializing the style or the manner in which a person walks or moves. For instance *zɔ lugulugu* referred to walking as if drunk; walking *kadzakadza* implied the majestic movement of a lion.[11]

Walking is not merely a method of transport or a purely practical thing. It involves movement and gestures that emanate from the whole body. As Geurts learned, there is a *proper* manner for an Anlo woman to walk, for instance. *Azɔlizɔzɔ* is not limited to the propelling action of the legs, but involves choreographic dynamics implicating the whole body. For many Anlo-Ewe a person's character and moral fiber are revealed, embodied, and expressed in his or her walk or mode of comportment. "The term *azɔlime* referred literally to the way or style in which a person moved and behaved, while it also denoted manner or course of life, deportment, nature, and disposition."[12] Geurts's conclusion aptly sums up the matter: "[I]n Anlo epistemological traditions and ontological practices, bodily movements specifically in the form of reified kinds of walks are instrumentally tied to forms of thinking and reasoning, especially about moral character."[13]

Bodily movement then is a vehicle that transmits knowledge concerning humanity. The movement of our bodies conveys ethical and ontological knowledge which can be valuable in all arenas of human life. The African Traditional healers in my research concur with this Anlo-Ewe insight. Many speak very expressively about the "wisdom of the body,"[14] and utilize their knowledge of "body language" in both diagnostic and therapeutic treatment of patients in their care. Africa's sacred healers recognize the somatization of psychic illness in diseased or dysfunctional movement patterns. They prescribe forms of movement, including dance and ritual performance, to correct what has gone awry in the souls and bodies of patients, often to very beneficial effect. In the African Diaspora in the Americas these insights appear in the innovative religious activities evident in the new geographical locations of Africa's peoples.

AFRICAN RELIGIOUS DIASPORA

Yvonne Daniel, anthropologist, ethnomusicologist, and professor of Dance and African American Studies has for over thirty-five years been studying the religious practices of diasporan Africans in Haiti, Cuba, and Bahia, Brazil. In a well-researched and carefully documented book titled

Dancing Wisdom: Embodied Knowledge in Haitian Vodou, Cuban Yoruba, and Bahian Candomblé, she presents the fruits of persistent participant observation of three faith communities of African origins in the Americas since 1974. She directs researchers and others interested in these religious phenomena to the dance/music practices found in their worship rituals. Daniel declares, "for the communities I study . . . it is most often the dance/music behavior within ritual behavior that continually reties the worshipping community to its spiritual affinity."[15] Daniel shows how the "divinities of these African American religions receive dance/music offerings within religious rites, and come to dance with the believing community."[16]

Brazil, which demographically is the nation with the largest number of persons of African origins outside of the African continent, is home to the religious tradition known as *Candomblé,* a Yoruba-based religious practice that is also called Nago/Ketu because of the prominence of particular Yoruba peoples within the practice. The term *Candomblé* itself is variously traced to Central Africa as well as Portuguese language and is said to refer both to "ritual drum music" and to "dance in honor of the deities." It is, of course, the case that many different forms of religious faith are practiced within Haiti, Cuba, and Brazil, including orthodox and reform variants of Catholicism, Islam, Judaism, Protestantism, and Hinduism, as well as African–derived religions such as Winti (Surinam); Rastafarianism, Obeah, Kumina (Jamaica); Caboclo, Umbanda (Brazil); Espiritismo (Puerto Rico, Cuba, Brazil).

Yvonne Daniel correctly directs us to the centrality of dance movement and music in any description or appropriation of African American life, pointing out that dance movement and music interconnect and, while making reference to dimensions of the social life, are pivotal to spirituality and spiritual development in African diasporan cultures.[17] She points out that dance and music performances in the contexts of these religious rituals, far from being engaged in exclusively for their entertainment value, have multiple levels of meaning embedded within them. Says Daniel,

> Patterns of movement and body rhythms are organized and integrated formulaically with specific instrumentation and call-and-response singing. Performance spaces are washed, decorated, and blessed—often with chalked or painted artistic lines or circular configurations that are drawn on objects, on earthen floors, or in the air.[18]

"Dance and music," she continues, "communicate through multiple sensory channels and thereby contain, symbolize, and emit many levels of meaning." Daniel confirms Ajayi's finding that, similar to the Anlo-Ewes (of Ghana and Togo), "to discover meaning in normal communication, Yorubas (of Nigeria) concentrate on keen scrutiny of the body."[19] In her ethnographic studies, Daniel too found that "Yoruba-derived and Fon-derived Americans regularly sense and adjudicate the meanings of the dancing body."[20] Daniel discovers that for the worshippers in the communities she studied, "dance rituals create religious, social, and galactic (of the entire cosmos) harmony."[21]

To my amazement, delight, and enlightenment, Daniel expresses out of the American contexts she has been involved with the very same things I, as well as other researchers such as Marion Kilson and Margaret Field, discovered in my research among Gã and Akan traditional priest/ healers in West Africa.[22] Daniel articulates this discovery in words deserving of extensive quotation:

> In the process of dance/music performances in Haitian Vodou, Cuban Yoruba, and Bahian Candomblé, social cohesion results among the living, the ancestors, and the cosmological divinities. Ritual performances are filled with what I call 'social medicine:' power, authority, and community relations are affected, re-arranged, or affirmed; social wounds are healed; each community member is accounted for; and the ritual community continues with strong bonds. The spiritual dimension of performance is connected to the social well-being of individuals and to the solidarity of a social community. Regular, repetitive ceremonial performances function as holistic medicine for community members.[23]

In these religious traditions worshippers generally view ritual dance/ music performances as "sacred offerings."[24] The congregation performs the dances until diviners or specialists in expressing and interpreting divine manifestation begin to emerge among the worshipping community. These adepts then lead and intensify the performance, moving the ceremony forward from ritual behavior through toward transcendence and transformation. From the perspective of the worshippers, Daniel found that the dance/music performances are presented simultaneously to the human and the communities of the divinities in the hope of transformations that will bring dancing divinities from the spiritual world into the worshipping community. Human dancers at this point dance in sync with the divinities expressing in their bodily movement divine messages.

Yvonne Daniel pointedly observes that the religious communities she has been studying have encouraged attention to both cognitive (theoretical) and kinesthetic (embodied) knowledge. Because they do not subscribe to Euro-American mind/body dualism, which emphasizes the mental and theoretical over the experiential and kinesthetic, these African American ritual communities do not reject science and theoretical knowledge for experiential knowledge. Instead they incorporate all sorts of knowledge within bodily and ritual practice. In fact some Candomblé priestesses cited by anthropologist Sheila Walker refer to the Candomblé as both a religious system and a science.[25] Afro-Bahian philosopher Edson Nunes da Silva recognizes, discusses, and analyzes the Candomblé as a religious system, "the foundation of which is a complex science of life and nature . . . some of which is yet unknown to present day science."[26] In her fieldwork, Daniel found that leaders referred to an understanding of the forces of nature and the universe as *orichas, orixãs,* or *lwas.* This parallels Yoruba understandings of the divine beings called the *orishas* as being both spiritual entities and forces of nature.

In the religious communities Daniel studied in Haiti, Cuba, and Bahia, regular, routine ceremonial performances have been developed that concentrate heavily on the human body and on what she terms "the suprahuman body." This is how she characterizes the suprahuman body:

> A suprahuman body is the result of spiritual transformation, when the worshipping, believing, and dancing human body is prepared for or overwhelmed by the arrival of spiritual force. The dancing human body proceeds to unfold spiritual energy, or in believers' understanding, to present or manifest divinities, who are aspects of a Supreme Divinity. Beauty salon operators and truck drivers, as well as journalists and lawyers, are transformed in the ritual setting into suprahuman bodies; they dance beautifully and forcefully in order to give expression to spiritual forces, which then give advice to the community.[27]

Daniel identifies two distinct tendencies in African American ritual dance. In one, there is a reliance on gestures and movement sequences that come from the heritage of a particular ethnic group such as the Fon, Yoruba, Gã, or Kongo-Angola; in the other, the reliance is upon abstract expressions within the dancing body. In both cases ritual performance involves movement vocabulary that is structured. Particular gestures and movement phrases occur with the sounding of specific rhythms and have a specific cultural or religious meaning. For example, in African communities that possess and play "talking drums," dancers and musicians relate stories, parables, and myths from their understanding of the drums in combination with specific movement sequences and their relationship to tonal languages. This is possible because the tones of the talking drums relate to linguistic structures and replicate speech patterns. Yet, as observed by several ethnomusicologists, the alternative practice of abstract or non-codified movement and non-talking, drum-based dance is also part of the African heritage. Both kinds of drumming practices and both kinds of movement sequences can and do lead dancers to convey various aspects of myth, history, and narrative.

Daniel observes that in religious and secular settings dancers and musicians are placed together in "deep, improvisational performance" such as in instrumental jazz music.[28] Jazz dance, for instance, participates in a theme in sound and movement, an overarching series of rhythms, an accumulating series of movements, and changing and projected emotional states, all of which are abstracted and combined to constitute meaning. Similarly, in Haitian Vodou, Cuban Yoruba, and Bahian Candomblé, "some gestures and movement sequences signal a literal meaning, but more often the social circumstances of performers have created a deep reliance on the abstracted expressiveness of the dancing body and on non-verbal communication procedures."[29] Meaning registers within visceral responses to kinesthetic and musical affect. Meaning, realizations, and knowledge are thus abstractly embodied.

Daniel recognizes how most of the movement sequences and motifs for the divinities conform to identifiable patterns that are recognizable across the African Diaspora. The dance for and of the deity Ogun is an example of this because it contains both explicit, literal meanings and implied, abstracted meanings that are common in all three ritual communities. In all three sites, the dance's movement patterns denote a fierce male entity that fights as he dances with a sword or machete. With minimal variation, this dance is performed in Haitian Vodou as the dance for the *lwa*, Ogou; in Cuban Yoruba as the dance of the *oricha*, Ogún; and in Bahian Candomblé as the dance of the *orixá*, Ogun. It is also performed in Nigeria as the dance of the orisha, Ogùn, and in Benin as the dance for the vodun, Gu.

In each community, the dance for Ogou, Ogún, or Ogun involves aggressive warrior stances, rigorous traveling movement sequences, and an emphasis on slicing or cutting with the sword or some sort of metal. The codified gestures within the dance performance show a warrior traveling through areas of obstruction, kicking and fighting an opponent, chopping with and cleaning his sword, and reigning triumphant. The abstracted meanings converge within the image of a warrior/hunter archetype and are drawn from symbolic colors, forceful body movements with closed fists, argumentative grunts and growls, intimidating facial expression, stories and myths about a powerful warrior whose force is as impenetrable as iron, richly animated song melodies, thickly textured drumming patterns, percussive actions, accents, and outbursts. Performance elements combine and result in cultural understandings not only about performance and the performer but also about their relationship with the viewer. The whole performance embodies power and protection and urges the Haitian, Cuban, and Bahian worshipper toward courage, strength, and appropriate protective action.

In her interviews and interactions with worshippers in Haiti, Cuba, and Brazil, Daniel learned that as worshippers perform, they sense and learn. As they continue to perform over time, in the process of music-making and dance performance, they consult, gain, and express embodied knowledge. It is a dynamic, practical referencing that can mean different things within a lifetime. Some ritual performers are concerned mainly with the musical and dance products that result in transformation and manifestation of the divinities. Others are interested in the meaning of the transformation and the related embodied knowledge that is conveyed. In particular embodied transformation appears to chiefly mediate three forms of knowledge:

1. Healing of the self
2. Healing of the community
3. Balancing relationships between the cosmos and the ritual community

Daniel realizes that "over time, performers become consciously aware of the knowledge that exists within sacred performance."[30] So fulsome and encompassing are Daniel's conclusions as to bear extensive quotation:

> The total wisdom within African American chanting, drumming, and dancing can be viewed as an accumulation and transposition of many different kinds of knowledge. African–derived performance is easily a transposing of philosophy, religion, or belief, as well as natural, technological, and social sciences into the aesthetic and artistic arena of primarily non-verbal, communicative forms. Embodied botany is revealed in an open state within the sacred chant texts that survived in the minds and healed the bodies of African and African American performers. Embodied physiology is revealed in the associations of divinities with particular parts of the human body, and embodied psychology emerges from within a history of skilled and effective performance. Embodied philosophy is read within the performance behaviors of worshippers and reveals cultural understanding of a suprahuman and interactive world within ritual performance. Embodied mathematical knowledge is buried and assumed within codified drum orchestrations. Dance performances of Haitian Vodou, Cuban Yoruba, and Bahian Candomblé are more than music and dance; in these religions, more than singing, drumming, and dancing are present. Praise performance practices have guarded embodied knowledges for centuries.[31]

PRACTICAL THEOLOGICAL REFLECTION

In place of the dismissiveness which has so often characterized Western Christian encounters of other, especially African religious practice, I suggest that much is to be gained through respectful dialog with these traditions.[32] It seems to me that in practical Christian theological terms what we are confronted with in the religious observances and everyday practices of Africans on the continent and in the diaspora can be discussed under three main headings, namely, incarnation, hermeneutics, and healing.

Incarnation

Christian doctrine is founded upon an understanding that Jesus, the Christ, was and is the Divine in human flesh, *par excellence*. Pivotal for an appreciation of the life, teaching, and works of Jesus, the Christ is the appropriation of his presence as embodying the Divine. According to the Christian narrative and understanding, all of human life is taken up into the Divine by the life, death, and resurrection of Jesus. And conversely all of the Divine realm is made available to humanity through Jesus, the Christ. Through Jesus all of humanity attains salvation and acceptance within the spiritual realm. The acts and words of Jesus are the very actions and communications of the Divine Creator. This way of thinking concerning the Jewish human person Jesus of Nazareth finds easy and ready acceptance within an African epistemology. The human being can mediate the divine within our bodily presence through close communion with the human Jesus. The Divine can readily communicate with the human, then, through the bodily expression of the human. It behooves us, then, to pay closer attention to the "wisdom of the body" for within it may be contained both that which enhances human flourishing and what the divine may be communicating with the human community.

Hermeneutics

The art of interpretation is characterized in Christian theology through the word "hermeneutics" that etymologically entails an embodiment of the Greek god of communication known as *Hermes*. Hermes is the "messenger" who conveys the words of the gods to humankind. Hermeneutics is the art and science of correctly deciphering and explaining the message of God, especially as contained in the words of Holy Scripture. However, the exclusive location of the messages of God in what is written has rendered Christianity in the West the preserve of the literate, and the art of interpretation a matter of words and titles. What these African religious adepts teach us is that the communication of God may also come to humanity through the bodies of human beings, especially the movements of these bodies under inspiration. As such, hermeneutics has to include the ability to "read" the movements of human bodies as they operate in concert with the impulses and rhythms of the spiritual universe. African religious practitioners affirm that movement, rhythm, and sound may also be divine communication needing to be understood if the whole counsel of God is to be appreciated. Such embodied hermeneutics would seem to follow from any doctrine of incarnation. If the "word became flesh and dwelt among us" (John 1:14), then are we not directed to the flesh (the body) in order to understand the "word." Has not the flesh (body) much to teach us? Should we not pay attention to the body and its messages to us in movement and artistic performances? Christian liturgical dance has largely been a human response and praise performance to God. The African insight here invites us to consider that Divine communication to humanity may come in the form of bodily movement. In the dance not only may humans speak to God but more poignantly God may be speaking to the human community. The task of the hermeneutician then becomes interpreting what the Divine communication may actually be in the dance. Such is the art of the "dancers of the gods" in African religious contexts. They are engaged in rhythmic bodily movement which is in sync with and embodies the movement of the divine. They prepare and present themselves to the Divine and become open vessels through which the divine may inscribe her/his messages. Their bodies then become the texts of the Spirit to be read by all. Inspired by the divine realm they become the embodied and living "word" of the living God available not exclusively to the literate (in particular languages) but to all of humanity.

Healing

The primary message of Jesus the Christ, attested to with word and sign, was one of healing and reconciliation. In fact healing was to be understood as reconciliation with oneself (body-soul-spirit), with others (love of neighbor), and above all with God (salvation). In similar fashion African and African Diasporan ritual as observed especially by Yvonne Daniel is engaged to be a means of healing on all three of these levels. Physical bodily movement is recognized as a necessary means of enhancing physical health. Worship, if it incorporates physical movement on the part of congregants, can thus in itself be a means of community and individual well-being. Through participation in the dance rituals that invite the manifestations of the divine, worshippers may not only receive the benefits of physical movement but also enter into communion with the spiritual realm thus embodying the inspiration of Spirit.

CONCLUSION

A more respectful engagement with the beliefs, rituals, and practices of African religions may have much to teach us about the nature of the divine (theology), the nature of humanity (anthropology), and the relationship between these, especially in terms of the embodied nature of all dimensions of reality. African religious communities may teach us that much can be known about the Divine through attention to the moving bodies of human persons as these bodies move under inspiration.

NOTES

1. Kathryn Linn Guerts, *Culture and the Senses: Bodily Ways of Knowing in an African Community* (Berkeley: University of California Press, 2002), 40.
2. Ibid.
3. Ibid., 41.
4. Ibid.
5. Ibid.
6. Ibid., 52.
7. Ibid., 55.
8. Ibid., 49.

9. Ibid., 49.
10. Ibid., 50.
11. Ibid., 51.
12. Ibid., 51.
13. Ibid., 69.
14. This particular expression, which very well captures the language of the healers I have talked with, comes from Barnaby B. Barrett, *The Emergence of Somatic Psychology and Bodymind Therapy* (New York: Palgrave Macmillan, 2013), 21.
15. Yvonne Daniel, *Dancing Wisdom: Embodied Knowledge in Haitian Vodou, Cuban Yoruba, and Bahian Candomblé* (Urbana/Chicago: University of Illinois Press, 2005), 2.
16. Ibid., 1.
17. Ibid., 51.
18. Ibid., 52.
19. Ibid., 53.
20. Ibid.
21. Ibid., 54.
22. See for example, Marion Kilson, *Dancing with the Gods: Essays in Ga Ritual*, (New York: University Press of America, 2013), especially chapters 2-5.
23. Daniel, 55.
24. Ibid., 55.
25. Ibid., 58.
26. Ibid.
27. Ibid., 61.
28. Ibid., 62.
29. Ibid., 63.
30. Ibid., 66.
31. Ibid., 93.
32. For a fuller statement and argument of the theological imperative of engagement with African religious cultures see Emmanuel Y. Lartey, *Postcolonializing God: An African Practical Theology* (London: SCM Press, 2013), 124–129.

REFERENCES

Barratt, Barnaby B. *The Emergence of Somatic Psychology and BodyMind Therapy*. London/New York: Palgrave Macmillan, 2013.
Daniel, Yvonne. *Dancing Wisdom: Embodied Knowledge in Haitian Vodou, Cuban Yoruba, and Bahian Candomblé*. Urbana/Chicago: University of Illinois Press, 2005.
Guerts, Kathryn Linn. *Culture and the Senses: Bodily Ways of Knowing in an African Community*. Berkeley/Los Angeles/London: University of California Press, 2002.
Kilson, Marion. *Dancing with the Gods: Essays in Ga Ritual*. New York: University Press of America, 2013.
Lartey, Emmanuel Y. *Postcolonializing God: An African Practical Theology*. London: SCM Press, 2013.

Part II

Sensing Religious Practices

SEVEN

Use of a Hot Tub as Spiritual Practice

Three Decades of Daily Baptism by Immersion

John C. Carr

My first experience of being in a hot tub was at a workshop following the Annual Conference of the American Association of Pastoral Counselors (AAPC) in Denver, Colorado, USA. High in the Rockies, two dozen pastoral counselors soaked in the hot water of an outdoor twenty-four-foot cedar tub, occasionally leaving the heat of the tub to roll in the snow. Not long after that experience, I acquired my own indoor cedar hot tub, subsequently replaced by one made of acrylic. After three decades of beginning my day in a hot tub, that practice has become a core spiritual practice for me—and especially because of the intense body focus of the experience.

In *Embodiment*, his groundbreaking work on body theology,[1] James Nelson writes about how D. H. Lawrence, in *Lady Chatterley's Lover*, was attempting to "restore belief in the basic goodness and importance of human embodiment."[2] Nelson goes on as follows:

> Christian theology ought to have an immensely positive bias toward embodiment. A great deal of Christian theology has tended to treat the body as something other than the essential person. Thus, the body has become inherently suspect. It might be redeemable by the grace of God, but more likely the carnal body is relegated to the domain of "this world" while the spiritual world is something qualitatively different.[3]

This "split" to which Nelson points in *Embodiment* can be found in many aspects of religious life, although that is gradually changing. For example, some denominations used to distinguish between the "spiritual"

117

leadership of congregations and leadership that was "not properly spiritual." The latter phrase was used, at the time of my graduation from theological college in 1962, to describe the responsibility of a Board of Managers in congregations of the Presbyterian Church in Canada (PCC). Those "not properly spiritual" responsibilities included management of the congregation's financial resources and care of its physical property — for example, activities that were characterized as being "of the flesh" rather than "of the spirit." The PCC has since found other "functional" language to describe the role of the Board of Managers—but attitudes change slowly because of the deeply embedded body-spirit split.

In *Body Theology*,[4] Nelson indicates that the body-spirit split is a factor in the ecological disasters that humans have visited upon planet Earth. When we treat Earth's natural resources as a commodity to be exploited, we are denying the presence of spirit in those resources and in ourselves and the rest of the human community. That is, humans are also commodified when they treat the Earth's resources as commodities. This is an error which aboriginal peoples, with their keen sense of the presence of "spirit" in all of life, do not make.

The Apostle Paul's use of the phrase "in the flesh,"[5] even though not intended to negate an "embodied spirituality," is almost universally understood to mean that there is no role for the human body in Christian spirituality. However, interpreting the usage in that way neglects a core Christian construct. "In the beginning was the Word . . . and the Word became flesh."[6]

While most Christians believe that, in Jesus, the enfleshment of the Divine was a non-repeatable event, it can be argued (paradoxically) that that non-repeatable event makes it possible for the imago dei to actualize itself in a new way—in the followers of Jesus and in communities of persons who gather together because they are followers of Jesus.

In this chapter I do not argue for the use of hot tubs as an essential condition of the spiritual life. In it I do propose, however, that the use of hot tubs may well, for some, be a core spiritual exercise—precisely because it is a practice that understands body and spirit as an integrated whole and also because it plays a role which is similar to the role of "smell" (so far as our neurological processes are concerned) as described by Martha Jacobi in the first chapter of this book.

Accordingly, I start by discussing the psychological and physiological benefits and risks attached to use of hot tubs. Then, after a discussion of what I mean by "spirituality," I write about the spirituality of caring for the body soul. I conclude with sections on the need for separation and withdrawal as a core spiritual practice, on the use of a hot tub as a spiritual practice, and on sacred space and ritual.

THE PHYSIOLOGICAL AND PSYCHOLOGICAL THERAPEUTIC VALUE OF HOT TUBS

Hot Tubs Offer Physiological and Psychological Therapeutic Value

Who doesn't think that relaxing in a hot tub after a stressful day isn't, in a word, sublime? Or who would deny the value of twenty to twenty-five minutes in a hot tub at the beginning of the day as a way of entering the day in a relaxed state?

Hot tubs are no longer just luxurious recreational items. They are practical.[7] Historically, hot springs have been used for many centuries and have proven to be beneficial for a range of ailments. Modern medicine, noticing the beneficial effects of natural hot springs, came up with a way to simulate these effects using hot tub therapy in clinical and care settings. Now hot tubs are widely available at least in North America.

The therapeutic values involved are heat, massage, and buoyancy, all of which lead to holistic benefits. Psychologically and physiologically, hot tubs and hot water therapy have made a significant contribution to human well-being. As complex as our bodies are, the simplicity of hot tub therapy can produce significant results. Of course, our bodies respond to hot tub therapy in unique ways. For some, the experience of the hot tub will be enhanced by use of aromas as described by Jennifer Baldwin in chapter 11 of this book.

Bliss

Soaking in a hot tub relaxes muscles and relieves stress. Relieving stress lowers blood pressure and creates endorphins that boost the immune system and detoxify the body. In turn, the mind is able to achieve clarity and calm. Hot tubs alleviate insomnia, which affects many North Americans. It allows the body to reach a deeper level of sleep that is more rehabilitative than average sleep.

Circulation

Hot water therapy raises the body's core temperature, which allows the blood vessels to dilate near the skin. This, in turn, aids in cardiac output. Diabetic patients may experience significant benefits from hot tub therapy because of increased blood flow which causes vein and artery dilation as well as a decrease in blood sugar levels.

Respiration

Acting as a bronchodilator,[8] hot tubs can relieve congestion and increase airway expansion, resulting in higher oxygen intake which is then distributed to the various systems of the body.

Physical Therapy

Hot tubs make physical therapy possible for some people who cannot otherwise obtain physical therapy. By taking a great deal of body weight pressure off joints, mobility is increased. Hot water therapy allows obese people to exercise without great distress to their joints. It is also used as an effective treatment for rehabilitation when joints have been damaged or replaced.

Chronic Pain and Disease

Sports medicine uses hot tub therapy to help rehabilitate joint and muscle stress and facilitate healing of injuries.

THE PHYSIOLOGICAL AND PSYCHOLOGICAL RISKS ASSOCIATED WITH HOT TUBS

Most forms of hydrotherapy or hot tub usage are well tolerated. However, there are some risks. These risks are described below, along with comments about how to minimize risk. An understanding of the spirituality of the hot tub experience that is grounded in a theology of embodied spirituality needs to include attention to potential harm to the body. Accordingly, it is important to discuss your hot tub use with your family physician—and especially so if you manifest symptoms that may be related to hot tub usage.[9]

Dermatitis

There is a risk of an allergic skin reaction (also known as contact dermatitis) for some people when they use essential oils and herbs in their bath water. People who experience an allergic skin reaction to an essential oil should discontinue its use and contact their healthcare professional for guidance.

Overheating

Another possible side effect of hydrotherapy is overheating, which may occur when a person spends too much time in a hot tub. The optimal amount of time in the hot tub needs to be determined in consultation with one's health professional, and when that has been done the risk is minimal.

Pseudomonas Bacteria

Pseudomonas bacteria grow in hot tubs that are not properly sanitized. Diabetes increases the risk of becoming infected with pseudomonas bacteria, resulting in a condition called hot tub folliculitis. Folliculitis, an infection of the hair follicles, is characterized by a red, bumpy rash and can cause hair loss and scars that are permanent. It can occur where the edges of your swimsuit rub against your skin, causing irritation. If the water is not properly sanitized, pseudomonas bacteria can infect you there. This particular risk is reduced when one does not wear a swimsuit.

Mycobacterium Avium

Mycobacterium avium is another bacterium that is found in hot tubs. Mycobacterium avium is related to the bacterium that causes tuberculosis. When it occurs in hot tubs, it causes a lung condition that has been named "hot tub lung." This condition can induce a fever, chills, a cough, and tightness in the chest of those infected. It also causes tiredness and fatigue. When people breathe in the air bubbles from the hot tub that contain the mycobacterium avium, they can become infected. This illness, if left untreated, can be fatal.

Legionnaire's Disease

Another infection of the lungs can occur in the same way as mycobacterium avium in hot tub usage. This bacteria is called legionella bacteria and can be inhaled from the warm moist air emitted by the hot tub. Antibiotics typically can manage the infection, but it also has been known to be fatal in some people.

Other Risks

Other risks you take when you step into a hot tub may depend on your gender. For example, if you are a woman and are pregnant, you could risk neural tube birth defects in your unborn child, particularly during the first three months of pregnancy. If you are a man, your sperm count may fall because of the excessive heat of a hot tub. This can cause problems if you and your partner are trying to conceive a child.

Taking Care of Your Body

The list above was reasonably complete at the time it was compiled. However, it is important to consult regularly with your family physician about any new problems that have been documented as being related to the use of hot tubs.

Minimizing Risk

Typically, public hot tubs use chlorine as a sanitizer. Private hot tubs use chlorine, bromine, or an ultraviolet (UV) light sanitizer. Consultation with a specialty hot tub products supplier and one's health professional is necessary in order to ascertain the best approach for you to take. It is relatively easy to test the water for bromine and chlorine levels in order to ascertain whether the levels are adequate to maintain the water at a sanitary level. There is no easily available test for ascertaining the sanitizing effectiveness of an ultraviolet light system. In addition, regular testing of the hot tub water for the level of chlorine or bromine, pH (potential of hydrogen), calcium hardness, phosphate levels, and total dissolved solids is essential. There are self-administered tests available—or one can have these tests carried out by taking a water sample to the supplier of the requisite chemicals.

Careful attention to the tub's cleanliness is also critical. The water needs to be changed at least once every three months although changing it monthly is probably safest. Frequent use of products designed to purge body oils and other residue from the tub and from the pipes is essential. Filters need to be cleaned and disinfected thoroughly at least as often as the water is changed.[10]

What Is "Spirituality"?

Although influenced by my Christian experience and belief system, my understanding of the nature of spirituality is not fully contained by that personal experience and the belief system which I share with other Christians. I understand "spirituality" as our groundedness in the Ground of our Being.[11] For some, "spirituality" will be experienced and imaged in ways that are recognizably Christian, Jewish, Muslim, Buddhist, Hindu, etcetera. For others, that will be imaged in highly idiosyncratic ways that may (or may not) have resonances with traditional European, Asian, African, or other "religious" experience and thought. For me, an understanding of spirituality as being grounded in the Ground of Being (God) has at least the following antecedents.

I grew up during the 1940s and 1950s in a home which was "spiritual but not religious"—a home infused with the spirituality of my mother and my maternal grandmother, whose spirituality was communicated in their singing of the popular Christian hymns of that period—"Old Rugged Cross" being a particular favorite.

I started attending church because, initially, an older cousin came by and walked with me to Sunday school. In both of the congregations of my childhood, the emphasis was on relationships and on one's embed-dedness in a community of persons who cared for and valued each other. The people of those congregations probably would not have articulated it this way—but, in my retrospective opinion, those folk were very much grounded in the Ground of their Being.

Although my original experience of vocation to ministry was to re-search and teaching in the field of First or Old Testament studies, I ended up in the parish and, in consequence, shifted my focus to Pastoral Theolo-gy and the Pastoral Arts (Pastoral Care, Psychotherapy, and Education). However, during the year of my graduation from theological college, when I was still intending to be a First/Old Testament scholar, I chose to do my critical exercise on the First/Old Testament passage which was assigned for that year, Psalm 73:23–26:[12]

> As for me, I am continually in Thy presence,
> Thou has taken my right hand,
> Thou dost guide me by Thy sovereign will,
> And afterwards shalt take me to glory.
> I have nothing in the heavens;
> Neither do I desire anything on the earth
> —for I have Thee.
> Though my flesh and my heart be in danger of perishing,
> My portion is Yahweh forever.[13]

So, for me, "spirituality" is a deeply felt and never absent relational expe-rience—with God, with others, and with self.

THE SPIRITUALITY OF HOT TUBS AS CARE OF THE BODY

The bodies in which we live out our spirituality are precious. Being grounded in the Ground of our Being inspires us to take care of our bodies, to do what is good for them, and not to do harm. Reciprocally, the physiological and psychological well-being that ensues from the use of properly maintained hot tubs potentiates our groundedness in the Ground of our Being. James Lapsley named this reality as "the interlock-ing processes of life."[14] For my essay in the course which Lapsley taught about the relationship between "salvation" and "health," I chose to ex-plore the use of those words in the Judaeo-Christian Scriptures, relating that usage to current languaging of the relationship between spirituality and health.[15]

THE SPIRITUALITY OF HOT TUBS AS CARE OF THE SOUL

According to the Encyclopedia Britannica, "soul" is used to describe . . . "the immaterial aspect or essence of a human being, that which confers individuality and humanity, often considered to be synonymous with the mind or the self. In theology, the soul is further defined as that part of the individual which partakes of divinity and often is considered to survive the death of the body."[16]

IS THE SOUL SEPARATE FROM THE BODY?

The *Encyclopedia Britannica* goes on to say that "the early Hebrews apparently had a concept of the soul but did not separate it from the body, although later Jewish writers developed the idea of the soul further. Biblical references to the soul are related to the concept of breath and establish no distinction between the ethereal soul and the corporeal body. Christian concepts of a body-soul dichotomy originated with the ancient Greeks and were introduced into Christian theology at an early date by St. Gregory of Nyssa [circa 335–395 AD/CE] and by St. Augustine [354–430 AD/CE]."[17] At least two authors who are widely referenced in the pastoral literature (McNeill and Williams)[18] appear to understand the history of soul care in Western Christendom as reflecting care for soul as distinct from body

I think that this is a misreading of history "on the ground." That is, the focus of pastoral/spiritual care may have been on the "religious" needs of the care receivers, understood as having nothing to do with the well-being of the body in the conceptualization regarding those practices. However, that care was, and continues to be, delivered in embodied ways (sitting with, smiling-crying with, putting an arm around a shoulder, sharing a Scripture passage etc.). Further, it is increasingly clear that embodied pastoral/spiritual care impacts soul and body in a holistic way. For example, John Florell describes his doctoral research project with 150 patients in a Midwestern USA city hospital as follows:

> Patients were assigned randomly to one of three groups called control, support, and support-information. The control group got regular hospital treatment; the support group got visits from clergy trained to give supportive relational visits that focused on emotional and religious questions; and the support-information group received special information about the hospital, rituals, staff, and administration, as well as the emotional and religious support of the relational method.[19]

Florell reports that patients in the support and support-information group left the hospital one to two days earlier than patients in the control group. Further, although the conversations that occurred with the support and support-information groups resulted in raising pre-surgical transitory anxiety[20] higher than that experienced by the control group prior to surgery, the support and support-information groups had significantly lower levels of anxiety than the control group post-surgery. Further, the support and support-information groups used significantly lower levels of pain medication post-surgery than did the control group. Florell's study is one of several which clearly indicate that soul care is delivered in embodied ways and that it has embodied outcomes.

I see hot tub use as embodied soul care. But how is that so?

NEED FOR WITHDRAWAL AND SEPARATION AS A WAY OF BEING PRESENT

We embodied souls need to have moments of solitude in order to engage fully with the world in which we live and move and have our being. The amount and kind of solitude that we need will depend on where we are on the continuum between introvertism and extravertism as understood by social psychology (for example, Hans Eysenk) and/or by depth psychology (Carl Jung[21]).

Henri Nouwen is one of many who write about the value of solitude.[22]

> The few times . . . that we . . . listen carefully to our restless hearts, we may start to sense that in the midst of our sadness there is joy, that in the midst of our fears there is peace, that in the midst of our greediness there is the possibility of compassion and that indeed in the midst of our irking loneliness we can find the beginnings of a quiet solitude.[23]

He goes on:

> It is probably difficult, if not impossible, to move from loneliness to solitude without any form of withdrawal from a distracting world, and therefore it is understandable that those who seriously try to develop their spiritual life are attracted to places and situations where they can be alone. . . . But the solitude that really counts is the solitude of the heart; it is an inner quality or attitude that does not depend on physical isolation. On occasion this isolation is necessary to develop this solitude of heart, but it would be sad if we considered this essential aspect of the spiritual life as a privilege of monks and hermits. It seems more important than ever to stress that solitude is one of the human capacities that can exist, be maintained and developed in the center of a big city, in the middle of a large crowd and in the context of a very active and productive life. A man or woman who has developed this solitude of heart is no longer pulled apart by the most divergent stimuli of the surrounding world but is able to perceive and understand this world from a quiet and creative center.[24]

A "quiet and creative center" indeed. That is what daily disciplines such as twenty to twenty-five minutes each day in a hot tub can help one to develop.

SPENDING TIME DAILY IN A HOT TUB AS SPIRITUAL PRACTICE

Marilyn Owen writes as follows:

> Can hot tubbing be seriously considered as a spiritual practice? . . .
> Spiritual practices come in a variety of denominations, structures, fre-
> quencies, and intensities. Most importantly, though, is that the practice
> fit the person: it should suit you. If your spiritual practice does not fit
> into your lifestyle, inspire, reflect, replenish and enliven you, it will
> ultimately fail. This is a truth I hold to be self-evident. I encourage
> dissidents to write their own essay.

For research into the important cultural and psychological roles played
by water in our lives in terms of history, architecture, nature writing, art,
environmental science and engineering, etcetera, the reader is referred to
the work of Robert Lawrence France.[25]

In my experience, water immersion, especially immersion in the hot
waters of a natural hot spring or hot tub, can be experienced as having
characteristics of the womb experience—a time of being enfolded and
protected and of being readied for "delivery" (back) into the ordinary
world.

SACRED SPACE

Marilyn Owen writes about sacred space as "tenemos."[26]

> Most spiritual practices occur in a particular place that has been set
> aside and protected specifically for that purpose. . . . The temenos, in
> this case, is created by the physical features of the place as well as the
> inclusion of the four Classical Elements (air, water, earth, and fire). In
> my particular location, the hot tubs are located on a natural hillside in a
> large county park, overlooking a lake and the wonderful San Gabriel
> Mountain range.[27]

Hot tubs located in homes or adjacent to homes and designated for personal or family use are usually seen as recreational or social equipment.
That need not limit their usefulness as spaces for sacred ritual. However,
small hot tubs intended for use by one or two persons can be obtained.

Location of hot tubs within homes has been problematic when the
space in which they are located is not constructed properly.[28] In any case,
many people will prefer an outdoor location so long as it has natural
beauty, is reasonably quiet and free of distractions, and is usable all year
round.[29]

What is important, above all else, is that the hot tub is experienced by
the user as "sacred space." That is, we "consecrate" the hot tub as "tenemos" by our intention in using it as an instrument for our spiritual
growth and development.

The subtitle of this chapter suggests an analogy between hot tub use and water baptism by immersion. My denominational tradition[30] does not practice water baptism by immersion although we do that when requested and when it is possible at the request of a person who was not baptized as an infant. Normally we sprinkle or pour the water, taking the position that the amount of water used is irrelevant because, although affirming the "real presence" of God's Spirit in the Sacrament, Baptism is seen as a symbolic act. That said, the analogy is useful—in that, as a result of the hot tub experience, as is the case in Baptism, one can experience being "cleansed, forgiven, healed, reborn"[31] through the spiritual practice of hot tubbing.

Again, in the PCC tradition, Baptism is not just about a preoccupation with the individual's personal spiritual well-being. It is a symbol of one's commitment to works of love and mercy, of justice-seeking, and of care of the earth. The PCC baptismal liturgy preface states that

> Baptism is the beginning of a new life in the world where ethical, social, and political decisions are made in the light of our response to God in Christ. Baptism is not a protection from the world but an initiation into the love and justice by which God seeks to redeem the world.[32]

One can make the choice to renew that sensibility daily through the spiritual practice of hot tub use.

NOTES

1. *Embodiment* was published in 1978. Nelson's *Body Theology* was published in 1992. In it he offers an incarnational way of doing theology. He takes body experiences seriously and views sexuality as central to the mystery of human experience and to the human relationship with God. He seeks to identify what scripture and tradition say about sexuality, focusing on three areas of concern: sexual theology, men's issues, and biomedical ethics. He blames a faulty dualism that separates body and spirit for distorting the meanings of masculinity, making modern medicine confusing, and fueling militarism, racism, and ecological abuse. See, also Miller-McLemore's introduction in this volume.

2. Ibid., 19.

3. Nelson, *Embodiment*.

4. Nelson, *Body Theology*.

5. The word "flesh" is used extensively in the writings attributed to Paul—but also can be found in most (twenty-two of twenty-seven) of the other Second (New) Testament books.

6. John 1:1, 14 (NRSV)

7. See section 5 below.

8. But take note, below, of the risks involved for the respiratory system when hot tubs are not properly cared for.

9. The material in this section has been gathered from several sources, including Internet sources. That original material has been assessed in light of the experience and knowledge of the author. The author has consulted several healthcare professionals and an environmental specialist, along with hot tub supplier staff members, con-

cerning safe hot tub practices—and the author expresses his appreciation to these persons for their contribution to his own healthy use of a hot tub and, indirectly, to the development of this chapter. However, in its present form, this chapter's author is responsible for what has been written here.

10. Once a month, after thoroughly rinsing the filters with the hot water tap wide open, I soak them for three to four hours in hot water with a strong concentration of bleach.

11. Paul Tillich. *Systematic Theology*, vol. 1 (Chicago: University of Chicago Press, 1951), 64, and throughout Tillich's many books.

12. The "critical exercise assignment" required that we write a paper indicating that we had consulted the relevant commentaries and theological writing deeply and broadly—a paper in which we also provided our translation of the assigned passage—with a choice of a passage from the First/Old Testament or from the Second/New Testament.

13. Author translation (Carr, 1962, unpublished): This is the translation at which I arrived in 1962 after my exploration of the commentaries and relevant theological works. Today, I would not use King James English and would make some other language changes.

14. James Lapsley, *Salvation and Health: The Interlocking Processes of Life* (Philadelphia: Westminster Press, 1972).

15. John Carr, unpublished Th.M. essay on "Salvation and Health in the Bible." Princeton Theological Seminary, Princeton, New Jersey, USA, 1971.

16. *Encyclopedia Britannica*, accessed online.

17. Ibid.

18. John T. McNeill, *A History of the Cure of Souls*, and Daniel Day Williams in *The Minister and the Care of Souls*.

19. John T. Florell, "Effective Pastoral Care in the Hospital," in James B. Ashbrook and John E. Hinkle, Jr., eds., *At the Point of Need: Living Human Experience—Essays in Honor of Carroll A. Wise* (University Press of America, 1988), 263 ff.

20. For example, anxiety specifically related to the hospitalization as contrasted with characterological anxiety

21. In *Memories, Dreams and Reflections*

22. In *Reaching Out: The Three Movements of the Christian Life*

23. Ibid, p. 36.

24. Ibid, pp. 37 and 38

25. *Deep Immersion: The Experience of Water*.

26. "Temenos" is Greek for a piece of land that is assigned as an official domain.

27. Internet source—see references.

28. There are risks of mold buildup if the wall and ceiling materials are not properly insulated and do not have the correct kind of vapor barriers—and if the walls are made of material into which hot tub emissions can be absorbed. And of course, the ventilation system must be adequate. A hot tub room in a home needs to be built using the same specifications as those used for a "steam room."

29. Rolling in snow, as I did during my first hot tub experience, is an added benefit when using an outdoor hot tub in an area where there is privacy and where the winter temperature drop is not too severe. It is not possible in the author's home location, where the winter temperature can dip below minus thirty degrees Celsius.

30. The Presbyterian Church in Canada (PCC).

31. Preface to the baptismal liturgy of the Presbyterian Church in Canada, p. 117 of *The Book of Common Worship*.

32. Ibid.

REFERENCES

Ashbrook, James B. and John E Hinkle, Jr. *At the Point of Need: Living Human Experience Essays in Honor of Carroll A. Wise*. Lanham, MD: University Press of America, 1988.

Baird, Carol L. "First-Line Treatment for Osteoarthritis: Part 2: Nonpharmacologic Interventions and Evaluation." *Orthopaedic Nursing* 20 (November-December 2001): 13–20.

Barker, K. L., H. Dawes, P. Hansford, and D. Shamley. "Perceived and Measured Levels of Exertion of Patients with Chronic Back Pain Exercising in a Hydrotherapy Pool." *Archives of Physical Medicine and Rehabilitation* 84 (September 2003): 1319–1323.

Carr, John C. Unpublished essay on "Salvation and Health in the Bible." *Princeton Theological Seminary*, Princeton, NJ: 1971.

Chaitow, Leon. *Hydrotherapy: Water Therapy for Health and Beauty*. Boston, MA: Element Books, 1999.

Cider, A., M. Schaufelberger, K. S. Sunnerhagen, and B. Andersson. "Hydrotherapy— A New Approach to Improve Function in the Older Patient with Chronic Heart Failure." *European Journal of Heart Failure* 5 (August 2003): 527–535.

Eysenck, H. J. *The Biological Basis of Personality*. Springfield, IL: Thomas Publishing, 1967.

France, Robert Lawrence. *Deep Immersion: The Experience of Water*. Winnipeg, MB, Canada: Green Frigate Books, 2003.

Johnson, Kate. "Hydrotherapy Greatly Eases Delivery Stress, Pain." *OB GYN News* 34 (November 1999): 27.

Jung, Carl. *Memories, Dreams, Reflections*. London: Fontana Press, 1995 (German first edition in 1962).

Keegan, L. "Therapies to Reduce Stress and Anxiety." *Critical Care Nursing Clinics of North America* 15 (September 2003): 321–327.

Lapsley, James. *Salvation and Health: The Interlocking Processes of Life*. Philadelphia: Westminster Press, 1972.

Lawrence, D. H. *Lady Chatterley's Lover*. New York, NY: Pocket Books, 1959.

Mayhall, C. G. "The Epidemiology of Burn Wound Infections: Then and Now." *Clinical Infectious Diseases* 37 (August 15, 2003): 543–550.

Molter, N. C. "Creating a Healing Environment for Critical Care." *Critical Care Nursing Clinics of North America* 15 (September 2003): 295–304.

Nelson, James. B. *Embodiment: An Approach to Sexuality and Christian Theology*. Minneapolis: Augsburg, 1978.

———. *Body Theology*. Louisville, KY: Westminster/John Knox Press, 1992.

Nouwen, Henri. *Reaching Out: The Three Movements of the Spiritual Life*. Colorado Springs, CO: Image Books, 1986.

Owen, Marilyn. "The Fully Realized Hot Tub Human." *Mythopoetry Scholar* (http://www.mythopoetry.com/mythopoetics/scholar11_owen_hottub.html), accessed on April 10, 2014).

Parish, Laura. "The Eysenck Personality Inventory by H. J. Eysenck and S. G. B. Eysenck." *British Journal of Educational Studies* 14 (1) (1965): 140.

Pelletier, Kenneth R. *The Best Alternative Medicine, Part I: Naturopathic Medicine*. New York: Simon and Schuster, 2002.

Taylor, S. "The Ventilated Patient Undergoing Hydrotherapy: A Case Study." *Australian Critical Care* 16 (2003): 111–115.

The Presbyterian Church in Canada. *Book of Common Worship*. Toronto, ON, Canada: The Presbyterian Church in Canada, 1991 (see http://presbyterian.ca/resources/).

Tillich, Paul. *Systematic Theology*, vol. 1. Chicago: University of Chicago Press, 1951 (1963 edition).

Tomlinson, Carole Anne. *Hot Tub Health Risks*. Livestrong.com at http://www.livestrong.com/article/80339-hot-tub-health-risks/, accessed April 10, 2014.

EIGHT

Word Made Flesh

*Using Visual Textuality of Sign Languages to Construct
Religious Meaning and Identity*

Jason Hays

Language is not merely a system of symbols and signs, it is the medium by which identity is constructed, meaning is made, and God is known. Narratives construct reality and identity in communal religious practices. In this sense, persons construct identities by "speaking" into being; at the same time being "heard" by another. Yet prevailing models of contemporary hermeneutics demonstrate a bias toward written and spoken texts to the neglect of visual languages.

This chapter explores the implications for a dialectical hermeneutic when the text is visual, the language is three-dimensional, and the narratives are not heard, but seen. I'll begin within the field of philosophical hermeneutics, with a brief engagement of Gadamer and Ricoeur in order to consider how the use of sign languages construct a visual "textual body," which Deaf[1] persons use to construct religious meaning and identity. I then turn to sociolinguistics, and the work of Bourdieu on symbolic power in order to consider the sociolinguistic oppression of signers by hegemonic systems of hearing/speaking power. This analysis will consider issues of relational power and privilege as Deaf signing communities' resistance to audism and other efforts to delegitimate sign language present opportunities for acts of subversive sociolinguistic identity construction. The chapter will conclude with several examples from Protestant religious ritual in North America.

I approach this exploration of visual narratives as a theologian who is shaped by poststructuralist, social constructionist, and critical theories. I engage this work with an intention to decenter my own assumptions so that I might bias experiences from those subjugated by dominant discourses of power—discourses which, by their very construction, provide me privilege. In the context of Deaf studies and linguistics of visual languages, I am even more so privileged by being hearing; which is to say that both my audiological and cultural-linguistic location is within the dominant hegemony of power. I am acutely aware of the oppressive liabilities inherent in writing about Deaf persons and their language as a hearing-identified scholar, particularly given the genealogy of hearing "professionals" engaging in discursive practices that exclude and perpetuate symbolic violence on persons who are d/Deaf.

Because I am a practical pastoral theologian, I seek to intentionally intersect my theological norms with the methodologies and epistemologies of language as they are practiced in the particularity of lived experience and community. I come to this work after several years as a bilingual hearing pastor working with a culturally Deaf congregation, professional teaching and campus ministry experience at Gallaudet University, and as one for whom American Sign Language (ASL) is a second language. While these professional experiences have shaped my interest in bringing together philosophical hermeneutics, Deaf cultural studies, and pastoral theology, it is my intention to decenter any assumptive "expertise" on my part. As such, while I bring a particular lived experience as a practical theologian working with Deaf communities, I am hesitant to "speak for" Deaf communities. This is a precarious place from which to engage in scholarship. I nevertheless acknowledge my privilege, and offer the following exploration tentatively and in conversation with Deaf scholars whom I hope will critique or contribute to the ideas posited here.

FOUNDATIONS IN PHILOSOPHICAL HERMENEUTIC

For Gadamer and Heidegger (as well as theorists in philosophical hermeneutics and social constructionist theory generally) language constructs the way in which we experience and constitute the world. Language is constitutive: it constructs and communicates ideas, and constructs representations of who we are as persons and how we represent the world. Humans are always constructing meaning through language.

But it is worth recognizing here the way in which "language" is used in philosophical hermeneutics to legitimate and perpetuate the dominant hearing hegemony. For example: Heidegger posits that speech, not mere expression, is the primary means of discourse. In doing so Heidegger, perhaps unintentionally, delegitimizes visual languages as a constitutive media. Indeed, the vocabulary of the field is encumbered with aural assumptions: speech, utterance, illocution. For persons who are Deaf and who have been subjugated by educational systems that emphasize speaking and speech skills over language acquisition; for those who have been punished for using their hands to develop their natural language; and for those whose intelligence has been evaluated solely on their ability to speak and visually speech read; this power dynamic is paramount.[2] Indeed, it is worth acknowledging that dominant schools in philosophical hermeneutics and linguistics have historically rejected the legitimacy of signed languages and some maintain such an epistemological stance today.[3]

Brenda Jo Brueggemann sums it up well:

> Language is humanspeech is language therefore Deaf people are inhuman and Deafness is a problem.[4]

Indeed, theorists in philosophical hermeneutics, linguistics, and theologians who maintain speech as the ultimate form of language perpetuate not only phonologist preferences toward spoken language, but engage in dehumanizing subjugation of sociolinguistic communities. If Heidegger is right, that only speech enables a person to be the living being one is as person, then those who do not speak are not human. This is unacceptable.

LANGUAGE AND SYMBOLIC POWER

We turn now to Bourdieu's work in *Language & Symbolic Power*.[5] Bourdieu posits that language is more than a method of communication; it is a means of engaging power. Everyday linguistic exchanges occur between language agents with particular social resources and competencies, and within socially structured frameworks of power. Through a complex historical process, especially in colonizing contexts, one language or set of linguistic practices emerges as the dominant and legitimate language, while other languages or dialects become eliminated or subordinated to it. Linguistic minorities are forced to enter into discursive relationships with the dominant language—on the dominant language's terms.

Many postcolonial theorists, particularly Bhabha and Spivak, note similar symbolic power exercised by the hegemony of dominant languages, and its serious threats to both cultural and linguistic diversity. Colonized and subaltern communities are delegitimated through the direct annihilation of their language or by the subjugation of their language to dominant English (or Spanish, or whatever the colonizing language happens to be). In this sense, Deaf signing communities embody a diglossic, hybrid subaltern status.[6]

Bourdieu offers two important insights for how we might critique the symbolic power of spoken language in their subjugation of sign languages. First is "competence." Bourdieu posits that without competence in the dominant/legitimate language one is condemned to "silence." Here persons who are Deaf are subjugated not only by means of linguistic *modality* (i.e., spoken languages are legitimate but sign languages are not), but also by *means* of being denied their natural language development through audist/oralist educational philosophies (in the United States) that deny the linguistic viability of American Sign Language and impose speech reading/Manually Coded English systems. Prevailing educational approaches, namely mainstreaming, often introduce sign language as a method of last resort when aural/oral methods have "failed," leaving d/Deaf students years behind in language development. In this sense Deaf students are not only subjugated because they don't have the language of the dominant group (i.e., hearing students), they are also denied access to the visual language that will, at the very least, provide them with linguistic minority status.

Bourdieu's second contribution is that competency in the dominant/ legitimate language is contingent upon "difference." (This is not unlike Derrida's discussion of "*differance*.") Indeed, the linguistic subjugation of Deaf persons cannot be dissociated from the social construction of "Deafness" as disability. There is significant scholarship in the area of disability as a social construction which is beyond our scope here. I will, however, highlight Branson & Miller's work which argues that disability, as a socially constructed category, is at its core necessary for the discursive construction of every other person's "normal" subjectivity. In other words, normal "able-bodied" persons construct their own sense of abled-ness by othering those who are different.

> The disabled, therefore, are not a tangible and unproblematic collection of people but, rather, a population that is assumed to exist, a category into which able-bodied people can slot others who pose a threat to their own normal view of the world and to those who inhabit it, and into which those who identify themselves as disabled can welcome those whom they see as suffering the same marginalization and oppression as themselves.[7]

Put another way, the medical model of "disability" constructs identities on arbitrary audiological categories predicated on the myth of bodily perfection: an etiological identity; the sociocultural model constructs identity on sociolinguistic affiliation: an emic identity. As Carol Padden reminds us: "The single most significant component of Deaf cultural identity in most societies is competence in a natural sign language, the community's vernacular language as well as a powerful marker of in-group membership and group solidarity."[8] Here we are dealing with two kinds of *differance:* While *differance* in the etiological construction of Deaf identity is manifested in paternalistic discourses of disability and pathology, based upon arbitrary and subjective discourses of normalcy; *differ-*

ance in the sociocultural construction of Deaf identity is manifested in linguistic discourses around the legitimacy of sign languages and the use of language in constructing a Deaf cultural identity.

SIGN LANGUAGES AND FOUCAULDIAN GAZE

It may be helpful here to note briefly Foucault's discussion of knowledge-power and gaze as we begin to synthesize Gadamar and Heidegger's philosophical hermeneutics and Bourdieu's discussion of language and symbolic power. Foucault's discussion of power is similar to Bourdieu's in so much as power is constituted by a network of relationships, not as a commodity or something which is merely omnidirectionally. Power is a relational dynamic of subjectivity and dominance. Though not specifically addressing language by Deaf communities, Foucault's discussion of the power of gaze offers an insightful metaphor for the power of language, particularly as constitutive of identity.

Two characteristics of the Foucauldian gaze may be helpful for our discussion here. First, his earlier work on "docile" bodies and the "clinical gaze" is particularly poignant for Deaf persons who have described the gaze of otolaryngologists, pediatricians, audiologists, speech-language pathologists, surgeons, and teachers of the Deaf (who are mostly hearing) who engage in discourse from an etiological and pathological stance. This gaze narrows the attention from the person to the *person's ear*: they became subjugated by being identified primarily with their body— their ears.

Second, Foucault's later work explored social discipline in the modern era and the normalizing gaze. This disciplinary watching is a metaphor for how modern discourses of language exercise control over systems of power-knowledge; the surveillance by those in power merely by their gaze upon another results in persons being subjected to the normalizing disciplines of acceptable behavior. This metaphor is also poignant for Deaf persons who have described the gaze of audism, which engages in disciplinary surveillance to perpetuate systems of power that normalizes and rewards Deaf persons behaving and speaking like Hearing persons,[9] by imposing institutional (e.g., educational) double-binds and by delegitimizing their natural language.

For generations, Deaf signing communities in North America have engaged in resistance against audism, particularly metaphysical audism, and other discourses of power that aim to delegitimate American Sign Language—both prior to and since the 1880 international conference on d/Deaf education in Milan, which (for all intents and purposes) banned sign language in d/Deaf education.[10] There is a long history of hearing oppression of the Deaf community by means of paternalistic pathology, symbolic violence, technologies of discipline, and linguistic genocide.[11]

With certain and noteworthy exceptions, I would argue that dominant Christian religious and theological discourses have, historically, conspired with the hegemonic medical establishment to perpetuate the insidious hearing gaze, subjugating Deaf persons, their cultural identity, and their language.

How might one give an account of a Deaf person's insistence upon using sign language and claiming one's cultural identity in light of this hearing gaze? Here I'm suggesting we turn Foucault's gaze on its head: that is, when Deaf signers insist upon being "seen" by the dominant hearing gaze, the Deaf signers are reclaiming subversive power to be the authors of their lives over and against dominant hearing discourses— discourses that deny the very language the Deaf signer is employing to create both a life narrative and to construct a vibrant cultural identity. In doing so, Deaf signers reject external etiological constructions of their identities and claim new sociocultural constructions based upon embodied language—text and grammar literally constructed by the hands, arms, face, and shoulder, in three dimensional space. This is the textual body.

An implication here is that Deaf persons resist submission and subjugation by claiming their linguistic agency. When Deaf persons insist that the dominant gaze redirects its orientation from the ear to the hands, when they insist upon being "seen" rather than "heard," they are resisting pathological and etiological categories of identity: a shift in identity from deaf to Deaf. The clinical gaze is now challenged to *see* the subjugated Deaf body with a different lens, literally gazing upon an embodied language. The technologies of discipline and surveillance of the normalizing gaze is now challenged to deconstruct normalcy in order to see sociolinguistic constructions of identity.

MEANINGFUL ACTION AND NARRATIVE IDENTITY THEORY

I am quick to impress that the Deaf communities' *meaningful action*— namely the insistence upon the dominant gaze to "listen" with its eyes to their visual and embodied language—is not merely a discursive act of relevance. As Ricœur reminds us, meaningful action of language is detached from its linguistic agent and develops consequences of its own. In this case, more than merely confronting prevailing discourses of pathology or hegemonic audism, the act of conversing in sign languages becomes an embodied constitutive act of narrative construction of identity.

I am suggesting that the construction of narrative identity (a la Ricœur) by means of the textual body—visual sign languages—is particularly unique to Deaf communities, and presents two significant hermeneutical implications.

First, the distinctive contribution of narrative identity theory is the critique of essentialist epistemologies of the self in favor of social constructionist theory, which argues that language through discourse constructs the self. This epistemological claim is crucial because it facilitates the deconstruction of etiologically and pathologically based categories of Deafness. Ironically, this deconstruction is done by using *visual* language, the very language that phonologist and metaphysical audism attempts to delegitimate. When Deaf persons use, teach, preserve, and linguistically analyze American Sign Language they do so not only to construct their narrative and cultural identities, but also to symbolically (a la Bourdieu) delegitimate essentialist claims of self and disability.

For example, a church member of a culturally Deaf Christian congregation says to me: "Heaven will be wonderful. I'll get to meet Jesus. . . . He'll sign to me 'Welcome home,' and I'll see all the angles singing songs in sign language." This is a powerful statement given hegemonic Protestant religious discourse that would be averse to making such a claim about Jesus and the angels. So here the church member is not only constructing an eschatology that legitimates a subjugated language with references to Jesus and angels fluent in ASL, but is also using the power of religious discourse to construct a religious identity using the very language that the hegemonic hearing religious establishment delegitimates in the first place. Moreover, the church member constructs an eschatology using sign language: a language that is mostly inaccessible to dominant Protestant systems of power and privilege. This presents a significant opportunity for subversive constructive theologizing because the hearing gaze of the religious hegemony has no idea what the church member is communicating. This not unlike other minority language groups that use subjugated languages in similar ways.

Second, narrative identity, when constructed in sign languages, is particularly unique because it occurs in a modality different than that of dominant languages (a modality not specifically addressed by Gadamer, Heidegger, Bourdieu, Foucault, or Ricœur). Thus, when religious identity narratives are authored and performed in a visual/manual modality, the textual body is "read" by being seen and witnessed. This is significant because visual narratives—stories constructed, authored, and signed in ASL (or other sign languages)—are constructed by unique semantical, grammatical, and syntactical methodologies distinctive to visual media. How one tells a story in ASL is different than how one would tell the same story in spoken English. This has important hermeneutical implications for how the visual narrative is "read" by others, particularly as Deaf persons claim their agency to author and tell their own stories in their own visual language

An example: in many Protestant worship services scripture is read, usually prior to the sermon. In culturally Deaf Protestant congregations, the scripture is often signed in ASL. But there are times when the scripture is enacted in dramatic form. While bible drama does occur within hearing Protestant congregations, it represents two important acts of resistance within the context of Deaf Protestant congregations: first, bible drama resists the logocentrism of many Protestant contexts in which the "word" of God is either inerrant or so reverently held that text itself becomes holy. In this sense, bible drama becomes, quite literally, "word made flesh." Second, bible dramas make the religious texts accessible to and transmitted by persons whose reading skills of the dominant language (e.g., written English) is limited, which is a direct result of the audist pedagogical decisions imposed by hearing hegemonic educational systems.

IMPLICATIONS

I've critiqued the inherent bias of philosophical hermeneutics toward spoken languages and have proposed a model of hermeneutics that takes into account the "textual body." I now offer a few implications for further study, particularly as they relate to the practice of hermeneutics within practical theology. First, it seems plausible that the contribution of visual narrative identity has significant implications for deconstructing dominant metaphors of "hearing," "Deaf," and "disability" in Christian communities. These metaphors have been used in a wide variety of ways by the hearing church: from cure and faith-healing practices which insist if one has enough faith one can be "healed" from Deafness; to mainline denominations participating in paternalistic Deaf ministry, framing it as "ministry *to* the disabled"; to reproducing liturgical and scriptural discourses that equate "Deaf" with ignoring God; or prayers of the people that petition God to "hear our prayer." These are acts of symbolic violence, and very well may constitute microaggressions.[12] At the very least, this is the hearing gaze well at work in the church, a gaze that necessitates ongoing critique and deconstructing.

Second, the logocentrism of contemporary Protestant theology, particularly as it relates to scripture, is challenged by visual textuality. Wrigley writes, "At least to the Hearing, the hermeneutical privileging of hearing and speech over sign seems related to traditions of the Reformation and its literal focus on 'the Word of God.' This bias remains embedded within the notions of textualization."[13] Regardless of whether one frames *Logos* exclusively within the text, or experientially through the text, significant theological concerns arise for the "people of the Book" when a language has no written form.[14] I am eager to learn what implications for the gaze of the hearing church may arise from the growing use of ASL (and other visual sign language) translation of Christian scripture into video media. I'm likewise curious what other Christian traditions, traditions that may emphasize proclaimed Word rather than written word, may offer insights in this regard.

Third, what is the role of community in the construction of visual textuality? I affirm the role of community in the communicative process, both as a market of discourse and as a gathering of hermeneuts who interpret and "read" narratives. But I am equally concerned about the question of power: Who in the community gets to determine which narratives become conventional or normative? Or which community? And who gets to decide in which language such narratives will be constructed? If we acknowledge the symbolic power of language presented by Bourdieu and affirm the discursive acts of subjugated Deaf persons to be "read" in their visual sign languages, communities of faith have an opportunity—even an obligation—to deconstruct pathologizing power located in our theological discourses. A poignant example of such deconstruction might be illustrated by subversive God-imaging. How might communities of faith invert the normalizing gaze of dominant audist images of God by proclaiming that God *signed* (rather than spoke) the world into being? Or by modifying our liturgical langue for prayer of the people by petitioning God to *receive* our prayer (rather than hear our prayer)?

CONCLUSION

I conclude by acknowledging the limits and liabilities of this work. First, my overarching epistemological commitment has been social constructionist, namely the discursive production of identity through language. Notwithstanding substantive critiques of this philosophical school, I posit that one does not need to be a social constructionist to affirm Ricœur's point that the importance of *meaningful actions* goes beyond its initial situation. That is, when Deaf persons engage in discourse using sign languages, particularly as language agents categorized, problematized and pathologized as "disabled," they are nevertheless engaging in symbolic acts of resistance over and against the dominant hearing hegemony.

Second, I acknowledge the implicit liabilities in engaging "gaze" as a metaphor of power (a la Foucault) and it being problematic for some who engage discourses of disability, vision, and blindness. I welcome this critique of Foucault's term, acknowledge its problematic implications, and invite engagement by scholars working in these discourses.

Lastly, given my social location as a hearing scholar working with intercultural methods of engagement in Deaf signing communities, I offer these conclusions quite tentatively, inviting collaborative engagement and critique of my ideas presented here, particularly from Deaf scholars, some of whose scholarship I have engaged in this work.

NOTES

1. Deaf with a capital *D* is used here to indicate those who consider themselves members of the sociolinguistic Deaf community; lower-case deaf indicates an audiological description (not a cultural and linguistic identity).

2. O. Wrigley, *The Politics of Deafness* (Washington, DC: Gallaudet University Press, 1996).

3. See T. Reagan, "Toward and 'Archeology of Deafness': Etic and Emic Constructions of Identity in Conflict," *Journal of Language, Identity, and Education* 1(1) (2002): 41–66.

4. Brenda J. Brueggemann, *Lend Me Your Ear Rhetorical Constructions of Deafness* (Washington, DC: Gallaudet University Press, 1999), 11.

5. Pierre Bourdieu, *Language and Symbolic Power*, ed. by B. Thompson, trans. by G. Raymond & M. Adamson (Cambridge, MA: Harvard University Press, 1991).

6. J. Davis, "Universalizing Marginality: How Europe Became Deaf in the Eighteenth Century," in *Genealogy and Literature*, ed. L. Quinby (Minneapolis: University of Minnesota Press, 1995).

7. J. Branson and D. Miller, *Damned for Their Difference: The Cultural Construction of Deaf People as "Disabled": A Sociological History* (Washington, DC: Gallaudet University Press, 2002), xiii.

8. C. Padden, "The Deaf Community and the Culture of Deaf People," in *Sign Language and the Deaf Community: Essays in Honor of William Stokoe*, ed. by Baker (Silver Spring, MD: National Association of the Deaf, 1980), 55.

9. H. L. Bauman, "Audism: Exploring the Metaphysics of Oppression," *Journal of Deaf Studies and Deaf Education* 9.2 (2004): 245.

10. The Milan Conference in 1880 was an international conference of Deaf educators (nearly all of whom were Hearing) which declared that oral methods of educating the Deaf were superior to "manual methods." In general terms, it led to the banning of sign language in schools of the Deaf across Europe and North America, the dismissal of large numbers of Deaf educators, and the introduction of speech therapy/speech reading (without sign language) as the primary pedagogical method.

11. T. Skutnabb-Kangas, *Linguistic Genocide in Education, or Worldwide Diversity and Human Rights?* (Mahwah: Lawrence Erlbaum Associates, 2000).

12. C. Pierce, "Psychiatric Problems of the Black Minority," in *American Handbook of Psychiatry*, ed. by S. Arieti (New York: Basic Books, 1974); D. W. Sue, *Microaggressions in Everyday Life: Race, Gender, and Sexual Orientation* (Hoboken, NJ: Wiley, 2010).

13. Wrigley, 224.

14. It is worth noting here two possible exceptions: 1) the transcription systems devised to schematically represent signs produced in three-dimensional space (e.g., Stokoe system, Liddell and Johnson Movement-Hold Model) (Valli et al., 2005); 2) the emerging use of video technology to record and "write" visual narratives.

REFERENCES

Bauman, H. L. "Audism: Exploring the Metaphysics of Oppression." *Journal of Deaf Studies and Deaf Education* 9.2 (2004): 239–246.

Bhabha, H. K. *The Location of Culture*. London/New York: Routledge, 1994.

Bourdieu, Pierre. *Distinction: A Social Critique of the Judgment of Taste*. Translated by Richard Nice. Cambridge, MA: Harvard University Press, 1984.

Branson, J and Miller, D. "Nationalism and the Linguistic Rights of Deaf Communities: Linguistic Imperialism and the Recognition and Development of Sign Languages." *Journal of Sociolinguistics* 2.1, 1998.

Branson, J. and Miller, D. "Sign Language and the Discursive Construction of Power Over the Deaf Through Education." In *Discourse and Power in Educational Organizations*. Edited by D. Corson. Cresskill, NJ: Hampton Press, 1998.

Branson, J. and Miller, D. *Damned for Their Difference: The Cultural Construction of Deaf People as "Disabled": A Sociological History*. Washington, DC: Gallaudet University Press, 2002.

Brueggemann, B. J. *Lend Me Your Ear Rhetorical Constructions of Deafness*. Washington, DC: Gallaudet University Press, 1999.

Case, B. A. "Using Analogy to Develop an Understanding of Deaf Culture. *Multicultural Education* 7.3,(2000): 41–44.

Davis, J. "Universalizing Marginality: How Europe Became Deaf in the Eighteenth Century." In *Genealogy and Literature*. Edited by L. Quinby. Minneapolis: University of Minnesota Press, 1995.

Derrida, Jacques. *Of Grammatology*. Translated by G. C. Spivak. Baltimore: Johns Hopkins University Press, 1976.

Eisland, Nancey. *The Disabled God: Toward a Liberatory Theology of Disability*. Nashville: Abingdon, 1994.

Foucault, Michael. *Madness and Civilization: A History of Insanity in the Age of Reason*. Translated by R. Howard. New York: Pantheon Books, 1965.

Foucault, Michael. *The Birth of the Clinic: An Archaeology of Medical Perception*. Translated by A. Sheridan. New York: Vintage Books, 1975.

Foucault, Michael. *Discipline and Punish: The Birth of the Prison*. Translated by A. Sheridan. New York: Pantheon Books, 1977.

Gadamer, Hans Georg. *Truth and Method*. Translated and Edited by G. Barden & J. Cumming. New York: Seabury Press, 1975.

Hahn, H. "Public Support for Rehabilitation Programs: The Analysis of U.S. Disability Policy." *Disability, Handicap & Society*, 1 (1986): 121–137.

Heidegger, Martin. *Poetry, Language, Thought*. Translated by A. Hofstadter. New York: Harper & Row, 1971.

Jankowski, K. "Empowerment from Within: The Deaf Social Movement Providing a Framework for a Multicultural Society." In *Sociolinguistics in Deaf Communities*. Edited by C. Lucas. Washington, DC: Gallaudet University Press, 1995.

Ong, Walter, J. "The Shifting Sensorium." In *The Varieties of Sensory Experience: A Sourcebook in the Anthropology of the Senses*. Edited by David Howes. Toronto: University of Toronto Press, 1991.

Padden, C. "The Deaf Community and the Culture of Deaf People. In *Sign Language and the Deaf Community: Essays in Honor of William Stokoe*. Edited by Baker. Silver Spring, MD: National Association of the Deaf, 1980.

Pierce, C. "Psychiatric Problems of the Black Minority." In *American Handbook of Psychiatry*. Edited by S. Arieti. New York: Basic Books, 1974.

Ricœur, Paul. *From Text to Action*. Translated by K. Blamey and J. B. Thompson. Evanston, IL: Northwestern University Press, 1991.

Ricœur, Paul. *Oneself as Another*. Translated by Kathleen Blamey. Chicago: University of Chicago Press, 1992.

Reagan, T. "Toward and 'Archeology of Deafness': Etic and Emic Constructions of Identity in Conflict." *Journal of Language, Identity, and Education* 1(1) (2002): 41–66.

Skutnabb-Kangas, T. *Linguistic Genocide in Education, or Worldwide Diversity and Human Rights?* Mahwah: Lawrence Erlbaum Associates, 2000.

Spivak, Gayatri. "Can the Subaltern Speak?" In *Marxism and the Interpretation of Culture*. Edited by Cary Nelson and Lawrence Grossberg. Urbana: University of Illinois Press, 1988.

Sue, D. W. *Microaggressions in Everyday Life: Race, Gender, and Sexual Orientation*. Hoboken, NJ: Wiley, 2010. Wrigley, O. The Politics of Deafness. Washington, DC: Galludet University Press, 1996.

Valli, C., Lucas, C., Mulrooney, K. J. *Linguistics of American Sign Language: An Introduction* (4th ed.). Washington, D.C: Clerc Books, 2005

NINE

A Laying On of Hands

Black Feminist Intimations of the Divine and Healing Touch in Religious Practice

Christina Jones Davis

Within Christian traditions, religious practices are patterns of communal action that create openings in our lives where the grace, mercy, and presence of God may be made known to us.[1] They are places where the power of God is experienced and, in the end, these are not ultimately our practices but forms of participation in the practice of God.[2] The body is ever-present in this human participation as those who practice religion are embodied persons. Within this work, I will explore ways in which certain experiences of the body shape and inform religious practices.

Exploring the influence of the body on religious experience is fitting due to the *pneuma-somatic*, or spirit-body, interconnection in religious practice. Within this connection, memories of bodily experience are often brought to bear when participating in religious practices. While they are not always accessible to the conscious mind, psychoanalysis forefather Carl Jung was convinced of a link between unconscious memory and religious experience.[3] Due to the trifold engagement of mind, body, and spirit, religious practices—particularly those involving physical touch— have the ability to invite powerful reincarnation-like recollections of the body as a conduit of life, a locus of healing, as well as evoke memories of the body as a location of harm. Physical touch that elicits experiences of the body as the location of harm is of particular concern in my exploration of the body and religious practice.

143

Among the most violating experiences of bodily harm is sexual abuse. Disturbingly, experiences of this form of violent touch are pervasive. According to the Center for Disease Control, one in three U.S. women and as many as one in four U.S. men will experience sexual abuse or intimate partner violence within their lifetimes.[4] This alarming ratio all but guarantees that sexual abuse survivors are present in large numbers within communities of faith since nearly 80 percent of people in the United States affiliate with a religion[5] and 70 percent of Americans say they attend a worship service at least once a month.[6]

The ways in which a history of sexual violence influences religious practice is also of particular concern to me because despite the aforementioned numbers, 74 percent of faith leaders surveyed in a recent study underestimate the level of sexual and domestic violence experienced within their congregations.[7] Furthermore, in-depth exploration of the relationship between the experience of survivors of sexual abuse and religious practices involving bodily touch is limited. There are several possible explanations for this deficiency of attention.

First, some religious leaders may wish to avoid the fact that so many people within their communities have experienced sexual violence because they feel ill equipped to adequately respond. As a result, the task of examining touch in religious practice and experiences of sexual abuse is evaded. Others may consider the use of social scientific inquiry to encounters with the transcendent too complicated or even inappropriate.[8] Thirdly, conversations about touch and the body within religious contexts are often solely focused on how clergy can maintain appropriate physical boundaries and avoid inappropriate touch. While physical boundaries are incredibly important, an unbalanced emphasis on avoidance can sometimes translate into evading physical touch in religious practices all together thereby eliminating the possibilities for enacting healing touch. Fourth, some may view an emphasis on the role of touch on the body an unworthy cause if one's religious doctrine focuses on seeking to escape the body in the name of sanctification.[9] In such cases, attention to engaging bodily sensations may be deemed contraindicated. Finally, discussions on the body can quickly be co-opted by dominant narratives within larger society which regard bodies as dismembered objects rather than membered subjects, or frame discussions about touch in ways that are instantaneously sexualized. Within this cacophony of views on physical touch and religious practice, it is tempting to conclude that conversations about touch and religious practice are fraught with too many challenges and are not worth having.

However, I maintain that it is imperative to examine the relationship between religious practice and experiences of both harmful and healing touch, even when sobering and difficult. Not to grapple with harmful touch, at best, carelessly neglects the suffering of those for whom histories of sexual violence impact their experience of religious practices and, at worse, colludes with a silence that serves abusers and further perpetuates a culture that supports an ongoing epidemic of sexual abuse. Furthermore, not to explore the role of healing touch is to deviate from a rich Judeo-Christian heritage that embraces touch and ignore the transformative potential of this vital communal resource. To be sure, great care is required in respecting the double-sided power and vulnerability involved in physical touch. As when holding a newborn, one simultaneously recognizes both the sacredness and the tremendous vulnerability of the body and that there is an intimate connection between the two.[10] It is important to both understand and revere the power of touch before one can harness its most healing potential.[11]

In response to the profound suffering caused by experiences of harming touch, a dearth of literature on the role of touch in religious experience, and a general lack of dialogue on the role of restorative touch in religious practice, what follows endeavors to present a pastoral theology of redemptive touch by exploring the healing role touch can have in religious experiences. The pastoral theological approach I provide is grounded in relational psychoanalytic principles of trauma and is further inspired by images described in black feminist Ntozake Shange's choreopoem "a laying on of hands" within the stage play, *for colored girls who have considered suicide/ when the rainbow is enuf.*[12]

As an ordained elder within a Protestant religious denomination, I locate much of my exploration of religious practices within this context. However, my pastoral theological approach in response to those suffering from the wounds of sexual abuse is not limited to a particular religion or denomination, nor is it necessarily theistic in nature. It may be applied within any context where there are practices that express an appreciation for a transcendent reality.

To organize the following discussion, I will first substantiate the claim that there is a historical intimate relationship between Judeo-Christian religious practices and the body. After supporting this connection, I will explore the problem of harmful touch by contextualizing it within the contemporary problem of sexual violence. Finally, I will end with providing a pastoral praxis of exercising healing touch inspired from images described Shange's choreopoem "a laying on of hands."

THE BODY AND TOUCH IN JUDEO-CHRISTIAN TRADITION

There is sufficient evidence that the body and religiosity are interrelated in Judeo-Christian history. Examples are found in both sacred texts and lived traditions. Biblical scripture supports the significance of the body in Timothy 3:16 which states, "God was manifest in the flesh."[13] Again in John 1:14, scripture reads "the Word was made flesh, and dwelt among us."[14] The Judeo-Christian narrative of an incarnate God and the phe-

nomenon of divine embodiment underscores a positive relationship between the body and religious experience.

Demonstrations in Judeo-Christian traditions of directly engaging the
body are found in its rituals. Baptism, for instance, can be understood as
the anointing of the body by the Holy Spirit in a way that unifies the
body and the Spirit. Irenaeus, along with other early church thinkers,
asserted that "our body receives unity by the washing which is for incor-
ruption also our souls by the Spirit."[15] The ritual of baptism can be
understood as a method by which the body and spirit deepen their connection through religious practice. As one can see, Judeo-Christian texts
and practices demonstrate a substantial tradition of an intimate connection between religion and the body.

Importantly, there are also vivid examples of healing touch illustrated
in the Bible. In Luke 7:36–50, a woman honors Jesus's body by washing
his feet, anointing them with oil, kissing them, and whipping them with
her hair. In this narrative, Jesus not only honors and affirms this woman's
acts of intimate physical touch, but the woman experiences profound
healing as her sins are forgiven and she is told to "go in peace."[16] In
another instance, a women with chronic bleeding is mentioned in three of
the synoptic gospels. This woman was described as being distressed
physically, spiritually, and relationally by this condition for twelve years.
When she courageously and desperately traversed social and cultural
rules to reach out and physically touch Jesus, she also experienced astonishing healing. Jesus tells her to "be comforted" and "go in peace."[17] In
both cases, Jesus affirms physical touch, and humanity experiences healing as a result.

Finally, the tradition of "laying on of hands" serves as another example of embodied religious practice found in Judeo-Christian history. This
tradition is referenced in sacred texts as *samkh* meaning "to lean upon"
and *sim* meaning "to touch."[18] Within the Dead Sea Scrolls, ancient texts
dating back to the first century and earlier, *samakh* is used to describe an
encounter between Abraham and Pharaoh, during which Abraham heals
Pharaoh by laying his hands on his head.[19] Biblical scholars note that
laying on of hands for the specific purpose of healing is not found in the
Old Testament or rabbinic literature; however, it is known to have been
practiced among pre-Christian Jews. One scholar states that laying on of
hands in the New Testament translates *samakh* in passages about healings.[20] The practice laying one's hands on another's body for the purpose
of healing is the tradition of healing touch in religious practice that inspired the illustrative images cast in Shange's final choreopoem that I
will later build upon within my pastoral praxis.

As we have seen, the body and healing touch are central images in
Judeo-Christian history, and many of its religious practices associate
touch with an extension of grace and divine healing. Touch, when violating, can cause the same action with sacred and restorative properties to

produce incredible injury. To know the truth about the prevalence of harmful touch in society is to begin to understand how it infiltrates our religious practice, and ultimately, discover what redemption looks like by means of these same practices.

THE PROBLEM OF HARMFUL TOUCH

When uninvited, physical touch can transmit great harm. Harmful touch in the form of sexual abuse plagues our society and is further supported by the cultures of sexism, secrecy, and shame that surround it. Sexual violence takes place in many forms including childhood sexual abuse, date rape, sex trafficking, and incest. Contrary to popular belief, most sexual violence is perpetuated by family members and by persons who are trusted leaders in communities—including clergy.[21]

The National Institute for Health projects that one in three American women will be sexually assaulted at some point during their lives.[22] Another source projects that by the age of eighteen, about 25 percent of girls and 10 percent of boys have been victims of sexual abuse.[23] Many would suggest the percentages are even higher because according to most estimates, 80 percent to 90 percent of rapes are not reported to police.[24] Sexual violence is organized at larger, systematic, and global levels as well. At least 20.9 million adults and children are bought and sold worldwide into commercial sexual servitude, forced labor, and bonded labor.[25] About 2 million children are exploited every year in the global commercial sex trade.[26] Sexual violence is a contemporary problem of epic proportions.

When discussing harmful touch, the body becomes a vehicle of evil rather than goodness. A common trauma symptom for survivors of sexual abuse is to see the body itself as evil as a result of the evil that was done to the body. This distorted view of the body represents one opportunity for healing to emerge. Communal rituals of healing that involve the body and touch can be redemptive in ways that restore understandings of the body's inherent worth and goodness by reclaiming the body as sacred and blessed.

In a society where there are professional counselors, social workers, and psychotherapists trained to attend to the trauma of sexual abuse, some may wonder why religious communities should also be concerned about a response. As I mentioned previously, many clergy are trained on the impact of boundary violation and are aware of its implications because of wanting to avoid re-traumatizing those we wish to help. However, the goal of religious communities is to not only strive to avoid harming one another, but also aim to offer transformational encounters that facilitate healing and wholeness. Therefore, the role of religious leaders is important and should not be minimized because its resources and tools do not mimic those of a professional counselor. Both vocations can have an essential part to play.

Moreover, religious leaders must refuse to be silent on this issue and instead speak out against the systems and structures that contribute to the perpetuation of such sexually abusive acts. Tragically, the church has been guilty of silence around issues of clergy perpetrators of abuse in particular.[27] When the church is silent, it raises questions about the nature and responsibilities of the Christian community.[28] The abuse of power that takes place in sexual abuse is a theological problem, and religion, when practiced responsibly, serves to define the nature of power and its appropriate uses.[29] I will now discuss how religious communities can provide redemptive religious practices that include healing forms of touch in ways that define and use power responsibly.

A PASTORAL THEOLOGICAL APPROACH TO HEALING TOUCH

Employing black feminist Ntozake Shange's choreopoem "a laying on of hands," I have developed a pastoral theological response to harming touch. A black feminist perspective on this issue is particularly appropriate. Black women have the highest numbers of sexual abuse among any other group in America making the wisdom and truth-telling that emerges out of black women's experiences extremely relevant. Engagement of the arts in my pastoral theology is also vital to this approach. The arts have a unique way of disarming the defenses, creating feelings of safety around difficult topics, and reaching beyond cognition to one's affective and emotional experiences.[30]

The stage play *for colored girls who have considered suicide/ when the rainbow is enuf* was first performed in 1975. Shange writes the play to outline the stories of seven women living in Harlem, New York, each represented by a color of the rainbow. These women struggle to find self-worth and meaning in life while living in a sexist, racist, and otherwise oppressive society within which some tell their stories of various forms of sexual trauma. The play is arranged into twenty choreopoems.

The term "choreopoems" refers to poetic monologues spoken while choreographed movements are performed simultaneously. Each word spoken is fully embodied and performed through the mediums of drama and dance. Included in the monologue stories are references to date rape, abortion performed on a teenage girl in an apartment by a non-medical neighbor, and intimate partner violence. The last choreopoem entitled "a laying on of hands" speaks directly about the need for healing touch that all seven of these women share. The images of the kinds of healing touch described in the final choreopoem are the interpretive basis for my pastoral theological approach.

I employ relational psychoanalytical perspective as a lens for understanding trauma because it represents well the notion that individuals
can have 'parts' of themselves that may or may not be attended to in
religious practices. I also appreciate its attention to what pastoral theologian Pamela Cooper-White describes as internal justice making. Internal
justice making supports a practice, such as the one put forth in this work,
in which individuals seek to bring to bear parts of themselves that need
healing into their religious contexts, even those parts that have been violated in cases of sexual violence.[31]

The first aspect of this pastoral praxis of healing touch highlights the
psychosocial, or relational, impact of harmful touch. In order to understand the nature of healing touch necessitated, it is important to first
understand the nature of the wound created by sexual violence. The effects of this kind of trauma are described in the following passage from
Shange's work:

> i sat up one nite walkin a boardin house
> screamin/cryin/the ghost of another woman
> who waz missin what i waz missin
> i wanted to jump up outta my bones
> & be done wit myself
> leave me alone
> & go on in the wind
> it waz too much
> i fell into a numbness[32]

This passage describing a woman feeling as though she was "missin"
something reflects well the overwhelming sense of loss, alienation, and
internal disconnection that often follows experiences of violating touch.
According to relational psychoanalytic thought, sexual trauma can produce unhealthy disassociation within an individual. Within this school of
thought, various degrees of dissociation are normal for every person to
have.[33] The healthy self is inevitably fragmented, containing accepted
parts of the self and fragmented or estranged parts of the self. However, a
relational psychoanalytic perspective distinguishes between healthy disassociation and unhealthy dissociation. The unhealthy dissociative effect
of trauma drives a wedge or wall between one's self states, making them
inaccessible to simultaneous consciousness.[34] When trauma drives a
wedge between multiple self states, certain parts of the self become cut-
off. An internal conflict emerges out of a need to internalize irreconcilable
identifications with ones that cannot be integrated into the more overarching organizational schemas and instead become unintegrated units.[35]
This happens because the existence of the self on whom the trauma was
inflicted is considered too threatening and psychically painful for the self
to manage. This would be considered unhealthy disassociation.

In cases of unintegrated self states, individuals are often unable to allow themselves to move into states that remind them of trauma and, at times, no longer have a conscious memory of these states. What is often conscious, however, is the fear individuals experience around whether or not they will still be an intact and recognizable self following the acknowledgment of these warded off parts of themselves. This disassociation can show up like it did in Shange's poem—"i wanted to jump up outta my bones & be done wit myself." This is the part of the self where healing is needed.

There is often a parallel process between the disassociation that happens within the individual and the disconnection that occurs to an individual within their faith community. It is not uncommon for sexual abuse survivors to find group settings difficult as encounters with others in a community can trigger wounds. As a result, isolation can feel safer than risking the vulnerability of connection as described by the resolute declaration in Shange's poem, "leave me alone." Despite the normalcy of this reaction to trauma, enduring disconnection and isolation can quickly lead persons into the despair reflected in the refrain, "it waz too much." For many survivors of sexual violence, these feelings of disconnection and despair can culminate into the psychologically protective defense mechanism of numbness—"i fell into a numbness." When feeling becomes too painful, numbness can feel like a preferred respite from suffering. When a fissure of this degree happens within self and community, the community holds the potential for the healing that enables a person to feel again. This community-possessed potential is described in the next part of this approach.

The second feature of my pastoral praxis asserts that persons long for experiences of healthy touch. There is often an innate knowing that touch holds the power to facilitate healing, and wholeness can function as a kind of healing reenactment. This assertion builds on the following passage:

> i waz missing somethin
> somethin so important
> somethin promised
> a layin on of hands
> fingers near my forehead
> strong
> cool
> movin
> makin me whole[36]

Shange's passage describes a woman harmed by touch who felt that what she was missing was something "so important" and "promised" that touch could provide. She was convinced that this touch would make her "whole." Wholeness, from a relational psychoanalytic perspective, is healing that occurs through reenactment and reintegration. To heal trauma, the goal is to reintegrate self-states dissociated by the trauma through healing enactments.

Enactment is the effort to be known with others in a way different from one's old self. Healing becomes possible for one who suffers when a version of the situation that led to the original need for dissociation is replayed in a way that allows the associated threat of potential trauma to be reprocessed.[37] Once reprocessed, the dissociated parts become less threatening and more tolerable allowing for them to become reintegrated with the other parts of a person's known self.

Religious communities can play an important role in these healing reenactments. Employing Martin Buber's "I-Thou" and "I-It" concepts, sexual trauma can be understood as an annihilation of connectivity between I and Thou resulting in the dulling and erasure of human relationality through objectification.[38] When religious communities provide healthy vulnerable touch in religious practices such as laying on of hands for prayer, the intimate washing of another's feet, the trustful holding of baptism immersion, or extending of caring arms when passing peace, we are able to reenact the physical vulnerability that was violated by honoring the body in a way that reintegrates and heals.[39] This restorative reenactment helps to repair the I-thou rupture in the experiences of sexual trauma survivors. Employing religious practices involving touch enables persons to co-construct a new reality with one another. One where vulnerability is invited, permission is given, and the embodied self is honored. Such an experience is supported and facilitated through the "we-ness" of God and community as illustrated by what pastoral theologian Pamela Cooper-White calls the I-Thou-We.[40]

The third aspect of this pastoral theological approach distinguishes between types of touch and further characterizes the nature of "holy touch." As stated earlier, survivors of sexual trauma often wrongly internalize the evil that was done to them as an indication that the body itself is evil. An appropriate pastoral response to a misappropriation of this nature builds on the following passage:

> i waz missing somethin
> a layin on of hands
> not a man
> layin on
> not my mama/holdin me tight/sayin
> i'm always gonna be her girl
> not a layin on of bosom and womb
> a layin on of hands
> the holiness of myself released[41]

The women portrayed in Shange's poem employ their instinctive ability to discern and distinguish between different types of touch. Throughout the entire choreopoem, the refrain "i missin somethin" is repeated, and now, the manner of touch needed is specified—touch from hands that cause "the holiness of [my]self" to be released. Religious practices involving physical touch can provide this kind of holy release by way of transcending the ordinary and ushering in the transcendent. As leaders and participants in faith communities, there are several ways one can help facilitate traditional and reimagined practices involving touch that may bring about this type of holiness-releasing experience.

For example, baptism can reinforce the understanding of the divine that is within each of us. Baptism holds the potential to focus less on our sinfulness and more on the notion that we have an inherent worthiness and goodness. Because survivors of sexual abuse often deal with feelings of shame in reference to the body, reinforcing the body's inherent goodness is a necessary part of healing. Rituals that employ intentional touch enact this new reality of the body as worthy of respect, good, and, indeed, holy.

To helpfully engage in forms of healing rituals, the concepts of power-over, power-within, and power-with are helpful.[42] Survivors of sexual abuse have been violated by power-over experiences. Religious practices involving healthy touch can remind survivors of their power-within as they are provided with opportunities to choose if, how, and when they engage in physical touch. For this reason, it is essential for religious leaders to foster a community culture that encourages members to make choices based on individually determined levels of comfort and preparedness for physical touch. This culture of valuing power-within can be created through a combination of teachings from the pulpit, statements reminding members of their power to choose included with the weekly bulletin, and modeling.

Enactments of power—with relationships in religious practices, also invite the holiness of the self to be released. For example, the religious practice of feet washing is particularly effective at reinforcing power-with dynamics. The restoration of the soul to the awareness of the community's power-with after individuals endure abuses of power is both theologically imperative and deeply healing for survivors of sexual abuse. This reenactment embodies what the Gospel of John refers to as the *eis telos*, or the full extent, of God's love for humanity. There are few more holiness-releasing experiences than to model Jesus's own enactments of divine love one to another.

CONCLUDING THOUGHTS

Care for one another within a community of faith is a person-to-person response that grows out of participation in a caring faith community and seeks to enable persons to give and receive care in community.[43] When we understand communities of faith in this way, sexual abuse survivors are those that sometimes struggle to fully participate in community due to the relationship rupturing and isolating ramifications of the trauma experienced. However, the church as a loving and responsive community has a responsibility to redeem appropriate uses for, and the power inherent in, touch within our religious practices in order to access the unique healing resources therein.

The pastoral theological approach presented here is not only for religious communities to (re)enact. Along with many postmodern and systemic thinkers, I believe that how we relate to one another on any micro level can change how power is understood and mitigated on a macro level. If individuals, family units, religious communities, and civic groups of many kinds within society could further embrace practices of healthy, transformative touch, perhaps we could impact a larger world plagued with violent, harmful touch and embark on a path toward healing and restoration together.

NOTES

1. Craig Dykstra, *Growing in the Life of Faith: Education and Christian Practices. 2nd ed.* (Louisville: Geneva Press, 2005), 80–100.
2. Dykstra, *Growing in the Life of Faith*, 20.
3. Carl Jung, *The Structure and Dynamics of the Psyche*, CW 8, par. 325.
4. Kathleen C. Basile, *National Intimate Partner and Sexual Violence Survey 2010 Summary Report*. Atlanta, GA: Centers for Disease Control and Prevention, National Center for Injury Prevention and Control, Division of Violence Prevention, 2011.
5. "'Nones' on the Rise." Pew Research Centers Religion Public Life Project RSS. October 8, 2012. Accessed September 15, 2015.
6. "What Surveys Say about Worship Attendance—and Why Some Stay Home." Pew Research Center RSS. September 13, 2013. Accessed September 15, 2015.
7. http://www.imaworldhealth.org/images/stories/technical-publications/Pastors-SurveyReport_final.pdf. 2014.
8. Susan Shooter, *How Survivors of Abuse Relate to God: The Authentic Spirituality of the Annihilated Soul*. Farnham, Surrey, England: Ashgate Publishing, 2012.
9. Dwight N. Hopkins, *Loving the Body: Black Religious Studies and the Erotic*. New York: Palgrave Macmillan, 2004, 112.
10. Stephanie Paulsell, *Honoring the Body: Meditations on a Christian Practice* (San Francisco: Jossey-Bass, 2002).
11. Shirley S. Guider provides a helpful discussion on the importance of touch as a basic human need in chapter 2, page 4 of this edited volume. She reminds us by citing classic and recent research findings that a lack of physical touch can cause a "failure to thrive" in humans and other animals.
12. Ntozake Shange, *for colored girls who have considered suicide/ when the rainbow is enuf: A Choreopoem* (New York: MacMillan, 1977).
13. Timothy 3:16. *The New American Standard Bible*.
14. John 1:14, *The New American Standard Bible*.
15. Everett Ferguson, *Baptism in the Early Church: History, Theology, and Liturgy in the First Five Centuries* (Wm. B. Eerdmans Publishing Co.: Grand Rapids, MI 2009), 117.
16. Luke 7:36–50, *New American Standard Bible*.
17. Luke 8:43–48, *New American Standard Bible*.

18. David Daube, *The New Testament and Rabbinic Judaism. London:* University of London, Athlone Press, 1956. pp. 224–46.

19. Everett Ferguson, "Laying on of Hands: Its Significance in Ordination," *The Journal of Theological Studies* (1975): 1–12.

20. David Flusser, "Healing through the Laying-on of Hands in a Dead Sea Scroll," *Israel Exploration Journal* 7 (1957), 107.

21. James Poling, *The Abuse of Power: A Theological Problem* (Nashville, TN: Abingdon Press, 1991), 11–12.

22. "Rape (Sexual Assault)—Overview: MedlinePlus Medical Encyclopedia." U.S National Library of Medicine. Accessed September 16, 2015.

23. Len Goettl and Bagby G. Daniel, *Sexual Abuse: Pastoral Responses.* Nashville: Abingdon Press, 2004. 12

24. Rape (sexual Assault)—Overview: MedlinePlus Medical Encyclopedia." U.S National Library of Medicine. Accessed September 16, 2015.

25. International Labour Organization, *ILO Global Estimate of Forced Labour: Results and Methodology* 2012, 13.

26. UNICEF, *Children Out of Sight, Out of Mind, Out of Reach; Abused and Neglected, Millions of Children Have Become Virtually Invisible* (Dec. 2005).

27. Poling, *The Abuse of Power*, 63.

28. Ibid., 14.

29. Ibid., 12.

30. Kelly Brown Douglas, *Sexuality and the Black Church: A Womanist Perspective* (Maryknoll, NY: Orbis Books, 1999), 133.

31. Pamela Cooper-White, *Braided Selves: Collected Essays on Multiplicity, God and Persons* (Eugene, OR: Cascade Books, 2011).

32. Ntozake, *for colored girls*, 61.

33. Jody Messier Davies and Mary Gail Frawley, "Dissociative Processes and Transference-countertransference Paradigms in the Psychoanalytically Oriented Treatment of Adult Survivors of Childhood Sexual Abuse," *Psychoanalytic Dialogues*: 5–36.

34. Jody Messler-Davies and Mary Gail Frawley. "Dissociative Processes and Transference-countertransference Paradigms in the Psychoanalytic Oriented Treatment of Adult Survivors of Childhood Sexual Abuse" (1991).

35. Jody Messier Davies and Mary Gail Frawley, "Dissociative Processes and Transference Countertransference Paradigms" in the Psychoanalytic Oriented Treatment of Adult Survivors of Childhood Sexual Abuse" (1991).

36. Ntozake, *for colored girls*, 58.

37. Philip Bromberg, "Shadow and Substance: A Relational Perspective on Clinical Process" (1993).

38. Pamela White, *The Cry of Tamar: Violence against Women and the Church's Response*, (Minneapolis, MN: Fortress Press, 1995), 18.

39. Additional references to the incorporation of healing touch within the Lutheran context provided by Shirley S. Guider in chapter 2 of this edited volume.

40. White, *The Cry of Tamar*.

41. Ntozake, *for colored girls*, 60.

42. White, *The Cry of Tamar*.

43. Joh Patton, *Pastoral Care in Context: An Introduction to Pastoral Care*, (Louisville, KY: Westminster/John Knox Press, 1993), 24.

REFERENCES

Basile, Kathleen C. *National Intimate Partner and Sexual Violence Survey 2010 Summary Report*. Atlanta, GA: Centers for Disease Control and Prevention, National Center for Injury Prevention and Control, Division of Violence Prevention, 2011.

Bromberg, Phillip M. *Standing in the Spaces: Essays on Clinical Process, Trauma, and Dissociation*, Hillsdale, NJ: Analytic Press, 1998.

Bromberg, Phillip M. "Shadow and Substance: A Relational Perspective on Clinical Process," *Psychoanalytic Psychology*, Volume 10(2) (1993) 147–168.

Brown Douglas, Kelly. *Sexuality and the Black Church: A Womanist Perspective*. Maryknoll, NY: Orbis Books, 1999.

Cooper-White, Pamela. *The Cry of Tamar: Violence Against Women and the Church's Response*. Minneapolis, MN: Fortress Press, 1995.

Cooper-White, Pamela. *Braided Selves: Collected Essays on Multiplicity, God and Persons*. Eugene, Oregon: Cascade Books, 2011.

Daube, David. *The New Testament and Rabbinic Judaism*. London: University of London, Athlone Press, 1956.

Dykstra, Craig R. *Growing in the Life of Faith: Education and Christian Practices*, 2nd ed. Louisville, KY: Geneva Press, 2005.

Ferguson, E. "Laying on of Hands: Its Significance in Ordination." *The Journal of Theological Studies* (1975): 1–12.

Flusser, David. "Healing through the Laying-on of Hands in a Dead Sea Scroll," *Israel Exploration Journal* 7 (1957).

Goettl, Len and Daniel, G. Bagby. *Sexual Abuse: Pastoral Responses*. Nashville, TN: Abingdon Press, 2004.

Hopkins, Dwight N. *Loving the Body Black Religious Studies and the Erotic*. New York, NY: Palgrave Macmillan, 2004.

International Labour Organization, *ILO global estimate of forced labour: results and methodology*, 2012.

Jung, Carl G. *The Structure and Dynamics of the Psyche* (Collected Works of C. G. Jung, Volume 8). Princeton, NJ: Princeton University Press, 1975.

Messler-Davies, Jody and Frawley, Mary Gail. "Dissociative Processes and Transference Countertransference in the Paradigms in the Psychoanalytically Oriented Treatment of Adult Survivors of Childhood Sexual Abuse." *Psychoanalytic Dialogues: The International Journal of Relational Perspective* 2.1 (1992): 5–36.

"Nones" on the Rise." *Pew Research Centers Religion Public Life Project RSS*. October 8, 2012. Accessed September 15, 2015.

Patton, John. *Pastoral Care in Context: An Introduction to Pastoral Care*. Louisville, KY: Westminster/John Knox Press, 1993.

Paulsell, Stephanie. *Honoring the Body: Meditations on a Christian Practice*. San Francisco: Jossey-Bass, 2002.

Pew Forum. "What Surveys Say about Worship Attendance—and Why Some Stay Home." *Pew Research Center RSS*. September 13, 2013. Accessed September 15, 2015.

Poling, James. *The Abuse of Power: A Theological Problem*. Nashville, TN: Abington Press, 1991.

"Rape (sexual Assault)—Overview: MedlinePlus Medical Encyclopedia." U.S National Library of Medicine. Accessed September 16, 2015.

Shange, Ntozake. "For Colored Girls Who Have Considered Suicide, When the Rainbow Is Enuf: A Choreopoem." New York: MacMillan, 1977.

Shooter, Susan. *How Survivors of Abuse Relate to God the Authentic Spirituality of the Soul*. Surrey: Ashgate Publishing, 2012.

UNICEF. *Children Out of Sight, Out of Mind, Out of Reach; Abused and Neglected, Millions of Children Have Become Virtually Invisible*. December 2005.

TEN

Have We Lost Our Taste?

Caring for Black Bodies through Food

Kenya J. Tuttle

In most cultures, both religious practices and food are ways to bring people together, and this is especially true for the African American community. Often people gather not only to enjoy the tasteful foods but also to enjoy social relationships. Food is used as a tool to maintain relationships and help people develop meaning through these important relationships. In many homes, these gatherings are one of the few times household members, and extended family and friends come together. Culturally, food, and the preference to particular types of food or taste, is what gives a group its ethnic distinction.

In my family we often gathered on Sunday afternoons after church to enjoy a meal together that included the entire family: aunts, uncles, cousins, and grandparents. The foods we ate were traditional Southern cuisine and unique to our culture and heritage. These types of foods shaped my taste, and I often associate family gatherings with the southern soul food we often shared. The dinner table was more than just about what we ate. As an emerging young adult, I found myself becoming more socially aware so that at the dinner table I could participate in the conversation. The dinner table taught me the importance of educating myself in the arena of public discourse. When our family sat down to eat, we talked about recent news events and shared stories about our family's history. These stories often included memories of my father and his siblings, as kids, and were complete with laughter and excitement. They shared stories of family trips down South when Jim Crow laws were operative. The dinner table taught me the reality of race in America and how to be critical about the nature of justice in our country. Food was the connector, the way we identified with our heritage and the traditions of our people. Thus, food and our taste toward certain preferences of food, proved to be more than just about nourishing our bodies but a way to reenact and live out cultural traditions.

In this way, taste is culturally shaped and eating habits are based on maintaining traditions. One's taste is largely shaped by the traditions and culture of one's family. Yet eating habits are critical to maintaining a healthy body. Thus, the health of one's body is based on the traditions of one's family and its cultural practices. Furthermore, taste and eating habits are largely based on one's socioeconomic status. Selecting foods for health is subordinate to both culture and socioeconomic status. Taste and access have been the primary factors in determining food selections at the expense of health. In this chapter, I ask, have we lost our taste toward healthy food selection? What has taken our taste away? I suggest that we have lost our taste and care for the body through healthy eating habits because we have devalued the health of the black bodies.

I begin with a discussion about religious beliefs and embodiment theology suggesting that one's religious and cultural beliefs shape how one views and cares for the body. I then move to a discussion about how we acquire taste through our cultural and familial practices and the affects food has on the health of our bodies. Utilizing psychoanalysis, I discuss taste as a cultural selfobject and move toward a theory of change using transmutation and internationalization. Finally, I conclude with the need for a theology of care for black bodies.

RELIGIOUS BELIEFS AND EMBODIMENT

Religion and culture inform how people understand the body and thus how one cares for the body. One's identity and beliefs about the self and the world around them are shaped through religious and cultural beliefs. In particular, one's religious and cultural beliefs about the body can significantly affect how one cares for the body. In turn, one's health and well-being are at stake given how they understand the body. Central to understanding how black people understand and care for the body, one must first understand what other people and faith traditions have said about black bodies and the effects of those—religious and nonreligious—beliefs. I contend that black people's religious and cultural understanding of the body has shaped their attitudes toward the care of the body.

Theologian Stephanie Y. Mitchem discusses African American theologians' and ethicists' exploration of the meaning of embodiment and its material consequences.[1] Mitchem recognizes the import of definitions of black bodies that have been detrimental to the health and well-being of black Americans. She proposes that social constructions that give meaning to black bodies have been tainted by religious denunciation of the body and religious appeals to otherworldly focus that have polluted black people's care of their bodies. Specifically, the controlled shaping of black bodies included beatings, threats, rapes, and lynching, and were all justified by accompanying white theological and cultural interpretations of those bodies.[2] Post-slavery, the white imagination stereotyped black bodies as lazy, stupid, and hypersexualized. In contemporary society, black bodies are used for entertainment without concern for health. Black bodies perform for their white audiences in minstrel shows, comedy acts, dancing, and by playing sports.[3] So much attention is given to the black women's hair texture, shape of nose, lips, and size of buttocks by white dominant culture that little time is spent on internal and holistic health. In this climate, care for the body in a healthy life-giving way is a radical act.

According to theologian Anthony Pinn, the body is a contested terrain—tablets upon which the power and practices of a given society are inscribed—and a biological reality—flesh through which and on which diasporic geography is mapped and developed.[4] Pinn asserts that the body is both metaphor and material. In addition, Pinn pushes black and womanist theology toward embodiment as the central reality of theological work and not just discussed in a discursive manner.[5] He extends the metaphorical discourse about the body to include the material reality (i.e., lived experience of black bodies) that must consider the ways in which power relationships are always at play in naming and giving meaning to the body.[6] Pinn argues, "The body becomes a proper source and framework for the exploration of our fundamental questions of existence and meaning. The body serves as both form and content of the religious."[7] Given this, the body is not only central to theological discourse but also central to the lived experiences of black people. Embodiment theology suggests that some bodies are valued more than others and more specifically black bodies continue to be devalued in detrimental ways thus delimiting one's ability to care for the self.

Embodiment and the effects of religious beliefs toward the care of the body are vital to flourishing. Religious and spiritual beliefs are reported to be of foremost importance among African Americans. According to Pew Research on religion and public life, African Americans are more religious than any other population on a variety of measures that include level of affiliation, attendance, frequency of prayer, and the importance of religion in life.[8] Furthermore, the vast majority of African Americans are Protestant (78 percent). African Americans also report that religion is very important to them, and it is demonstrated in their religious beliefs and habits. Therefore, religious beliefs about the body play a critical role in shaping black people's understanding and care of the body.

In *What's Faith Got to Do with It*, theologian Kelly Brown Douglas outlines the role of the Christian tradition on black bodies.[9] She finds that a platonized Christianity, most prominent in the American South and with black Christians in America, is inherently theologically flawed and inclined toward a disregard for certain human bodies, mainly black and female. Douglas provides a glimpse into how the Christian tradition plays an integral role in their understanding of black bodies. In particular, she focuses on the mind-body dichotomy and the ways in which sexuality is equated to the body. Douglas refers to a dualistic sexual ethic that informs the body and the ways in which the body has been sexualized and subsequently demonized is worth noting in length. She writes,

> This rigid dualistic approach invariably gives rise to the profound denigration of the body (the vehicle of sex) and sexuality (essentially defined in terms of sexual activity) that has come to characterize a platonized Christian tradition. Accordingly, it is platonized Christianity that gives rise to Christian participation in contemptible attacks against human bodies, like those against black bodies. Not only does platonized Christianity provide a foundation for easily disregarding certain bodies, but it also allows for the demonization of those persons who have been sexualized.[10]

Historically, black bodies have been demonized and treated inhumanly. Douglas believes that Christianity's disdain for certain bodies, and its role in the denigration of black bodies is born out of its theological core of closed monotheism and a Christological paradox that coalesced with Platonic and Stoic thought.[11]

Douglas uses the literary work of James Baldwin to express the troublesome disdain the flesh represents in a Protestant tradition in America, especially for black bodies. As she notes, black bodies have been overwhelmed and bear the burden of being hypersexualized in the white culture imagination and therefore dehumanized because of sexuality. This speaks to the effects that platonized theology and white culture have had on black people's attitudes toward their own bodies.

Douglas makes a connection between the parallel between Jesus's sacrifice of his body and black people's sacrifice of their sexual bodies. In this instance, as Jesus was willing to sacrifice his body even unto death for the sake of human salvation, black people are moved to sacrifice their black bodies for the sake of their particular salvation.[12] The sacrifice of the black body is considered crucial to attaining a white soul.

In a platonized Christian tradition, spirituality is revered and the body is abhorred, as the body is regarded as that which separates human beings from God. Platonized Christianity does not construct a theological paradigm in which the body and soul can equally coexist. Even as platonized Christianity purports to protect the integrity of the soul by vanquishing the body, it actually undermines divinity's very sacred authority. It concedes that the body overwhelms the soul; hence, divinity is enfeebled by humanity.[13]

As noted by Douglas, platonized Christianity, which has condoned the rape and lynching of black bodies, has also significantly shaped black faith subsequently impacting black people's regard for their own black bodies and the bodies of others. Because of the significance of religious beliefs in the lives of black people, black people's understanding of their bodies has been shaped by Christianity's views of their bodies. I claim that this negation or denunciation of the body, for the sake of salvation, has led black Christians to show little concern about the health and well-being of the physical bodies. More emphasis is placed on spirituality than on caring for the body. As noted, religious beliefs play a major role in one's understanding and the content of belief shapes care for the body.

ACQUIRING TASTE AND THE HEALTH OF THE BODY

In today's fast-paced society and convenience-driven eating, processed and fast food are often the most viable option. In poorer neighborhoods and urban city living, processed and fast foods are often the only option available. By eating a diet of mostly processed and fast food loaded with salt and sugar, the consumer loses the ability of taste to detect the excessive levels of added salt and sugar. Not only do we lose our ability to detect excessive levels of salt and sugar but also these products are addictive and we must consume more to reach desired levels, thus changing our body's biochemistry. Our taste changes and we crave even more salty and sugary foods to satisfy our hormones that have also changed. For this section, I address the challenge of how humans acquire taste and the sociocultural effects taste has on the health of the body.

Taste is one of the five[14] human senses in which we perceive the world around us. When we taste, we sense the flavor of what we are eating or drinking. Taste is necessary to help us nourish our body. Having a sense of taste is directly related to our survival and well-being. Foods that are poisonous often taste bitter or repugnant, and we avoid those foods because of the bad taste that protects us from eating it. The five[15] unique taste profiles we have through our tongue are sweet, sour, salt, bitter, and umami (savory or pleasant). Taste is important in what we choose to eat. Often people eat for taste or the culture it represents and lose the sense of eating for health. When individuals and communities have limited access to healthy food, I suggest that we have lost our taste and care for the body through healthy consumptions of food and we have devalued the health of the body.

With our ever-increasing need to spend more time working and less time preparing meals for our families, we have succumbed to eating fast "food" and packaged "food." The challenge is generated because people are now consuming large amounts of food outside of the home and leaving it up to the Food and Drug Administration (FDA) and food industry to regulate our food. We have outsourced our health, and it has left us sick. We are eating fast "foods" and packaged "foods" that have been approved as "safe" by the FDA yet are high in sugar, fat, and chemicals — all things that are poisonous to the human body. Furthermore, for those in the inner city and predominantly urban communities obtaining high-quality food is a challenge — thus creating food deserts. There is a huge class and race divide, and food security is an urgent and emblematic problem of systemic oppression. Access to information about healthy food consumption and the healthy food products are virtually nonexistent in urban communities. Only certain bodies are a part of the conversation about healthy food options and more importantly not all bodies have access to healthy food.

Taste largely determines the foods we choose to eat, and food availability and choice is a topic of much debate among doctors and nutritionists. The focus has primarily been on eating habits and the diseases that are a result of unhealthy eating habits. In the book *Fat Chance: Beating the Odds against Sugar, Processed Food, Obesity, and Disease,* pediatric endocrinologist Robert H. Lustig, M.D., argues that the biochemistry of the human body is altered by prolonged consumption of unhealthy food. Lustig's experience is in treating obese babies and young children who struggle to function daily due to their health. He states that the babies' struggle is not a result of their eating habits, since many of these babies are still drinking milk or eat limited amounts of food; rather Lustig concludes that the hormones driving behavior toward the American diet of excessive amounts of sugar have altered the biochemistry of the human body. A major consideration in the cases of obese babies is the health and biochemistry of the mother while the child is developing in utero. For adults, once biochemistry has changed, leptin and other hormones drive behavior toward larger consumptions of sugar and alter the body's state to decrease activity and exercise. As a result of the excessive sugar, which turns into insulin in the body, fat is accumulated.

Nutritionists warn Americans of the dangers of too much added sugar, and Lustig has taken it a step further to claim sugar as a poison to the body. Added sugar is a rampant concern in the American diet. People who are poor and people of color disproportionately consume processed foods with added sugar compared to other Americans. "Many poor neighborhoods throughout America lack farmers' markets, supermarkets, and grocery stores where 'healthy' foods can be purchased. Many supermarkets have pulled out of poor neighborhoods, mainly because of financial decisions based on revenue and fear of crime."[16] Food insecurity, the lack of ability to acquire health foods, as suggested above, is an issue that dramatically affects one's overall health. Lustig states, "The poor suffer from issues of food insecurity. People experience massive amounts of stress when they don't know where their next meal is coming from. They eat what is available, when they can—usually processed food."[17]

Additionally, stress levels among lower- and middle-class Americans and people of color are something to consider when analyzing one's health and eating habits. "50 percent of African Americans are obese—and are more likely to have associated medical problems, such as metabolic syndrome."[18] With a lack of access to healthy food options, lower- and middle-class people and people of color are disproportionately affected by degenerative diseases that can be reversed through dramatically altering one's eating habits. "Death rates and illness correlate with low social status, even after controlling for behavior (e.g., smoking). . . . The prevalence of disease such as diabetes, stroke, and heart disease are highest among those who suffer from the most stress, namely middle- and lower-class Americans."[19]

I argue that not only do lower- and middle-class people suffer because of a lack of access to health food options, but also culturally people of color suffer health conditions due to stress and a cultural preference or taste toward particular types of food that are unhealthy for the body.[20] "The data on insulin resistance and dementia show clear causation. African American and Latinos are the biggest fructose consumers and those with the highest waist circumference (a marker for insulin resistance). Coincidently, they also have the highest rate of dementia."[21] Consuming high doses of fructose, a form of sugar, is a known risk for many degenerative diseases in America that can be avoided through proper nutrition. The health of the body can be regulated by the foods we eat daily; yet, little attention has been given to the manner in which we acquire taste and the sociocultural dynamics of why we eat certain foods.

TASTE AS A CULTURAL SELFOBJECT

In this section, I utilize the work of womanist psychoanalyst Phyllis Sheppard to discuss how taste as a cultural selfobject is internalized. I claim that taste and how the self acquires eating habits is born through one's primary caregivers and the broader social context of those caregivers. Taste is based on foods common to one's cultural and familial preferences. Taste as a cultural object is internalized from one's family and culture. Taste and thus eating habits are passed down from primary caregivers and are often unconscious. Thus, the health of one's family and culture is a prediction of one's own health and eating habits. In a discussion about how one adopts one's eating habits and taste for particular foods, we must take seriously the dynamics of the familial context and its relationship to the broader social context.

In *Self, Culture and Others in Womanist Practical Theology*, Sheppard states,

> The self is always contextualized culturally, while it is also simultane-
> ously a psychic experience. This is an element to the discourse on self
> that a womanist contribution to psychoanalytic self-psychology makes.
> The implication is that the self cannot be understood outside its con-
> texts and contextual forces that either support or impede the formation
> and maintenance of the self. [22]

Sheppard points out and clarifies the importance of cultural dynamics on the formation of the self as experienced through primary relationships as well as through broader context such as media images and more. Shep-pard recognizes that womanist theology can contribute to psychoanalysis by broadening the scope of self psychology to include one's cultural con-text. She states,

> A womanist-informed self-psychology recenters the important location
> of the cultural and gendered embodiment and the social. This recenter-
> ing does not dismiss the familial, but rather suggests that the familial
> context is always in relationship to the broader social structures and
> that where there are faulty or even abusive selfobject experiences they
> are very often contiguous with the reflections in the broader culture. [23]

This suggests the importance of both family and culture in how taste is acquired. According to Sheppard, concepts of self and cultural selfobjects are cultural productions and are unique to the context. Sheppard draws on the work of psychoanalyst Heinz Kohut to discuss selfobjects and how they work. Kohut describes the selfobject as any person or object that has a need-fulfilling function. [24] Selfobjects function to provide essential psychological needs for the self. They are different from objects in that objects are separate from the one observing, while selfobjects are persons or objects that are experienced as part of the self and used for a particular purpose.

Kohut describes a two-step process involving transference of cultural selfobjects that he believes leads to change. This theory of change is im-portant to our discussion as we consider that the desire to change one's taste and eating habits is a complex and difficult dynamic, given that taste is both cultural and individual based. Furthermore, if primary care-givers have shaped one's taste and desires toward particular foods from early life experiences, these same eating habits may no longer serve the body in healthy ways. In *How Does Analysis Cure?*, Kohut proposes a theory of change or analytic cure that can be used to consider how one can change one's taste and ultimately eating habits. Kohut describes transmuting internalization as a process initiated by an optimum level of frustration in the patient. This frustration is used to strengthen the self through selfobject transference from the patient to the therapist. The ther-apist offers the patient a level of understanding after listening to the patient's inner life. Then the therapist explains how the patient's early life experiences are replayed in a current situation. This two-phased intervention fosters the patient's psychological strength and ultimately leads to change or cure.[25] This process of being understood and thinking through prior and current life experiences moves the patient toward strengthening the self and ultimately change. Furthermore, this process allows the patient to think through detrimental beliefs about the body and move toward more life-giving practices.

A THEOLOGY OF CARE FOR BLACK BODIES

Previously, I have suggested how religion and culture inform how one cares for the body. I have also discussed what bodies have the right to care for the self through food, given the discussion of food deserts present in urban and black communities. More emphasis must be given to the ways beliefs about the body help or hinder health and well-being. In the last chapter of her book, Douglas makes a claim for the ways in which black people, particularly womanist theology, have resisted the oppressive platonized Christianity and looked toward more life-giving ways the body can be understood and lived out.[26] A hermeneutic of appropriation is needed to push beyond the racist and sexist notions of which black bodies are sacred, as she notes that female and nonheterosexual bodies are terrorized and diminished even while others bodies are not.

There is a need for a theology of care for black bodies. Much has been said about the discursive manner in which black bodies are demonized and sexualized and therefore treated inhumanely. We have also turned to the way theology must consider the lived realities of black bodies, and I suggest ways to move toward a theology of care for black bodies. In black communities, great emphasis is placed on spirituality and cultural practices; but, do these traditions help or hinder the health of the body? Are we considering if our taste or eating habits bring our bodies health? Black Christians have adhered to a politics of respectability[27] in regard to the physical appearance of the body, adorning the body in "Sunday's best" but have spent little time and effort in maintaining the health of the body and ultimately caring for the soul.

Many other religious practices have regarded the dualistic split between spirit and body in more healthy ways that promote overall well-being. For example, in *African American Folk Healing*, Stephanie Y. Mitchem found how African Americans used folk knowledge and healing or traditional indigenous practices to nurture their bodies and souls despite their marginalized status.

> Black women's access to ideas of folk healing is due to the continued existence of embodied spirituality. This spirituality may be nurtured at

home or in church. African American women's embodied spirituality is more than charismatic expression. Embodied spirituality is grounded in a different perspective of the human person, a perspective that unifies body and soul within the life of the past, present, and future community in conversation with an ever-present God.[28]

Mitchem describes how African American women have used folk healing to heal their minds and bodies by countering the negative effects of racist ideology about their bodies. Yet, even the practice of folk healing was demonized as a lower class practice. Nonetheless, Mitchem suggests eight reasons for African American folk healings continuation:

> (1) the social marginalization of black Americans, which makes access to institutional medicine difficult; (2) cultural hybridity, which incorporates the remedies of other cultures; (3) racism within institutional medicine, which denies the humanity of black bodies; (4) adaptation of practices based on the availability of materials in new environments; (5) the development of commerce, which aids in making ingredients available if they cannot be found naturally; (6) pragmatism, which seeks the most direct line to healing; (7) efficacy, which offers a proven track record to those seeking cures; and (8) a holistic approach, which understands the whole person, not just isolated symptoms in line with black cultural conceptualizations of wellness.[29]

These reasons address why folk healing has been a practice continued today, in hybridity, as the culture and social structures change for black Americans. Furthermore, folk healing is a way African Americans can move toward more life-giving ways to understand and care for the body. Mitchem concludes her book by stating "black folk healing indicates how, culturally, African Americans act as agents in defining their own bodies, exerting some control over life, and constructing identity."[30] In this way, she gives affirmation to the ways black folk have pulled from various cultural practices and promoted their well-being in both spirit and body. Folk healing can be used as a model of self-care that provides healthy practices for the body that include aspects of religion and spirituality that were once demonized by Christianity.

Furthermore, overall well-being in both spirit and body must include food as a primary way toward health of the body.[31] An embodiment theology and care for the self includes caring for the types of food that give our bodies the ability to flourish. Eating based on taste, culture, or tradition no longer serves overall well-being. Change in our taste is especially difficult given that taste is a cultural selfobject we acquired from our primary caregivers early in life; yet, change is what is necessary to care for the body. Furthermore, change in cultural beliefs about black bodies is necessary to provide more life-giving ways to understand and care for black bodies.

NOTES

1. Embodiment in African American Theology, *Oxford Handbook of African American Theology* (NY: Oxford University Press, 2014).
2. Ibid., 309.
3. Ibid., 310.
4. Anthony Pinn, *Black Religion and Aestetics: Religious Thought and Life in Africa and the African Diaspora* (Palgrave MacMillan, 2009), 4.
5. Anthony Pinn, *Embodiment and the New Shape of Black Theological Thought* (New York: New York University Press, 2010).
6. Ibid., 5.
7. Ibid., xiv.
8. A Religious Portrait of African-Americans, January 30, 2009. http://www.pewforum.org/2009/01/30/a-religious-portrait-of-african-americans/.
9. Kelly Brown Douglas, *What's Faith Got to Do with It?: Black Bodies/Christian Souls* (New York: Orbis Books, 2005).
10. Ibid., 37.
11. Ibid., 38.
12. Ibid., 183.
13. Ibid., 79.
14. Perhaps six or nine human senses, some scientists, and other authors in this text, include: proprioception and kinestic, among others.
15. Scientists debate if there are more than five basic tastes. Some say there are six or seven unique taste humans can detect.
16. Robert H. Lustig, *Fat Chance: Beating the Odds against Sugar, Processed Food, Obesity, and Disease* (New York: Hudson Street Press, 2012), 28.
17. Ibid., 29.
18. Ibid., 28.
19. Ibid., 66.
20. As Bonnie Miller-McLemore, in the introduction of this volume, suggests the epistemology of literal bodies is a valuable resource left for further inquiry. Here Lustig's data shows how the literal body (and the hormones that drive behavior) provides valuable knowledge about the health of the body.
21. Ibid., 124.
22. Phyllis Sheppard, *Self, Culture and Others in Womanist Practical Theology* (New York: Palgrave MacMillan, 2011), 117.
23. Ibid., 120.
24. Allen M. Siegel, *Heinz Kohut and the Psychology of the Self* (New York: Routledge, 1996).
25. Heinz Kohut, *How Does Analysis Cure?* (Chicago: The University of Chicago Press, 1984), 69–71.
26. Douglas, 209.
27. Evelyn Brooks Higginbotham, *Righteous Discontent: The Women's Movement in the Black Baptist Church* (Harvard University Press, 1994).
28. Stephanie Y. Mitchem, *African American Folk Healing* (New York: New York University Press, 2007), 85.
29. Ibid., 72.
30. Ibid., 165.
31. Stephanie N. Arel in the third chapter of this volume establishes that "taste as both the actual act of eating food and taste as a metaphor function as powerful ways to connect with or perceive the divine." She utilizes "Christian examples to demonstrate how food functions metaphorically to convey relationship to the divine."

REFERENCES

Brown Douglas, Kelly. *What's Faith Got to Do With It? Black Bodies/Christian Souls*. New York: Orbis Books, 2005.

"Embodiment in African American Theology." *Oxford Handbook of African American Theology*. Oxford University Press, USA, 2014.

Higginbotham, Evelyn Brooks. *Righteous Discontent: The Women's Movement in the Black Baptist Church*. Cambridge, MA: Harvard University Press, 1994.

Kohut, Heinz. *How Does Analysis Cure?* Chicago: The University of Chicago Press, 1984.

Lustig, Robert H. *Fat Chance: Beating the Odds Against Sugar, Processed Food, Obesity, and Disease*. New York: Hudson Street Press, 2012.

Mitchem, Stephanie Y. *African American Folk Healing*. New York: New York University Press, 2007.

Pew Forum. "A Religious Portrait of African-Americans" (January 30, 2009). http://www.pewforum.org/2009/01/30/a-religious-portrait-of-african-americans/.

Pinn, Anthony. *Black Religion and Aesthetics: Religious Thought and Life in Africa and the African Diaspora*. Palgrave MacMillan, 2009.

Pinn, Anthony. *Embodiment and the New Shape of Black Theological Thought*. New York: New York University Press, 2010.

Sheppard, Phyllis. *Self, Culture and Others in Womanist Practical Theology*. New York: Palgrave MacMillan, 2011.

Siegel, Allen M. *Heinz Kohut and the Psychology of the Self*. New York: Routledge, 1996.

ELEVEN

Holy Transitional and Transcendent Smells

Aromatherapy as an Adjunctive Support for Trauma in Pastoral Care and Counseling

Jennifer Baldwin

I first discovered aromatherapy as a doctoral student struggling to write my dissertation. I have long known that writing generates anxiety for me; however, the writing-induced anxiety amplified so much with the added stakes of a dissertation that it became nearly incapacitating. I would carve out a full day to write and end up with maybe a paragraph. At that rate I knew I would never finish, and nearly a decade of work and expense would be for naught. In desperation and on a whim, I purchased a blend of "anxiety relief" at Whole Foods and diffused the oil the next time I attempted to write. Astonishingly to me, the anxiety abated enough that I could be productive . . . at least until the candle for the diffuser burned out and the anxiety and panic returned. Over the next few months, I noticed that diffusing the "anxiety relief" oil held the anxiety and panic at bay, and I was able to complete my dissertation.

My initial experience using essential oils was formative for my interest in utilizing essential oils personally and convincing in the efficacy of essential oils and aromatherapy for the support of mental health concerns. In addition to my (now completed) doctoral work in religion and science, I was and am a practicing psychotherapist in Illinois (LCPC). Over the few years since my personal introduction to aromatherapy, I have noticed that many clients in my clinical practice struggle with symptoms of anxiety, posttraumatic stress disorder (PTSD), and depression that impede their full functioning but do not meet the level of dysfunction that warrants psychotropic medication.[1] As I worked with these individuals, I began to wonder if aromatherapy could offer an appropriate level of symptom support that could enhance our therapeutic work. I began offering aromatherapy blends designed for the individual as an adjunctive support to clients in private practice as clinically appropriate and at the request of individual clients. I have received very positive feedback from many clients particularly with regard to symptoms of anxiety and PTSD. Consequently, I am convinced that aromatherapy can be utilized as a clinically appropriate adjunctive support for mental health care as practiced by a certified aromatherapy practitioner and licensed clinician.

As a professor and mentor to seminary and social work students, I have also come to believe in, and argue for, the utility of essential oils in the care of souls through a variety of expressions of pastoral or spiritual care. My first lead on the intentional utility of essential oils for pastoral care and their historical use of incense in the churches liturgy[2] came from a study published in 2008.[3] The study argues that burning incense of frankincense releases incensole acetate which activates ion receptors in the brain that result in lowered anxiety and depression. This study was both a pleasant surprise and, upon reflection. liturgically ingenious and care-full. The use of incense by the historical church was not only a way to keep the smell of body odor masked in a pre-deodorant period but was also a caring act that alleviated anxiety and reduced depression in the congregation. It turns out that, in many ways, this "new age-y" practice of aromatherapy is actually quite traditional and established.

The resins and corresponding aromas of frankincense and myrrh have a lofty presence in Christian scripture as two of the three gifts given to Jesus at his birth. However, as time has marched on, the healing properties of plant-derived oils and resins have been forsaken for the marvels of the pharmacological labs of the postenlightenment scientific world. While modern medicine is a powerful helping and healing agent with an important function in life and society, pharmacological science has become an uncontested king in providing support in physiological and psychological health. This uncontested dominance is problematic, especially for mental health care when pills are dished out like candy and the underlying life stressors and traumas are left unattended under the mask of pharmacology. While psychotherapy is primarily tasked with the care of minds and relationships, pastoral care and counseling utilizes some of the same resources but is tasked with the care of relationships and souls. Aromatherapy, when directed by a certified or clinical practitioner,[4] can be a helpful adjunctive support for attending to many of the sufferings presented in the context of pastoral care and counseling.

The current chapter explores the use of essential oils in aromatherapy by pastoral and spiritual care professionals through four movements. Recognizing that the postmodern church exists within a social matrix marked by traumatic experiences, direct and indirect exposure to traumatic stimuli, and the pervasive presence of traumatic response at the personal and societal level, theological reflection and pastoral praxis can no longer remain ignorant of traumatic response and how it impacts individuals, communities, and society. The first section discusses the primary, secondary, and cultural experiences of trauma and the profound need for religious professionals to employ a "Trauma Sensitive Theology"[5] in the realm of pastoral care. The second part provides pastoral and spiritual caregivers with information that is essential to understanding the neurological dimensions that undergird symptoms of posttraumatic response. The third section discusses aromatherapy and two theories of efficacy and offers benefits for the skillful use of aromatherapy as a non-pharmacological assist for trauma survivors that can augment pastoral care and counseling. This final section explores the use of aromatherapy with essential oils in the context of pastoral care and spiritual care to individuals or communities who have experienced trauma.

TRAUMA SENSITIVE THEOLOGY AND PASTORAL CARE

Judith Herman notes in her classic text on trauma that clinical and popular acknowledgment of experiences and the sequelea of traumatic responses wax and wane over time. She notes,

> The study of psychological trauma has a curious history—one of episodic amnesia. Periods of active investigation has alternated with periods of oblivion. . . . This intermittent amnesia is not the result of the ordinary changes in fashion that affect any intellectual pursuit. The study of psychological trauma does not languish for lack of interest. Rather, the subject provokes such intense controversy that it periodically becomes anathema. The study of psychological trauma has repeatedly led into the realms of the unthinkable and foundered on *fundamental questions of belief* (emphasis added).[6]

While survivors of traumatic experiences have not always garnered the care and attention they deserve from the psychological community, they have equally been neglected by religious communities who have been ignorantly dismissive at best or spiritually abusive in their misunderstanding and misappropriation of traumatic experience at worst. While Herman's recognition of "fundamental questions of belief" primarily is directed toward professional and community acknowledgment and validation of survivors' experiences of traumatic events, it can also be read as an invitation for religious scholars to attend to the spiritual and communal disruptions inherent in traumatic experience.

The current revival of scholarly attention to traumatic experience and response thankfully includes scholars of religion and theology; however, there remains a fatal imbalance in the awareness of traumatic response and informed care of trauma survivors by scholars. Too often, theological scholars, pastoral counselors, and pastors engage survivors of trauma with a "thick theology and thin traumatology." In their desire to "help," religious professionals too frequently skip the necessary step of educating themselves in the area of traumatic response, resolution, and resiliency.[7] This oversight, at best, or arrogant ignorance, at worst, can not only fail to help but can also retraumatize survivors or unwittingly engage in theologically abusive behavior by blaming posttraumatic symptoms on a lack of faith. This occurs when pastors advise a congregant to pray more in order to cope with flashbacks or nightmares or to have faith that God will handle everything when faced with the anxiety of hyperarousal while failing to recognize these distressing experiences as symptoms of traumatic response. The risk of increasing the wound of traumatic experience is present in the ignorant blaming of symptoms on a lack of faith as well as in the temptation to see the survivor as only a victim thereby robbing them of support in their resiliency.

Pastors and theologians rob survivors of their innate resiliency when they place their theological anthropologies of original sin and "rot-gut sinner" or theologies of sacrificial atonement as the measure of human nature and capacity for recovery. Additionally, religious professionals fail survivors of trauma when they view the survivor as a victim who is "existentially undone," "shattered," "broken," or "annihilated."[8] Rather than adding to wounds of relational, psychological, and bodily trauma, theologians and spiritual care providers must invest in proclaiming an atonement theology of accountability for abuses of relational power and a theological anthropology that retains space for the goodness and empowering grace of resiliency. Practices of pastoral care across the activities of counseling, preaching, liturgy, teaching, and/or spiritual accompaniment or direction must engage from a foundation of trauma sensitive theology.

What is trauma sensitive theology and pastoral care? Trauma sensitive theology is a lens for theological reflection that can be applied to nearly any theological system. At its core, trauma sensitive theology and pastoral care acknowledge the insipid prevalence of trauma exposure, with symptoms presenting on both the clinical and subclinical levels, in our current social location. "Trauma" is most broadly defined as experience/s that threaten one's life or the life of a loved one. Trauma is widely acknowledged to include experiences of bodily assault, catastrophic accidents, natural disasters, and/or war survival. However, it is less the content of the experience that leads to traumatic response and more how the individual experienced the incident/s. Experiences that generate feelings of helplessness, worthlessness, perceived or actual threat to life, and/or powerlessness all have the potential to be traumatizing. These experiences with corresponding affect and interpretation lead to a fundamental questioning of one's safety and capability to life safely enough in the world. At its deepest, there is a learning from experiences of trauma that the world is no longer as safe as one thought it was and offers less security. For many people, these experiences lead to a re-evaluation of many dimensions of life once assumed to be true, including theological and spiritual learnings and practices.

Theology and praxis informed towards and sensitive to the lived experiences of trauma survivors is not only relevant to the individuals who have directly encountered trauma (e.g., war veterans, rape survivors, abuse survivors, car accident victims, etc.). Traumatic experiences do significantly alter one's sense of safety, stability, and trust in the world, others, and the divine; however, traumatic experiences also impact people and communities secondarily and culturally. Consequently, the population of people impacted by traumatic experience is far more vast than ordinarily thought. Secondary trauma occurs when traumatic response symptoms occur when a loved one's life or well-being is threatened. Secondary trauma is the primary culprit in compassion fatigue or burnout among people in the helping professions. To broaden the net further, due to the rapid proliferation of media technology, news and images of traumatic events spread among the population and into cultural awareness and parlance at an astonishing rate (e.g., news of the destruction of the World Trade Center in 2001, images and video of abuses of power by law enforcement officials and subsequent community outcry, news of mass shooting events, and images of crime scenes and photographs of the victims). The increased awareness of traumatic events pervades cultural awareness, memes, rhetoric, and behavior. The pervasiveness of traumatic awareness increases subclinical presentations of traumatic response in the general population making very few of us untouched by traumatic events and experiences.

TRAUMATIC RESPONSE AND PTSD

Posttraumatic stress disorder (PTSD) is a chronic anxiety disorder characterized by hyper- and hypo-arousal of the central nervous system caused by exposure to a traumatic event/s that threaten the life or well-being of the individual or the individual's loved one. Traumatic events leading to the development of PTSD can alter an individual's behavior, affect, and cognition; however, neuroscience is increasingly able to identify the ways in which traumatic events, particularly prolonged traumatic events such as abuse, may alter brain structure/s and memory formation. Awareness of the biological and neurological impacts of trauma are essential for assisting pastoral care providers and spiritual caregivers in gaining a "thick traumatology" necessary to compassionately attend to survivors of primary, secondary, or cultural trauma.

Dangerous, and potentially traumatizing, situations prompt a series of neurological and physiological changes designed to facilitate the best possible survival outcome. During a traumatic experience, mammals have three fundamental neurobiological system responses/options that are selected subconsciously based on the perceived degree of risk and safety. Internationally recognized leader in traumatology Bessel van der Kolk writes,

> The level of safety determines which one of these is activated at any particular time. Whenever we feel threatened, we instinctively turn to the first level, *social engagement* (activation of ventral vagal complex). We call out for help, support, and comfort from the people around us. But if no one comes to our aid, or we're in immediate danger, the organism reverts to a more primitive way to survive: *fight or flight* (activation of the sympathetic nervous system). We fight off our attacker, or we run to a safe place. However, if this fails—we can't get away, we're held down or trapped—the organism tries to preserve itself by shutting down and expending as little energy as possible. We are then in a state of *freeze* or *collapse* (activation of the dorsal vagal complex). [9]

It is important to highlight for pastoral care providers and spiritual leaders that the first line of protection is social engagement. If a community or individual is able to be attentive, empathetic, compassionate, and present during or immediately after experiences of trauma, the survivor of trauma is less likely to develop more prolonged symptoms of distress. This first line of protection is one of the key places in which religious communities can either offer great support or increase the damage initiated by traumatic experiences. If the victim/survivors' appeal to the community for help is unsuccessful, the person's system employs other survival mechanisms that more directly correspond to the salient symptoms of posttraumatic response.

The symptoms present as a result of unresolved trauma correspond to the survival mechanisms that are automatically employed during traumatic survival according to degree of perceived threat. By definition, traumatic stimuli overwhelm an organism's ability to respond and incorporate the experience into narrative memory. In other words, the survival mechanisms glitch and some elements of the traumatic experience get stuck and retain a "here-and-now" quality as the event moves into the temporal past. As a result, many of the clinical features of primary trauma responses are essentially the ghosts of adaptive survival responses. Hypervigilance and activation of the SNS, in the immediacy of trauma, allows the organism to attend to a breadth of external and internal stimuli that facilitates a greater chance of survival. The ghosts of hypervigilance haunt in the form of nightmares, flashbacks, and a hypersensitive startle response. Hypoarousal and the numbing of body sensation due to activation of the DVC at the time of trauma permit the organism to separate awareness from bodily pain allowing for either the persistence of movement to escape or to employ a freeze response that minimizes further bodily injury. The ghosts of hypoarousal are present in dissociation.

In her article "Neurobiological Alterations Associated with Traumatic Stress," Sandra Weiss delineates several neurobiological alterations found in individuals diagnosed with PTSD that are important for the use of essential oils as a supportive component of pastoral/spiritual care.[10] She writes, "A traumatic experience activates numerous brain regions, primarily the limbic system, a network of neural regions and processes that work together to achieve homeostasis in response to external events."[11] The role of the limbic system is essential for understanding traumatic memory formation, the temporal displacement of affect and sensation connected to traumatic symptoms, and the role of aromatherapy in assisting trauma recovery and resolution. The limbic system is comprised of the amygdala, which is primarily responsible for attention, emotions, and social processing; the hippocampus, which corresponds to spatial memory and learning; the hypothalamus, which connects the limbic system to the prefrontal cortex; and the olfactory bulbs. Traumatic experience largely impacts the limbic system and its connection to the prefrontal cortex (meaning making resources).[12] During a traumatic event, the individual's (or community's collective) limbic system and corresponding prefrontal cortex are overwhelmed and thrown off-balance. A large challenge in promoting resolution of traumatic experience and memory is the reconnection and balance among the affective and content of traumatic dimensions of traumatic encounters.

Unresolved traumatic experiences result in a misplacing of experience, sensation, affect, and behavior. The components of attention, emotion, social cueing, learning, and meaning, making that were hijacked during the traumatic event/s and essential in surviving the threatening experience in the past re-emerge in the present. This reliving of the past in the now-safe-enough present occurs when incompletely processed experiences are reactivated by sensory stimuli or memories. When sensations ignite incompletely processed experiences, survivors of trauma experience the past in the present which activates the three survival strategies described by van der Kolk and can result in a fight/flight response initiated by the amygdala or a dissociative experience or flooding of the DVC.

Sensory information reaches the amygdala via three routes. In the first route, olfactory information is connected to the amygdala through the olfactory nerves. The second route allows sensory information except olfaction to directly connect to the amygdala from the thalamus, which is the grand central station of sensory information. Third, sensory information is passed through the cortex, which fills in context and risk assessment, and hippocampus, which promotes learning, before reaching the amygdala.[13] In terms of speed of impact, scent sensations will trigger most quickly followed by other sensory information. The brain's provision of context to determine safe/not safe is the slowest of the routes. Consequently, support through olfaction can calm the amygdala most quickly, care via other forms of sensation (touch, sight, hearing, taste, proprioception) will be slower, and compassion offered through meaning-making, contextualization, learning, or narrative will be slowest.

HOW AROMATHERAPY HELPS: TWO THEORIES OF EFFICACY

One of the first questions clients and interested care providers ask is: how does aromatherapy work? Or stated more bluntly: how does smelling stuff help? Aromatherapists routinely note two means of utilizing essential oils, topically and via inhalation. For the purposes of this chapter, I will focus on the inhalation of essential oils as the most useful application of essential oils for pastoral and spiritual care providers. The inhalation of essential oils depends on the olfactory system and its connection to the limbic system. In her literature review of eighteen studies focusing on the use of essential oils and their impact on mood and behavior, Rachel Herz notes that there is "credible evidence that odors can affect mood, physiology and behavior" and offers two mechanisms to explain the efficacy of odor to alter mood, "the pharmacological and psychological mechanisms."[14] She writes,

> The pharmacological hypothesis proposes that the effects of various aromas on mood, physiology and behavior are due to the odor's direct and intrinsic ability to interact and affect the autonomic nervous system/central nervous system and/or endocrine systems. . . . In order for a volatile compound to act pharmacologically it must enter the bloodstream by way of the nasal or lung mucosa, or diffuse directly into the olfactory nerves and the limbic system of the brain.[15]

For mental health and spiritual support, the olfaction/limbic system pathway is the more desirable option given the important role of the limbic system in sensory and emotional processing irrespective of the pharmacological or psychological mechanisms of activation. Marcello Spinella discusses the connection between smell and empathy, or aroma and emotion.[16] He notes, "Olfaction is a chemical sense that has powerful relationships with emotion. The central olfactory system has projections to the limbic and paralimbic structures . . . and orbitofrontal cortex. Orbitofrontal cortex is activated during olfactory identification tasks."[17] Connections between the olfactory system and the amygdala, thalamus, and orbitofrontal cortex provide neuroanatomical support for the efficacy of aromatherapy for care providers, specifically for mood disorders including PTSD.

The second of Herz's hypotheses is the psychological hypothesis. The psychology hypothesis posits "that odors exert their effects through emotional learning, conscious perception, and belief/expectation. The central claim of the psychological hypothesis is that responses to odors are learned through association with emotional experiences, and that odors consequently take on the properties of the associated emotions and exert the concordant emotional, cognitive, behavioral, and physiological effects themselves." [18] The psychological hypothesis is built on the idea of learned association and Hebb's theory that "neurons that fire together wire together." Hebb's theory basically indicates that if a scent is paired with a positive, safe, and supportive environment, then encountering that scent will neurologically and physiologically re-enact a positive, safe, and supportive effect. Likewise, and more strongly, a scent associated with a traumatic experience can strongly trigger memories of the trauma when the individual encounters the scent again. Evolutionarily, it makes sense that scents paired with experiences of danger would be more strongly encoded than those paired with experiences of safety. However, the clinically beneficial correlate is that aromatherapy can partner with the trust and safety created through the community of faith, spiritual care-giver, or therapeutic alliance between client and caregiver, behavioral modification and breathing exercises to create a portable "touch stone" or "transitional scent" [19] to ground and soothe during moments of emotional hyper- or hypo-activation. Additionally, inhalation of essential oils requires a degree of mindful attention on breathing and somatic awareness that assists in regulating dysregulation of arousal.

Herz's two hypothesis of how essential oils can assist in the regulation of mood, physiology, and behavior both show supportive possibilities to care for individuals and communities that have experienced traumatic event/s. While there is additional focused and standardized work to be done in researching the pharmacological mechanisms of action and benefits of essential oils, there already exists the testimony of centuries of use of essential oils for emotional and health wellness as well as some research demonstrating the efficacy of aromatherapy for decreasing anxiety, insomnia, depression, and pain. Additionally, given the areas of the brain most influenced by the olfactory system, it is reasonable to conclude that mental and spiritual health could be positively supported by the informed use of aromatherapy and essential oils. Aromatherapy is also a supportive adjunct to mental health care via the psychological hypothesis. Pastoral counselors, spiritual care-givers and psychotherapists already regularly utilize transitional objects, mindfulness, behavioral modification, breathing exercises, and the therapeutic alliance of safety and support to assist clients in processing experiences that become "stuck" and generate dis-ease. Utilizing essential oils, regardless of the pharmacological benefits (which there is evidence of significant benefit), is assistive to the overall process of mental wellness by extending the boundaries of the pastoral care connection via aromatherapy as a "holy transitional scent." Supportive blends can be established by diffusing the blend in the congregational or pastoral care space thereby establishing a non-cortically dependent transitional bridge via scent.

The inhalation of essential oils in aromatherapy can be a powerful support for individuals struggling with symptoms of PTSD. As noted above, traumatic experiences have the capacity to alter structures in the limbic system of the brain. These changes correspond to the symptoms of PTSD that inhibit full functioning of memory consolidation and balanced responses to environmental and relational stimuli. Wu et al., Chen et al., Haze, Namazi et al., and Choi et al. each cite data indicating that essential oils (lavender and geranium, neroli and lavender, rose or patchouli, and neroli respectively) all assist in decreasing anxiety or physiological indicators of anxiety.[20]

Aromatherapy is an ancient and multicultural practice for the care of physical, emotional, and spiritual dis-ease. While it has been eclipsed in the development of modern, Western medicine and pharmaceuticals, the art and science of utilizing plant essential oils for health and wellness is resurging. This resurgence is ripe for research to strengthen the validity of the efficacy of essential oils that could support and clarify Herz's pharmacological hypothesis. Identifying the pharmacological mechanisms of action that underlie the psychological benefits of essential oils will further ingratiate the use of essential oils into more standard treatment practices. In the meantime, pastoral care and counseling and psychotherapy is well-suited to utilize essential oils as an adjunct to current treatments because it can incorporate the benefits of aromatherapy either through the pharmacological mechanism or the psychological mechanism. More importantly, aromatherapy can function as an appropriate and beneficial bridge for managing symptoms of emotional distress while pursuing more long-term understanding and processing of a variety of distressing affects and experiences.

AROMATHERAPY IN PASTORAL CARE

Trauma does, to some degree, touch us all. The wide-reaching scope of traumatic experience and response cries out for skillful and informed care across the helping professions. While each of the helping professions has a role to play, religious care-givers are uniquely equipped to tend to the rupture of faith in community and the divine. Religious professionals need to be informed about traumatic responses as well as have a sensitivity to the impact of their theological statements and implicit messages within those very hallowed confessions. Additionally, religious care-givers need supportive strategies to augment their primary means of care, pastoral counseling, preaching, and liturgy. The use of essential oils through aromatherapy already has a robust, though largely unidentified, history of application in the liturgy of some religious communities. Intentional amplification and explicit embracing of the tradition of lighting incense during the liturgy of the community is a ready-made avenue for the use of essential oils and aromatherapy as an adjunctive care of the community.

Aromatherapy and the use of essential oils could offer a tremendous enhancement of pastoral care in the areas of liturgy and counseling. The tradition of utilizing incense in liturgical gatherings to foster a mood of reflection and openness to the divine. A brief survey of the components of liturgical incense reveal that the most frequently utilized components (frankincense, sandalwood, rose, lavender, myrrh, and vanilla) are resins with a low volatility (base notes). Additionally, most of these resins are helpful in the reduction of anxiety, grief and loss, and depression while providing a feeling of groundedness, stability, calming of mind, and introspection. It is easy to connect the qualities encouraged by these resins with their utility in creating and fostering a worship community. The resin blends available on the market offer a robust base of aromatherapy that could be tailored to the specific needs of the congregation through the addition of other top and middle note essential oils. For instance, the addition of neroli could further support a congregation that has experienced a traumatic loss in the community while the addition of gingergrass or geranium could increase the energy, vitality, and imagination of the congregation that is becoming weary and stagnant.

The most tailored benefit of aromatherapy is in the area of pastoral counseling and mirrors many of the benefits of essential oil use by psychotherapists. While pastoral counselors would be unlikely to create blends for specific individuals to utilize as an adjunct to mental health care, it would be appropriate for pastors and pastoral counselors to use aromatherapy to create a space that fosters care, stability, and connection.

For many people across faith traditions, their religious leader is often one of the individuals gifted with access to the most significant events in their lives. Religious care-givers are often present to celebrate new life in a family through baptism, as new family bonds through marriage, as well as to mourn tragedy and death through funerals. All of life's major milestones come with the stress of transition, and many of life's most formative experiences are silently accompanied by a form of traumatic experience. A care provider's most vulnerable and essential work comes in joining with people and communities through their valleys of darkness and crises of faith. During these journeys, the caregivers most likely to accompany the individual or community through the darkness and into health are those who are aware of the terrain of traumatic experience, response, and recovery and those who are equipped with a variety of assistive tools. The use of essential oils through trained and thoughtful aromatherapy is one of the many tools available to pastoral care and counseling providers as truly holy transitional and transcendent smells.

NOTES

1. Please note I do not advocate aromatherapy as a replacement for medication as appropriately prescribed by a psychiatrist.

2. For more information see Edward Godfrey Cuthbert Frederic Atchley, *A History of the Use of Incense in Divine Worship* (NewYork: Langmans, Green and Co., 1909), reprinted Nabu Press, 2010.

3. Federation of American Societies for Experimental Biology. "Burning Incense Is Psychoactive: New Class of Antidepressants Might Be Right Under Our Noses," *ScienceDaily*. ScienceDaily, May 20, 2008. www.sciencedaily.com/releases/2008/05/080520110415.htm. Site accessed September 6, 2015.

4. As of 2015, aromatherapy is not a protected, licensed professional title. While there are not state or federal levels of professional qualifications, there are several professional organizations that provide standards for education, experience, ethics, and professionalization. The two most significant organizations are the National Association of Holistic Aromatherapy (NAHA) and the Alliance of International Aromatherapists (AIA). These organizations regulate training programs and provide certification requirements and professional standards and maintain a list of approved training programs. In recent years, Young Living and DoTerra have grown in popularity. These companies are multi-level marketing companies that provide limited training to sellers for the purpose of distribution of essential oils for home use, and this training should not be mistaken for professional certification and does not in itself qualify the seller to use or direct the use of essential oils clinically.

5. A fuller exposition of the term "Trauma Sensitive Theology" will be developed in the upcoming monograph *Trauma Sensitive Theology: Thinking Theologically in the Era of Trauma* (Eugene: Cascade Books), under contract. The term "Trauma Sensitive Theology" was initially developed in my doctoral dissertation. It has since been carried over as a specific lens for theological reflection in praxis through various workshops and chapters. For more information see Jennifer Baldwin, *Injured But Not Broken: Constructing a Trauma Sensitive Theology*, PhD diss., Lutheran School of Theology at Chicago, 2013; Jennifer Baldwin, "From Traumatic Disruption to Resilient Creativity: How Hermeneutics, Feminism, and Postmodernism Provide Grounds for the Development of a Trauma Sensitive Theology," in *Embracing the Ivory Tower and Stained Glass Windows: A Festschrift in Honor of Archbishop Antje Jackelen*, ed. by Jennifer Baldwin (Springer, 2016).

6. Judith Herman, *Trauma and Recovery* (New York: Basic Books, 1992), 7.

7. For an additional perspective on trauma and religion, see Christina Davis's chapter in this volume.

8. These terms have been utilized by established and well-respected theologians who purport to write with authority in the areas of theology and trauma to describe survivors of trauma. See Serene Jones, *Trauma and Grace: Theology in a Ruptured World* (Louisville: Westminster John Knox Press, 2009); Shelly Rambo, *Spirit and Trauma: A Theology of Remaining* (Louisville: Westminster John Knox Press, 2010); Shelly Shooter, *How Survivors of Abuse Relate to God: The Authentic Spirituality of the Annihilated Soul* (Burlington: Ashgate Publishing Company, 2012).

9. Bessel van der Kolk, *The Body Keeps the Score* (Penguin Books, 2014), 80–81.

10. Sandra Weiss, "Neurobiological Alterations Associated with Traumatic Stress," *Perspectives in Psychiatric Care* 43.3 (2007): 114–122.

11. Ibid., 114.

12. Ibid., 116.

13. Louis Cozolino, *The Neuroscience of Psychotherapy: Building and Rebuilding the Human Brain* (New York: W. W. Norton & Company, 2002).

14. Rachel Herz, "Aromatherapy Facts and Fictions: A Scientific Analysis of Olfactory Effects on Mood, Physiology and Behavior," *International Journal of Neuroscience* 119: (2009) 263–290, 263.

15. Ibid., 271.

16. Marcello Spinella, "A Relationship between Smell Identification and Empathy," *International Journal of Neuroscience* 112: (2012) 605–612.

17. Ibid., 605–606.

18. Herz, 276.

19. The notion of a "transitional scent" is a derivative of Winnicott's "transitional object." "Transitional objects" are utilized by children in normal human development to increase a sense of security and confidence when encountering a new or challenging situation. "Transitional objects" are frequently small blankets, a favorite toy or stuffed animal, etc.

20. An aromatherapy blend that includes *Lavandula angustifolia, Pelargonium roseum x asperum, Pogostemom cablin,* and *Citrus aurantium var. amara* is particularly appropriate as an adjunctive support for PTSD mental health care. *Lavandula angustifolia* and *Pelargonium roseum x asperum* are shown to decrease salivary cortisol, thereby supporting the movement of traumatic memory from the limbic system into the cortical structures that support long-term, non-emotionally reactive memory. *Pogostemom cablin* supports deactivation of the sympathetic nervous system which remains hyperactive in traumatic response. Research on the impact of neroli (*Citrus aurantium var. amara*) on anxiety is optimistic indicating that neroli has anxiolytic properties similar to xanax and can assist in lowering blood pressure and serum cortisol. While there is not currently a standard pharmacological regimen for assisting with PTSD symptom management, there is a strong likelihood that aromatherapy blends including the aforementioned essential oils could support symptom relief in individuals with PTSD while also in the care of licensed therapists trained in the treatment of trauma resolution.

REFERENCES

Atchley, Edward Godfrey Cuthbert Frederic. *A History of the Use of Incense in Divine Worship.* New York: Langmans, Green and Co., 1909, reprinted Nabu Press, 2010.

Baldwin, Jennifer. "From Traumatic Disruption to Resilient Creativity: How Hermeneutics, Feminism, and Postmodernism provide grounds for the development of a Trauma Sensitive Theology," In *Embracing the Ivory Tower and Stained Glass Windows: A Festschrift in Honor of Archbishop Antje Jackelen,* ed. by Jennifer Baldwin, Springer, 2016.

Baldwin, Jennifer. "Injured But Not Broken: Constructing a Trauma Sensitive Theology." PhD diss., Lutheran School of Theology at Chicago, 2013.

Cozolino, Louis. *The Neuroscience of Psychotherapy: Building and Rebuilding the Human Brain.* New York: W. W. Norton & Company, 2002.

Federation of American Societies for Experimental Biology. "Burning Incense Is Psychoactive: New Class Of Antidepressants Might Be Right Under Our Noses." *ScienceDaily,* 2008, fromhttp://www.sciencedaily.com/releases/2008/05/080520110415. Retrieved August 31, 2013.

Herman, Judith. *Trauma and Recovery.* New York: Basic Books, 1992.

Herz, Rachel. "Aromatherapy Facts and Fictions: A Scientific Analysis of Olfactory Effects on Mood, Physiology and Behavior." *International Journal of Neuroscience* 119 (2009): 263–290.

Jones, Serene. *Trauma and Grace: Theology in a Ruptured World.* Louisville: Westminster John Knox Press, 2009.

Rambo, Shelly. *Spirit and Trauma: A Theology of Remaining.* Louisville: Westminster John Knox Press, 2010.

Shooter, Susan. *How Survivors of Abuse Relate to God the Authentic Spirituality of the Soul*. Surrey: Ashgate Publishing, 2012.

Spinella, Marcello. "A Relationship Between Smell Identification and Empathy." *International Journal of Neuroscience* 112 (2012): 605–612.

Van der Kolk, Bessel. *The Body Keeps Score*. Penguin Books, 2014.

Weiss, Sandra. "Neurobiological Alterations Associated with Traumatic Stress." *Perspectives in Psychiatric Care* 43.3 (2007): 114–122.

Index

About the Contributors

Dr. Stephanie N. Arel locates her research at the intersection of theology, trauma, and affect theory, in its philosophical and psychological conceptions. She holds a certificate in trauma modalities for clinical treatment from the New York Institute for the Psychotherapies, and she has taught college courses in comparative religion and on death and dying. She is also interested in the ontogeny of shame and the role of violence in spiritual formation, especially as these relate to sex and gender.

Rev. Dr. Jennifer Baldwin, LCPC is currently adjunct professor at Elmhurst College, executive director and clinician at Grounding Flight Wellness Center in Atlanta, founder and executive director of Vertical Exploration Foundation, and senior editor of Vertical Exploration Journal, an interdisciplinary online journal fostering research into the pole and aerial movement arts. She is a certified aromatherapist specializing in the use of essential oils to support mental health.

Rev. Dr. John C. Carr is a semi-retired pastoral theologian and pastoral psychotherapist and educator. During his professional life he has been a congregational minister, executive director of a freestanding ecumenical center for pastoral counseling and family life education, pastoral/spiritual care staff in a psychiatric hospital, community-based pastoral psychotherapist, and associate faculty in a theological college.

Rev. Dr. Christina Jones Davis, LMFT is clinic director and assistant professor of pastoral care and counseling at Christian Theological Seminary in Indianapolis, Indiana. Her research and professional interests include spiritually integrated counseling, relational psychoanalytical approaches to therapy, and culturally appropriate counseling interventions. In addition to her scholarship, Dr. Davis has experience as a marriage and family therapist, hospital chaplain, and associate minister.

Rev. Dr. Shirley S. Guider holds a doctorate in theology and practice of ministry with a focus/concentration in pastoral theology from the Lutheran Theological Seminary at Philadelphia and a master's of science in nursing in psychiatric-mental health nursing from Yale University. She is currently an adjunct professor at Moravian School of Nursing and serves as an intentional interim minister in the Southeastern Pennsylvania Synod. Shirley is an ordained pastor in the Evangelical Lutheran Church in America.

Rev. Dr. Jason Hays has been pastoring and teaching in congregational and community settings for more than twenty years. He is a pastoral counselor in private practice and serves as associate minister for Pastoral Care at First Congregational UCC Church in Boulder, CO. Jason is also an adjunct professor of pastoral care and counseling at Lexington Theological Seminary where he teaches courses on constructive theology, embodiment, and pastoral/spiritual care. His research interests include postmodern approaches to pastoral/spiritual care, gender and sexuality, and congregational leadership.

Rev. Martha S. Jacobi, LCSW is a minister of the ELCA, serving in a specialized ministry of pastoral psychotherapy since 1994. She is currently a pastoral associate at the St. Luke's Lutheran Church, Manhattan. She also maintains a private practice in Manhattan and Queens. She specializes in trauma and spirituality, has been a consultant to the MNYS Domestic Violence Task Force, and was a clinical supervisor for the New Ground Day Camp mental health staff.

Dr. Emmanuel Y. Lartey is the L. Bevel Jones III Professor of pastoral theology, care, and counseling at Candler School of Theology at Emory University. Dr. Lartey is interested in pastoral care, counseling, and theology in different cultural contexts, with particular reference to African, British, and American expressions. He is researching the theological implications and practical effects of pastoral care in a diversity of cultures. He also teaches in Emory's Graduate Division of Religion in the person, community, and religious life program.

Rev. Dr. Bonnie Miller-McLemore is E. Rhodes and Leona B. Carpenter professor of religion, psychology, and culture at the Divinity School and Graduate Department of Religion of Vanderbilt University. A national and international leader in pastoral and practical theologies, widely recognized for work on families, women, and children, and recipient of a Henry Luce III Fellow in Theology award, she is author and editor of numerous publications.

Kenya J. Tuttle holds two master's degrees in religion with an emphasis in ethics and society from Vanderbilt University and an undergraduate degree in psychology from Rice University. She is currently the creative writing and journalism teacher for a junior high public charter school in Houston, Texas. Prior to teaching, she was an editor for upper elementary and youth Sunday school quarterlies at a denominational publishing house in Nashville, Tennessee.

Dr. Sonia E. Waters is an Episcopal priest and the assistant professor of pastoral theology at Princeton Theological Seminary. Her interests include visual culture studies, critical theory, contemporary relational psychoanalysis, addictions, embodiment, and feminist and womanist theology. She served in parish ministry for ten years before teaching. She has a background in domestic violence advocacy and shelter work. She is especially interested in how the affective and relational elements of faith communities constitute the Christian subject.

Made in the USA
Monee, IL
19 September 2020